# Improve Your Chess Tactics

Yakov Neishtadt

# Improve Your Chess Tactics

## 700 Practical Lessons & Exercises

Second, improved edition

New In Chess 2024

© New In Chess
~~First edition 2010~~
Second, improved edition 2024

Published by New In Chess, Alkmaar, The Netherlands
www.newinchess.com

Cover design: Volken Beck
Translation: Steve Giddins
Editing, supervision: Peter Boel
Typesetting: Sandra Keetman
Engine check, proofreading: Michaël van Liempt
Production: Anton Schermer, Sandra Keetman

Have you found any errors in this book?
Please send your remarks to editors@newinchess.com. We will collect all
relevant corrections on the Errata page of our website www.newinchess.
com and implement them in a possible next edition.

ISBN hardcover: 978-90-833788-4-8
ISBN softcover: 978-90-833788-5-5

# Contents

## Solutions

# Concerning chess improvement, and this book

It is well-known that the best form of training is practical play, and taking part in tournaments. In order to play better, one must play more, and with strong opponents wherever possible. However, this axiomatic advice requires a little amendment.

Every game is an examination in itself. But it is an examination without precise model answers to the questions that are most important. Did we (and our opponent) handle the changing situation from move to move correctly? Which moment was the turning point – where was the decisive mistake made, and was it exploited in the best way?

'To know that, we have to analyse the game,' – the reader will doubtlessly tell us. Indeed, but it would be very useful to compare our conclusions with those of a more qualified judge, a player who is significantly stronger than ourselves. Your analysis, no matter how serious it may be, is limited by the level of your chess understanding. Suppose that you have found the place where, it seems to you, your play departed from the best line, where you committed some inaccuracies and mistakes, and now you know how you should have played. But have you found the best moves for sure? How accurate is your tactical vision? Can you be sure you have not missed any combinative possibilities for yourself or your opponent? Finally, no matter how well-developed your feeling for position may be, are your assessments totally objective? In a word, aren't you taking on too much, and setting yourself a task that is unfulfillable? Have you missed a decisive continuation, before you are convinced that the position cannot possibly contain anything out of the ordinary?

But even if you have an experienced helper on hand, you are unlikely to achieve great successes if you only study your own games. You also have to study others' games, both classical and modern: instructive master games, typical and original combinations and characteristic plans. Added to that is the required basic knowledge of opening and endgame theory.

We can find all of this (or, at least, we should be able to find it) in the traditional chess textbooks. When playing over the games given, one remembers what one has seen, and tries in similar situations to implement the knowledge obtained. However, it is hard to judge how and to what extent the material is mastered, since there is no direct contact between the book's author and its reader. In general, both methods of self-improvement –

analysing one's games (not only won games, but losses as well) and working with textbooks, have their pluses and minuses, and complement each other.

But isn't it important to bring together knowledge and practical play?

In your hands, you have a textbook (a schooling in combinations) and a collection of exercises (practice). In short, a self-tutor and a sparring-partner.

These positions, taken from the games of masters and grandmasters, as well as lesser players, are given immediately before the decisive moment in the game. You have to find the winning line, or, in the case of difficult positions, the saving resource. A few of the positions are compositions, or are taken from compositions, close in style to practical play. A number of them have also featured in my book *Test Your Tactical Ability* (Batsford 1981), but I have reorganized the material and added many new examples in this new book.

In the first part of this book, the positions are grouped by theme, which, of course, makes them easier to solve. In the second part, the themes are not indicated, and so the reader has no extra hints in this 'Finishing School'. However, the basic fact that all of the positions require a combinative solution is itself a sufficient hint for the experienced player to find the correct path.

Try at first to solve the questions without moving the pieces, and go over to detailed analysis only when you are convinced that you cannot solve the exercise in your head.

The reader will no doubt notice that far from all of the famous grandmasters are represented here. But the book is not intended as an anthology of combinations by the great, and the examples have not been chosen on the principle of being representative, but for their instructional value. The level of the event in which the game was played has also not been used as a factor in the selection. Alongside fragments from the games of the most famous masters, you will meet examples from simultaneous displays and quite insignificant competitions.

And so, in conclusion: this book, which is aimed at a wide range of chess amateurs, may also be used by an experienced player, a master, or even a grandmaster. Even he will find many positions that are unknown to him, and which he can use to show to his own pupils.

*Yakov Neishtadt*
*November 2010*

**Editor's note to this second edition:** We have updated this edition and checked all the exercises with modern engines. As a result, many of them have been corrected, and a few have even been removed.

# The Alpha and Omega of chess

### Strategy and tactics. The definition of a combination. Classification.

Right from the very first page of most chess books, in almost every comment we encounter special terminology, without thinking much about their derivation and basic meaning.

A chess game is an ideal representation of war, in which the sides (as distinct from a real war) follow clearly-defined rules. The majority of the terms we use in chess are derived from military lexicon. Tactics and strategy. Attack and defence. Counter-attack. Flanks and the rear. Fortress, siege, blockade, breakthrough, penetration, etc.

**STRATEGY** is the most important part of the art of war, devoted to the preparation and carrying out of military actions, and the planning of operations. **TACTICS** is the art of conducting a specific battle. Because the specific battle is part of the overall (strategic) operation, tactics serve strategy, and fulfil its tasks.

In this sense, chess strategy should occupy itself with planning, and the selection of the targets at which our play should be directed in the given position. Tactics are the specific concrete actions which we have to carry out to achieve our desired aims. In the words of Max Euwe, the distinction is between 'what to do' and 'how to do it'.

In a word, tactics serve strategy and depend on it. Compared with a war situation, the chess definitions have a slightly different sense.

Tactics do not embrace all concrete operations (for example, exchanges), but only actions of a sharp, combinative character, intended to change significantly the picture on the board, or to decide the game's outcome. In this sense, it does not matter whether the tactical operation is the logical outcome of events (i.e. whether it fits in with the strategic plan) or whether it is unconnected with the general flow of the game, and arises randomly (for example, because of a blunder by the opponent in a position that is better for him).

In other words, tactics in chess do not always serve strategy – sometimes they exist of their own accord. Separate manoeuvres, aimed at fulfilling the strategic plan, are not usually regarded as part of tactics. In general, the terms 'tactics' and 'strategy' and, correspondingly, 'tactical play' and 'strategic play' are used almost as synonyms. When starting out using chess literature, it is worth remembering this change in military (and even political) terminology.

And now we turn to the play itself.
**Note**: Throughout the book, we will use squares to the left of every diagram to indicate which side is to move.

Position 1
**Manca**
**Braga**
Reggio Emilia, 1992/93

The queen was sacrificed – **1.♕c7+!**, and the game ended. Black is mated: 1...♘xc7 2.♘b6+ axb6 3.♖d8#.

Position 2
**Siegel**
**V. Mikhalevski**
Neuchatel, 1996

White thought his opponent had nothing better than to take the knight. However, there followed **1...♗h4+! 2.♔xh4** 2.♔f3 ♕f2#.

**2...♕f2+ 3.♔g5 h6+ 4.♔xh6 ♕h4#**

In the following examples, after the sacrifice, there follow only checks and forced replies.

Position 3
**Durao**
**Catozzi**
Dublin, 1957

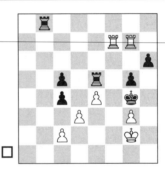

Black was mated elegantly:
**1.♖f4+ ♔h5 2.♖h4+! gxh4 3.g4#**

Position 4
**Cruz Lima**
**A. Hernandez**
Cuba, 1994

Here Black announced mate in five:
**1...♕xh2+! 2.♔xh2 ♘f4+ 3.♔g3 ♖h3+ 4.♔g4 h5+ 5.♔g5 ♖f5#**

In the following example, the king is mated after two sacrifices.

Position 5
**Geller**
**Novotelnov**
Moscow, 1951

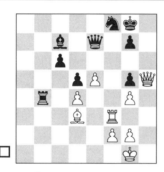

**1.♖xf8+! ♔xf8**

If 1...♕xf8 2.♗h7+ ♔h8 3.♗g6+ and 4.♕h7#.
**2.♕h8+ ♔f7**

**3.♗g6+!**
Luring the king into the mating net.
**3...♔xg6**
3...♔e6 4.♕c8+ (or 4.♕g8+ ♔d7 5.♗f5+ ♕e6 6.♕xe6+ ♔d8 7.♕d7#)
4...♕d7 5.♕g8+ ♔e7 6.♕f7+ ♔d8 7.♕f8+ ♕e8 8.♕xe8# does not change things.
**4.♕h5#**

Moves (or series of moves) connected by a general idea and logically connected with one another, are called **a variation**. When one side forces the other's moves, this is **a forcing variation**. In all of the examples we have seen, the forcing character of the struggle resulted from a sacrifice. **A combination is a forced variation with a sacrifice**.

Arguments about formulae have no real connection with practical play. But these definitions are the basis for the classification of combinations, and, correspondingly, for the construction of our account of this important theme.

So far, we have deliberately chosen combinations in which every move is a check. Checks are a powerful means of control, of limiting the opponent's choice of replies. Calculating a combination in which the enemy king is continually chased around with checks (especially if the main line has few, if any, deviations) is usually quite easy. However, such chances occur relatively rarely. Other means of control are threats and captures (exchanges). Decisive threats can also be set up by 'quiet' (i.e. outwardly unremarkable) moves.

Here are a few examples.

## Position 6
**Spielmann**
**Landau**
The Netherlands, 1932

The game continued **1.♘f6+! gxf6 2.♕g4+ ♚h8**. Mate became inevitable after the 'quiet' move **3.♚g2!**.

## Position 7
**Hort**
**Portisch**
Madrid, 1973

**1.♖g4+!** So as to open the bishop's diagonal. **1...fxg4 2.♕g5+ ♚h8 3.♕h6!**
There is a threat not only of mate on h7, but also of 4.♕xf8# (hence the check on g5). Black resigned.

## Position 8
**Botvinnik**
**Keres**
The Hague/Moscow, 1948

After **1.♖xg7+! ♚xg7 2.♘h5+ ♚g6** (on 2...♚f8 there is 3.♘xf6 ♘xf6 4.♕xf6), the game was ended with the 'quiet' move **3.♕e3!**.

In the following fragment, the means used to draw the opponent into a forcing variation was an exchange of pieces.

## Position 9
**Kubicek**
**Privara**
Ostrava, 1976

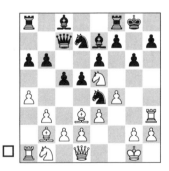

White has brought his rook to h3, to attack the opponent's castled position. To defend against the threat of ♕d1-h5, Black has played ...g7-g6. How can we continue the assault?

An exchange of minor pieces opens the possibility of a decisive sacrifice:

**1.♗xe4** Ensuring the rook has access to the square g3. **1...dxe4 2.♘xd7** Removing the knight that could go to f6. **2...♕xd7** (or 2...♗xd7) and now the decisive blow: **3.♕h5!**, and Black resigned. After 3...gxh5 the game is ended by 4.♖g3+, and otherwise the h7-square cannot be defended.

Now we see a combination devoted to material gain.

Position 10
**Rosenblatt**
**Volk**
Biel, 1977

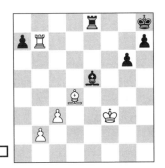

The simple combination **1.♖b8** (1...♖xb8 2.♗xe5+; 1...♗xd4 2.♖xe8+) ended the game.

Position 11
**Beliavsky**
**Tavadian**
Yaroslavl, 1982

There followed **1.♖xe5! ♕xe5** (1...♗xe5 2.♖d8#) **2.♖d8+ ♗xd8 3.♕xe5+ ♔d7 4.♕d4+** with a great material advantage (4...♔e6 5.♗xd8; 4...♔e7 5.♗c5+ and 6.♕xh8).

Position 12
**Sliwa**
**Stoltz**
Bucharest, 1953

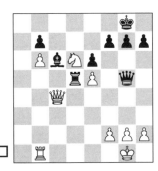

White sacrificed his queen for the sake of forcing his pawns through: **1.♕xc6 bxc6 2.b7 ♕d8 3.b8♕ ♖d1+** Is this the refutation of the combination?...

**4.♖xd1 ♕xb8**

White has only rook and knight for the queen, but his next 'quiet' move radically clarifies the situation:
**5.♘b7!**
Black resigned.

Besides mating the enemy king and gaining material, any favourable change in the position can be the object of a combination (for example strengthening an attack, improving piece coordination, transposing into a promising endgame, etc.), and in a bad position, a combination may be the basis for saving the game (e.g. by setting up perpetual check, stalemate, re-establishing material equality, reaching a theoretically drawn ending, etc.), obtaining counterplay and even weakening the enemy attack.

A combination is the strongest means of achieving the aim. It is an extraordinary way of reaching the goal, a breakthrough that clarifies the situation on the board in a short time-frame, reveals the truth about the position, and exposes false values.

Now let us look at combinations through the eyes of the spectator. Sacrifices and the subsequent extreme follow-ups create a strong emotional effect, whether we are watching the game in the tournament hall, or reading a book in which a game from long ago is presented. Original thoughts (not, in the final analysis, the amount sacrificed), accurate calculation, 'quiet' intermediate moves, and the final victory of a relatively small force have a striking effect on us.

Aesthetic appreciation of a combination depends, of course, on the class of a player. A typical combination, using a hackneyed theme, can be a real revelation to one player, but little more than an element of technique to another. The main point, though, is that the scope for original combinative ideas is almost inexhaustible. This is the nature of chess. Even with respect to typical combinations, all chess positions are concrete and have their own unique characteristics, and so experience, although it helps, can never insure anyone against mistakes.

There are as many combinations as there are chess positions. After the reform of the moves of queen and bishop (in the 15th-16th centuries), the role of combinations greatly increased. It is precisely in the existence and extent of combinations that other games invented by the human mind are unable to compare with chess.

Thus, **a combination is a forcing variation with a sacrifice, in pursuit of a positive aim, and leading to a significant change in the situation on the board**.

Combinations can be classified by intention, and also by other formal attributes: the material which is sacrificed, the pieces taking part in the combination and playing the major role therein, and the object against which the combination is directed.

However, the most important of all is the classification of combinations by **content**.

The **MOTIF** is the characteristic of the position, on which the player fastens in his search for a combination. This may be the cramped position of the enemy king, or, on the contrary, the distance by which its pieces are cut off from the defence, the weakness of the back rank, or of the squares in the immediate vicinity of the king, or the undefended position of a certain piece, or the lack of coordination between the pieces. The motif is nothing other than the initial signpost which directs the player's attention to the right area in his search for a combination.

The **THEME** of a combination (sometimes called the 'idea') is the answer to the question of what the combination consists of. For example, the deflection of the queen from the defence of a key square (the deflection theme), the breaking of the connection between enemy pieces, the presence of pieces on a single line, etc.

# COMBINATIVE THEMES

# Deflection

In combinations on the theme of deflection, an enemy piece or pawn which is performing an important function is forced (or induced) to leave its position, thereby exposing a key line or square, or leaving another piece undefended. The final aim of the operation can vary.

We start with a simple textbook example from the endgame.

Position 13

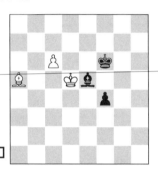

The black bishop has to control c7. With **1.♗c3** White deflects the bishop from the key diagonal and after **1...♗xc3 2.c7** he wins.

Position 14
**Popov**
**Emelyanenko**
Correspondence game, 1984-85

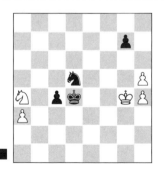

White is prepared to give his knight for the c-pawn, which leads to a draw after 1...c3 2.♘xc3 ♘xc3 3.♔g5 ♘e2 4.♔g6 ♘g3.
However, after the deflection **1...♘b6!** he has to resign – the pawn cannot be stopped.

Position 15
**Abrahams**
**Winter**
London, 1946

**1.♖h5+ ♔xh5 2.♕xf5+ ♔h6** (2...♔h4 3.g3#) **3.♕xe4 ♖xe4 4.d7** and Black cannot stop the pawn promoting. As a result of his combination, White turns an apparently complicated position into a clear one, in which he has a winning advantage.

Now we will look at some examples where the deflection is followed by a knight fork.

As in the previous examples, the final aim is to secure a material advantage.

## Position 16
**Alexander**
**Cordingley**
England, 1947

**1.♗xb7 ♛xb7 2.♛d5!**
Black resigned, because he loses a piece: 2...♛xd5 3.♘xe7+ and 4.♘xd5; 2...♘c6 3.♛xc6!.

## Position 17
**Atlas**
**Wirthensohn**
Wohlen, 1993

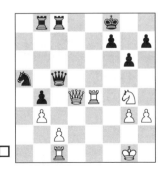

After **1.♖e8+! ♚xe8 2.♘f6+ ♚e7** (2...♚f8 3.♘d7+) **3.♖e1+ ♚f8 4.♘d7+** Black loses his queen to a fork. This combination did not occur in the game, but was found in analysis.

## Position 18
**Panczyk**
**Schurade**
Zakopane, 1978

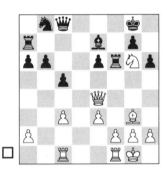

The simple 1.♗e5 ♖f7 2.♗xb8 ♛xb8 3.♛xe6 or 3.♘e5 and ♘c6 is strong, but the game ended with the remarkable long move **1.♛a8!!**. If the queen is taken, there follows 2.♘xe7+ and 3.♘xc8, remaining with an extra piece. If 1...♖b7, then 2.♘xe7+ ♖xe7 3.♛xb8. After 1...♖xg6 2.♛xa7, and also 1...♗d8 2.♛xa7 ♘c6 3.♘e7+! ♘xe7 (3...♗xe7 4.♛xb6) 4.♖fd1, the realisation of the extra exchange should not be too difficult. In the last variation, White also wins the exchange after 2.♛xb8 (instead of 2.♛xa7) 2...♛xb8 3.♗xb8 ♖b7, by playing 4.♘e5 ♖xb8 5.♘d7.

Now let us acquaint ourselves with some of the many different motifs involving the hidden weakness of the back rank.

If the king does not have a bolthole (or he cannot make use of it because the square is attacked), the deflection of a piece which is defending the back rank can result in catastrophe.

Position 19
**Füster**
**Balogh**
Budapest, 1946

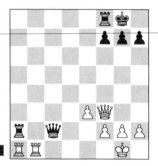

After **1...♕b2!** ('mating the rook'!) White acknowledged defeat.

Position 20
**Mechkarov**
**Kaikamdzozov**
Bulgaria, 1969

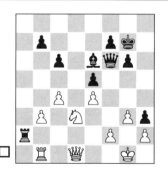

By playing **1.♖b2**, White prepared to exchange rooks. The reply **1...♕f3!** forced him to resign.

Position 21
**Mikenas**
**Bronstein**
Tallinn, 1965

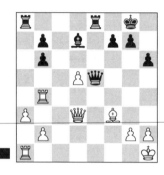

White did not detect any danger: on 1...♕e1+ he does not take the queen, but continues 2.♕f1.

However, with the move **1...♖xa3!** Black captured an apparently well-defended pawn, after which White had to resign.

Position 22
**Reshevsky**
**Fischer**
Palma de Mallorca, 1970

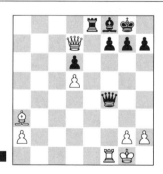

After **1...♕d4+ 2.♔h1 ♕f2!** White resigned. On 3.♕b5, and also 3.♖g1, there follows 3...♖e1.

## Position 23
**Mileika**
**Vojtkevics**

Riga, 1963

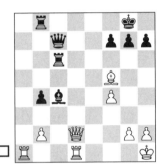

The key square d8, at which the white queen, supported by the rook, is looking, is defended twice. It would be good to deflect one of the pieces that defend this square, which can be done by means of **1.♖a7!**. After **1...♕b6** (it is easy to see that there is no other move) the white rook places itself under a double attack – **2.♖b7!**.

After any capture, 3.♕d8+ decides. Black resigned.

## Position 24
**Lepek**
**Koonen**

Correspondence game, 1962

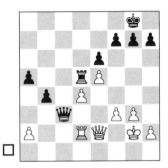

**1.♖c2! ♕xd4 2.♖c4 ♕b6** There is no other reply – otherwise the 8th rank will be undefended. **3.♖c8+ ♖d8 4.♕b5!** (or 4.♕e3!). The deflection of the queen decides the game.

## Position 25
**Madsen**
**Napolitano**

Correspondence game, 1953

A decisive advantage could be obtained without any fuss by 1...♖e2 2.♔f1 ♕e6. What instead happened has a direct connection with our theme (as well as with chess aesthetics): **1...♖e1+! 2.♖xe1 ♕d4+! 3.♕xd4 dxe1♕#**

## Position 26
**Teschner**
**Portisch**
Monaco, 1969

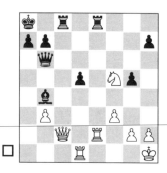

Black is not threatening to take the queen, and so White re-established material equality by means of **1.♖xd5**. In reply, Portisch could have decided the game with the deflection **1...♕f2!**. White can stop the mate on f1 and at the same time defend his rook by means of **2.♘g3**, but then **2...♕e1+** leads to mate. The Hungarian GM played 1...♕a6. The reply 2.♘g3 allowed White to liquidate the danger and the game was drawn.

It can also happen that a piece is overloaded with responsibilities – it has to defend two or even more important objects (pieces, squares or lines). Deflection of the overloaded piece can result in one of the objects being left undefended.

## Position 27
**Ragozin**
**Panov**
Moscow, 1940

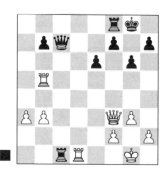

The move **1...♕c6!** deflects the queen, and after 2.♕e2, the exploitation of its overload and need to defend the rook (2...♖xd1+ 3.♕xd1 ♕xb5) forced White to resign.

A few more examples of deflecting sacrifices.

## Position 28
**Byvshev**
**Tolush**
Leningrad, 1954

The move **1...♛a7!**, deflecting the queen from the defence of c3, ended the game.

Position 29
**Alexeev**
**Razuvaev**
Moscow, 1969

The pawn on e4 defends against the powerful bishops, so: **1...♛d8!** Or the 'simple' 1...♛d6. **2.♛f3 ♛d1!** **3.♔g2** Again the queen cannot be taken because of mate. **3...♛c2+** **4.♔h3 ♝xe4** White resigned.

Position 30
**Petkevich**
**Castaneda**
Russia, 1994

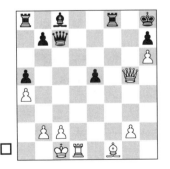

Deflecting the rook from the f-file (or the queen from the defence of g7) renders mate unavoidable: **1.♖d8! ♖xd8** If 1...♝e6 or 1...♝f5, then 2.♛f6+ and 3.♛xf8#. And after 1...♛f7 – 2.♛xe5+ ♔g8 3.♝c4!, and Black is mated on g7. **2.♛f6+ ♔g8** **3.♝c4+** with mate.

Position 31
**Höfer**
**Felmy**
Hamburg, 1975

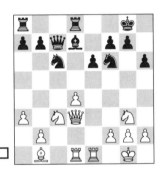

**1.♘h5!** Deflecting the knight from the defence of h7. **1...♘xh5** After the new deflection blow **2.♘d5!**

the king is deprived of e7 – Black resigned. White could also have first played 2.♛h7+ and after 2...♔f8 – 3.♘d5!, with the same result.

**Position 32**
**Zakic**
**Miljanic**

Budva, 1996

**1.♖d8+!** and Black resigned in view of the following variation: 1...♕xd8 2.♗xb7+ ♔c7 (Black is also lost after 2...♔xb7 3.♕xd8 ♖xg4+ 4. ♔f1 ♗c6) 3.♕a5+ ♔d7 4.♗c6+ ♔c8 (4...♔e7 5.♕xc5+) 5.♕a6+ ♔b8 6.♕b7#.

**Position 33**
**Polugaevsky**
**Szilagyi**

Moscow, 1960

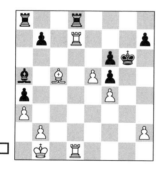

White has the advantage, of course. He could play, say, 1.e6 followed by 1...♖xd7 2.♖g1+, and on 2...♔h5 or 2...♔h6 – 3.exd7 ♖d8 4.♖d1.

However, Polugaevsky found an original mating combination: **1.♖g1+ ♔h6 2.♗f8+!** Deflecting the rook from the d-file allows the decisive manoeuvre (note that 2.♖f7 was also enough to win). **2...♖xf8 3.♖d3!,**

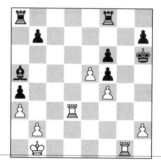

and the mate is unstoppable.

**Position 34**
**Mackenzie**
**NN**

Manchester, 1889

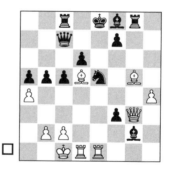

Black will be mated on d8! To do so, White needs to open and clear the d-file and deflect the enemy queen and rook. Thus, **1.♖xe5+! dxe5 2.♕xe5+! ♕xe5 3.♗c6+ ♖xc6 4.♖d8#**.

# Exercises

Position 35

Position 36

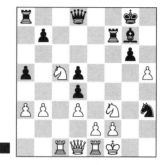

Position 37

Position 38

Position 39

Position 40

Position 41

Position 42

Position 43

Position 44

Position 45

Position 46

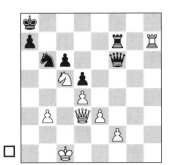

Position 47

Position 48

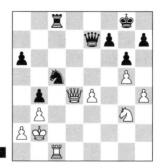

Position 49

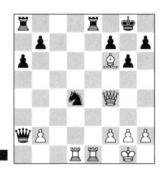

Position 50

Position 51

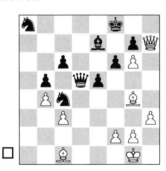

Position 52

Position 53

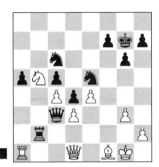

Position 54

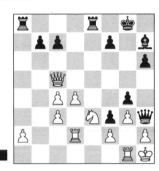

Position 55

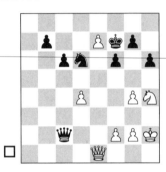

Position 56

Position 57

Position 58

Position 59

Position 60

Position 61

Position 62

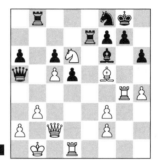

Position 63

Position 64

Position 65

Position 66

Position 67

Position 68

Position 69

Position 70

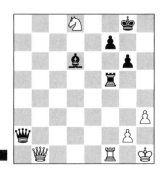

Position 71

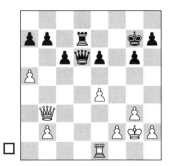

On **1.♕c3+** Black blocked the check with **1...♕d4**. Assess this move.

Position 72

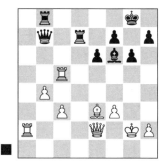

What is your reply to **1...♖c8** ?

Position 73

Black's last move was ...♘f6-g4. How should it be met?

Position 74

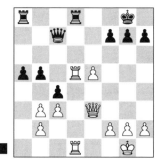

Black did not want to give up the d-file (1...♖xd5 2.♖xd5 cxb3 3.♕d3 or 3.♕d4 with advantage to White) and took the pawn at once – **1...cxb3**. Was he right?

Position 75

White defended against mate by means of **1.f4**. Continue the attack.

Position 76

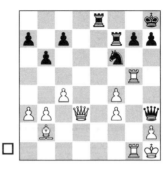

Assess the continuation **1.♖xg7 ♖xg7 2.♗xf6**.

Position 77

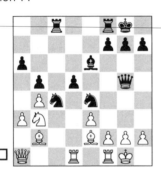

White played **1.♗d4**, deciding that a direct attack on the kingside is not dangerous for him: **1...♗h3 2.♗f3 ♖c6 3.♔h1**, and the bishop on h3 must retreat. Were his calculations correct?

Position 78

By putting his queen on c3, White threatened mate and attacked the bishop at the same time. Is Black obliged to return the bishop to f8?

Position 79

How should White's last move
1.♖d1-d6 be met?

Position 80

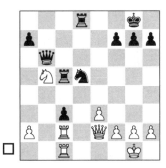

Can the pawn on c3 be taken?

Position 81

By sacrificing a pawn, Black went
into the variation **1...♗xg5 2.♗xf7+
♔h8 3.♗xe8 ♗xc1 4.♗xg6 ♗xb2**.
Assess it.

Position 82

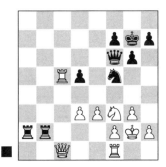

The black rooks have burst onto the
7th rank. Continue the attack.

Position 83

Mate is threatened on c2, and the bishop on c8 is attacked. What should White do?

Position 84

On **1.♖h8+** Black plays **1...♔d7**, in order after 2.♖xc8 to reply 2...♖xg7, and after 2.♖xf7 – 2...♖xh8. Has he seen everything?

Position 85

White has an extra pawn, but is well behind in development, and with the move **1...f4** Black went over to the attack.
What happens after **2.♗xd7 ♕xd7 3.♕xe5** ? Analyse the position.

Position 86

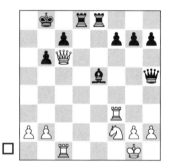

White refrained from the move 1.♖a3 with the threat of mate on a8 (first question: why?) and played **1.♖h3**, on which there followed **1...♕g5**.
Question two: how should the move **2.♖a3** be assessed now, the queen having been driven away?

# Decoying

In combinations on this theme, an enemy piece is again induced to leave its position, but in this case, it is lured to a specific position. In this position, the piece then turns out to be badly placed, either for itself, or in relation to other pieces.

We begin with a textbook position.

Position 87

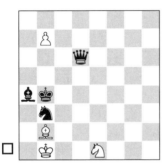

By continuing **1.♗a3+!** White either entices the king to a3 and gives mate with 2.♘c2, or (if the king retreats) wins the queen.

Position 88
**Stanciu**
**Drimer**
Bucharest, 1969

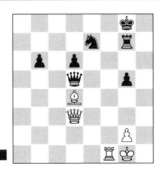

With the tempting move **1...♘c6?** Black attacked the pinned bishop. However, after **2.♖f8+!** he had to resign. The king is lured to f8, allowing the pinned bishop to land a deadly blow (2...♔xf8 3.♗xg7+).

Now several examples in which the king is lured into a fork.

Position 89
**Raitza**
**Casper**
Brandenburg, 1973

**1...d4+!** After every capture of the pawn, as well as a king retreat, White loses his queen: 2.♕xd4 ♘f5+; 2.♔xd4 ♘c6+; 2.♔f4 ♘g6+;

2.♔e4 ♕e2+ 3.♔f4 ♘g6+ or 3.♔xd4 ♘c6+.

Position 90

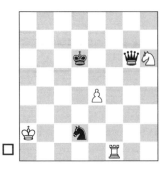

In this textbook example, Black has queen for rook, but **1.♖f6+! ♕xf6 2.e5+** saves White (2...♔xe5 3.♘g4+ or 2...♕xe5 3.♘f7+).

Position 91

**Przepiorka**

**Ahues**

Kecskemet, 1927

**1...♖d1+ 2.♔g2 ♖g1+! 3.♔xg1 ♘f3+** and **4...♘xe5** – the white queen is lost.

Position 92

**Euwe**

**Davidson**

Amsterdam, 1925

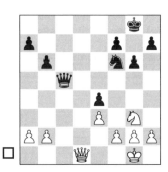

**1.♕d8+ ♔g7 2.♕xf6+! ♔xf6 3.♘xe4+ ♔e5 4.♘xc5 bxc5 5.♔f1** and **1-0**.

Position 93

**Pirc**

**R. Byrne**

Helsinki ol, 1952

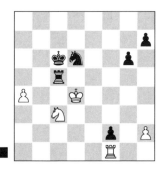

Byrne forced a transposition into a winning endgame by means of **1...♘f5+ 2.♔d3 ♖xc3+! 3.♔xc3 ♘e3! 4.♖xf2 ♘d1+ 5.♔d4 ♘xf2**. The king cannot cope with the pawns – 6.♔e5 ♘g4+, and after 6.h4

the simplest is 6...♘g4 7.♔e4 ♘h6
8.♔f4 ♘f7 or 8.♔e5 ♘f5.

## Position 94
**Oszvath**
**Honfi**
Budapest, 1953

**1...♕xc1! 2.♕xc1 ♖xc3 3.♕e1** If
3.♕xc3, then 3...♘e2+, but now too,
the queen is lost to a fork: **3...♖c1!**
**4.♕xc1 ♘e2+** and 5...♘xc1 with an
extra piece for Black.

Now, some examples of luring the
king into a mating net.

## Position 95
**Ustinov**
**Ilivitsky**
Frunze, 1959

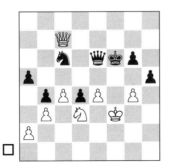

The 'modest' check **1.g5+!** turned
out to be a shock for Black. On
1...♔xg5 there follows 2.♕f4#. He
had to resign.

## Position 96
**Eckhardt**
**Tarrasch**
Nuremburg, 1887

The king is lured into a deadly
discovered check: **1...♕f2+! 2.♔xf2**
**♖d1+**, and mate next move.

In the next two fragments, the king
is lured into a double check.

## Position 97
**S. Anderson**
**Knutsen**
Sweden, 1974

**1...♕d1+! 2.♔xd1 ♗g4+** and
**3...♖d1#.**

## Position 98
**Glass**
**Russell**

Belfast, 1958

Black responded to the queen
exchange offer by mating in three:
**1...♕g2+! 2.♔xg2 ♘f4+ 3.♔g1**
**♘h3#** A standard combination,
repeated many times.

## Position 99
**Sunni**
**Alivirta**

Helsinki, 1957

Black's position is winning, and
after the tempting 1...♕h7 (2.♖f3

♕h2+ 3.♔f2 ♘xf3 4.♔xf3 ♕g3+
5.♔e2 ♖he8 or 5...♖h2), and also
1...♕xg4 he would win. Instead, the
final combination seen in the game
showed two decoy sacrifices:
**1...♖h1+! 2.♔xh1 ♕h7+ 3.♔g1**

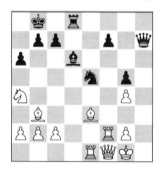

**3...♕h2+ 4.♔xh2 ♘f3+ 5.♔h1** (or
5.♔h3) Now, when the king no
longer has the square g1, there
followed **5...♖h8#.**

## Position 100
**Nette**
**Abente**

Paraguay, 1983

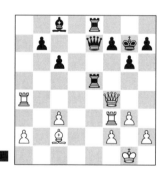

Instead of the prosaic 1...♗h3
2.♖e3 ♖xe3 3.fxe3 ♕xe3+ 4.♕xe3
♖xe3 with a technically winning
endgame, Black preferred mate in
six: **1...♖e1+ 2.♔g2 ♖g1+! 3.♔xg1**

♕e1+ 4.♔g2 ♕f1+! 5.♔xf1 ♗h3+, and mate next move.

## Position 101
**Heemsoth**
**Weber**
Correspondence game, 1973-74

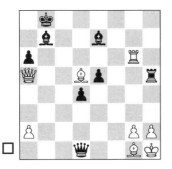

The threat is 1...♖xh2+ 2.♔xh2 ♕h5+ 3.♔g3 ♗h4+ and mate. However, it is White's move, and he can give mate more quickly:
**1.♖g8+ ♔a7** 1...♗c8 2.♕b6#.
**2.♖a8+! ♔xa8** 2...♗xa8 3.♕c7+.
**3.♕xa6+** and **4.♕xb7#**.

## Position 102
**Vidmar**
**Euwe**
Carlsbad, 1929

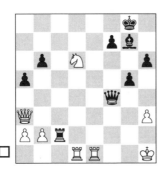

White's material advantage is irrelevant, as he is threatened with mate. However, it is Black who gets mated: **1.♖e8+ ♗f8** 1...♔h7 2.♕d3+. **2.♖xf8+!** The first decoying sacrifice. **2...♔xf8** Or 2...♔g7 3.♘e8+ ♔g6 4.♖d6+ mating. **3.♘f5+ ♔g8 4.♕f8+!** Only this second decoying sacrifice leads to victory. After 4.♖d8+ ♔h7 5.♖h8+ Black is not obliged to take the rook, and thereby get mated – he can retreat the king to g6. **4...♔xf8 5.♖d8#**

## Position 103
**Levitina**
**Gaprindashvili**
Tbilisi, 1979

Black has just played her queen to f3, to threaten mate. In reply to **1.♕c6** (or 1.♕xe5+ ♗f6 2.♕e4 ♖fe8), Gaprindashvili's original calculations had gone **1...e4** and after **2.♕xe4** the decoy sacrifice **2...♖fe8 3.♘xe8+ ♖xe8**. But when the white queen appeared on c6, she realised that at the end of this variation, White in her turn can attack the queen with **4.♘d4**

(4...♖xe4 5.♘xf3), and Gaprindashvili was forced to abandon her original intention. Instead of 1...e4 she played 1...♕f5 and soon lost.
However, the new decoy sacrifice **4...♕g2+!** leads to mate!

A special place amongst decoy sacrifices is occupied by those cases where the king is forced to flee towards the enemy camp, and meets his end there.

Position 104
**Filip**
**Bajar**
Czechoslovakia, 1957

**1...♖xe4! 2.♔xe4 ♘xc5+ 3.♔d4 ♖d8+ 4.♔c3 ♖d3+** It was possible

to give mate in one with 4...♘e4#.
**5.♔b4 ♖xb3+ 6.♔a5 ♘xc4#**

Position 105
**Voitsekhovsky**
**Gabaidullin**
Kaluga, 2003

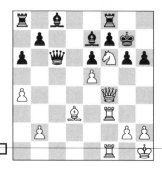

**1.♕xh6+!**
The follow-up moves 1...♔xh6 2.♖h3+ ♔g5 (else mate on h7) 3.♘h7+ ♔g4 4.♗e2+ were not played; Black resigned.

Position 106
**Rödl**
**Blümich**
Wiesbaden, 1934

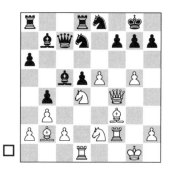

The king hunt begins with a queen sacrifice, to set up a discovered

check: **1.♕xf7+! ♔xf7 2.♗xd5+
♔g6** 2...♔e7 3.♖f7#. **3.♗f7+ ♔xg5
4.♗c1+ ♔g4** Or 4...♔h4. **5.♖f4+
♔g5** 5...♔h3 6.♖d3#. **6.♖e4#**
If Black had retreated his king
instead of taking the queen, then
after 2.♗g4 his position would have
been hopeless (e.g. 2...♕xe5 3.♗xd7
♕xg5+ 4.♖g2).

Position 107
**Kasparian**
**Manvelian**
Yerevan, 1936

**1.♕xc6+!** 'Come into my parlour!'
**1...♔xc6 2.♘e5+ ♔c5 3.♘d3+ ♔d4**.

**4.♔d2!**
A striking finish to the combination. There is no defence to 5.c3#,
so Black resigned.

Position 108
**S. Farago**
**Bigaliev**
Budapest, 1996

There followed:
**1...♘xf2! 2.♔xf2 ♕c5+ 3.♔f3**
If 3.♔e1, then 3...♕e3+ 4.♔d1 ♗g4+
5.♔c1 ♖fc8 6.♔b2 b4.

**3...♗g4+! 4.♔xg4**
When calculating the combination,
Black also had to reckon with the
retreat of the king. After 4.♔g3
he can set up decisive threats by
4...♕e3+ 5.♘f3 (5.♔xg4 h5+ and
5.♔h4 ♘g6+ end in mate) 5...♗xf3,
and after 6.gxf3, the inclusion of
the rook in the attack – 6...♖a6!.
**4...♕f2!**
Cutting off the king's retreat.
**5.g3**

Leads to mate. However, there was no way out. If 5.♗xe5, then 5...h5+ 6.♔g5 (6.♔f5 ♘xg2+) 6...f6+ 7.♗xf6 (7.♔f5 g6#) 7...gxf3+, and mate after 8.♔f5 ♕h4 (9.e5 ♘d3!) or 8.♔h6 ♕a7. **5...h5+ 6.♔h4 f6 0-1**

A triumph for accurate calculation. If White had seen what was to follow, he could have declined the knight and, with a heavy heart, have played 2.♘c4. In this case, after 2...bxc3 3.♕xf2 f5 Black would have had an extra pawn and a large advantage.

Position 109

**Tietz**
**Römisch**

Carlsbad, 1898

By sacrificing rook, queen and bishop (!), White draws the enemy king from d7 to f5:
**1.♖xc6 ♔xc6 2.♕xb5+ ♔xb5 3.♗a4+! ♔c4**
3...♔xa4 leads to mate in two – 4.♘c3+ ♔b3 5.♘d2#.
**4.b3+ ♔d3 5.♗b5+ ♔e4 6.♖g4+ ♔f5 7.♘e3#**
This striking combination by the well-known chess organizer, who

ran the international tournaments in Carlsbad, has been published many times. However, there was not actually any need to chase the black king all round the board. Firstly, the move 1.♕c2! (threatening to take the bishop on c6, and at the same time breaking the pin on the rook) would end the game. Secondly, after 1.♖xc6 ♔xc6 instead of the queen sacrifice, it was also possible to play 2.♕c2+, in order then to take the rook and remain with an extra knight.

Thirdly, Black could also decline the queen, and instead of 2...♔xb5? retreat the king. After 2...♔b7 3.♕xe8 ♘c7 4.♕a4 ♖xf1 5.♕b3 White has the advantage, but the game would continue.

Now we see a position from a more recent game.

Position 110

**Karjakin**
**Malinin**

Sudak, 2002

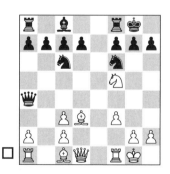

With such an undeveloped black queenside, White's first move, breaking into the king's defences, simply begs to be played – **1.♘xg7.** But what then?

Answer: on **1...♚xg7 – 2.♗h6+!** **♚xh6.**

If 2...♚g8, then 3.♕d2 ♕a5 (after 3...♕h4 there is 4.♗g5 ♕h5 5.♗xf6) 4.♗xf8 ♚xf8 5.♕h6+ ♚e7 6.♖ae1+ ♘e5 7.f4 ♕c5+ 8.♚h1 ♘g4 9.♕h4+.

**3.♕d2+ ♚h5**

**4.g4+!**

It is impossible to believe that such a king can escape mate after 4.c4, isolating the queen. But Karjakin accurately calculates the variation in the game. By allowing the enemy queen into play, he includes his rook in the attack, and concludes the game by force.

**4...♘xg4 5.fxg4+ ♕xg4+ 6.♚h1**

The queen's presence cannot save the black king. The threat is 7.♗e2, which follows after 6...f6 or 6...♘e5. If instead 6...♖e8, then 7.♖f6! ♕g5 8.♗e2+ with mate in a few moves. Also hopeless is 6...♕g5 7.♖f5 ♕xf5 8.♗xf5.

In the game, there followed **6...d6 7.♖f6! ♕g5 8.♗e2+ ♗g4 9.♗xg4+.** Black is mated.

**Position 111**
**Bouaziz**
**Miles**
Riga, 1979

White has an extra exchange, and the c-pawn is one step from promoting. It seems that all approaches to the king are well defended. However, there followed:

**1...♖xh3! 2.♚xh3**

White thought his opponent's move was just a desperation sacrifice, else he would have refused the gift and played 2.♕f1. After 2...♖g3+ 3.♚f2 ♖xf3+ 4.♚xf3 ♕xf1+ 5.♚e4 the game would probably have ended in perpetual check.

But why not take the rook?

**2...♕h1+ 3.♕h2 ♕xf3+ 4.♚xh4 ♗e7+ 5.g5**

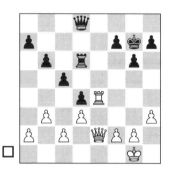

In calculating the combination, Black had to foresee the final decoy sacrifice:

**5...♗xg5+!**

Despite having two extra rooks, White is mated after 6.♔xg5 f6+.

Decoy sacrifices can also be made with a view to blockading.

In mating combinations of this type, with a decoy sacrifice, an enemy piece is lured to a square on which it blockades its king's only escape route.

Position 112
**Polyansky**
**Gerchikov**
Arkhangelsk, 1949

Black has an extra rook, and after 1.♕h7+ ♔f8 2.♕h8+ ♔e7 3.♕xg7+ ♔d8 4.♕xf6+ ♔c8 or 4.♘f7+ ♖xf7 5.♕xf7 ♕xf7 6.exf7 ♔d7 he would be ready to realise his material advantage.

The moves **1.♕h7+ ♔f8** were played, but now the king's escape route was blocked by **2.e7+! ♖xe7 3.♕h8#**.

Position 113
**Kwilecki**
**Reslinski**
Poznan, 1963

After **1.♖e7**, Black, without delving into the subtleties, played **1...♖d7** and after **2.♕e5+** was probably very distressed: **2...♔f8** (2...♔g8? 3.♖e8+; 2...♔h6? 3.♕f4+)

**3.♖xd7 ♕xd7 4.♕h8+** and 5.♕xh7 leads to a pawn-down queen ending. But White has no need to take the endgame. With the 'quiet' move **3.♕f6!**, putting the rook en prise, he attacks f7. The rook is untouchable, since if it is taken, Black blocks his king's escape and is mated on h8. The f7-square can only be defended by 3...♕e8, giving up the queen. He had to resign.

Instead of 1...♖d7? he should have played 1...a5, and if 2.♕e5+, then 2...♖f6.

It sometimes happens that the only defence to a kingside attack is to move a pawn in front of the king. In that case, a blockading sacrifice, preventing the pawn moving, may force mate.

With kingside castling, it is usually the pawn on f7 (f2) that is blockaded.

Position 114
**Fischer**
**Benko**
New York, 1963/64

On **1.♕h5** Black replied **1...♕e8**, intending 2...f7-f5. There followed **2.♗xd4 exd4**.

The mate threat 3.e5 is defeated by 3...f5 (4.♕xe8 ♖axe8 5.exd6 dxc3). But Benko had failed to see the striking move **3.♖f6!**, 'freezing' the f-pawn: now 3...♗xf6 (3...dxc3) 4.e5 leads to mate.

In the game, Black played **3...♔g8 4.e5 h6**, and now not 5.♖xd6? because of 5...♕xe5, after which the game would still continue, but **5.♘e2!**, which forced Black to resign.

If he takes the rook, then 6.♕xh6, whilst in the event of the knight retreating, there is 6.♕f5. After other replies, White simply takes the knight on d6.

As Fischer pointed out, instead of 1...♕e8? Black should have played 1...c5 or 1...♘e6.

Position 115
**Ravinsky**
**Ilivitsky**
Riga, 1952

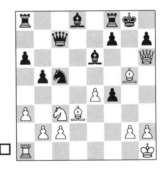

Black has an extra rook. On 1.e5 the reply 1...f5 deals with all the threats. However, 'freezing' the f7-pawn by **1.♗f6!** leads to a forced mate after **1...♗xf6 2.e5! ♘xd3 3.exf6**

45

♘f2+ 4.♔g1 ♘h3+ 5.♔f1 ♗c4+ (if 5...♕c4+, then 6.♔e1) 6.♘e2 ♗xe2+.

**7.♔e1!**
If it were not for this 'quiet' move, the combination would be mistaken (7.♔xe2? ♕xc2+, and White is mated). Now after the only check 7...♕a5+ there follows 8.b4. Black resigned.

Position 116
**Schäffer**
**Kalinitschew**
Münster, 1990

The immediate 1.♗e4 gives nothing, because of 1...f5. However, barricading the f-pawn by **1.♘f6!** (because of the double threat, there is no time for ...♗e6-f5 and the sacrifice has to be accepted), White

creates an unstoppable threat of mate after **1...♗xf6 2.♗e4**.

The freezing of the pawn on e7 (e2) occurs rather more rarely.

Position 117
**Friedman**
**Thornblom**
Stockholm, 1973

Black has sacrificed a piece for two pawns, and must find a way to crown his attack. But after 1...♘h3 there follows 2.e3, opening a bolthole for the king.
The move **1...♖e3!** prevents this, and carries the threats of both 2...♘h3, and 2...♖xf3 with mate on g2 or h1. After **2.fxe3 ♘h3** it is mate on g1.

It would be hard indeed to find a textbook which did not feature some examples of the famous 'smothered mate' combination, which was known as far back as the early days after the reform of the rules of *shatranj*.
One historical example comes from the end of a short game quoted by

Giacomo Greco, from the beginning of the 17th century.

Position 118

**1...♘xd4! 2.♘xd4 ♛h4 3.♘f3?**
3.♗e3 was compulsory. **3...♛xf2+**
**4.♔h1 ♛g1+** The blocking sacrifice.
**5.♖xg1 ♘f2#**

In the final position, the king is completely hemmed in by his own pieces and pawns, hence the name 'smothered mate'.

After a classic example, a more subtle, modern-day interpretation.

Position 119
**Kondolin**
**Ojanen**
Helsinki, 1952

**1...♘g4** was played. Believing this move to be simply an offer to exchange bishops, White replied
**2.♗xe7**.
But in reality, the knight manoeuvre was the prelude to the famous combination. There followed **2...♛b6!**.
The threat is 3...♘f3+ (or 3...♘e2+) and 4...♘f2# (or 4...♛g1#).
White moved his king away –
**3.♔h1**, but Black still carried out his idea, by inverting the moves:
**3...♘f2+ 4.♔g1 ♘e2+! 5.♗xe2**
Other captures also result in mate.
**5...♘h3+ 6.♔h1 ♛g1+ 7.♖xg1 ♘f2#**

# Exercises

Position 120

Position 121

Position 122

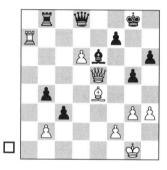

Position 123

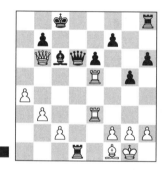

Position 124

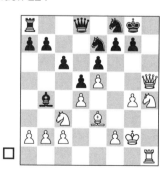

Position 125

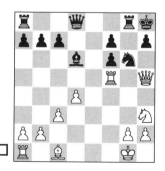

Position 126

Position 127

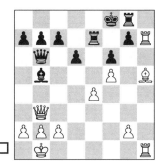

Position 128

Position 129

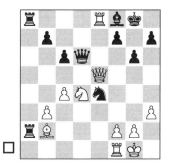

Position 130

Position 131

Position 132

Position 133

Find the quickest win for White.

Position 134

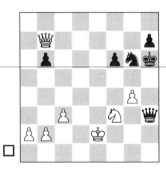

Position 135

Position 136

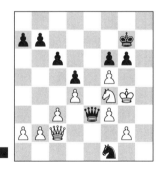

Position 137

Position 138

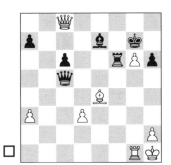

Position 139

Position 140

Position 141

Position 142

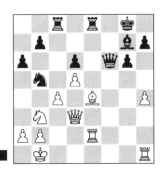

Position 143

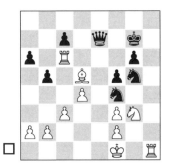

Position 144

How should we answer **1.♕b3** ?

Position 145

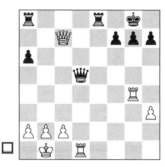

Black has put his queen under attack. What would you do?

Position 146

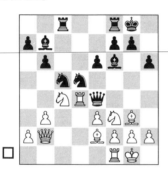

Assess the continuation **1.♘fe5**.

Position 147

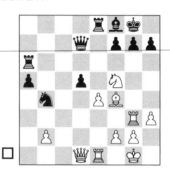

After 1...♖g6, White's initiative on the kingside will be liquidated. What should he do?

Position 148

Does Black have to exchange on d3?

Position 149

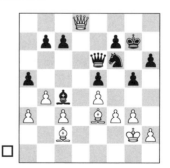

Can the pawn on c7 be taken?

Position 150

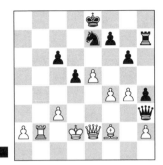

Assess the move **1...♕xh2**.

Position 151

White went into this position, counting on meeting **1...♘xb5** or **1...♘xd1** with **2.♗xf6**. What would you advise Black to do?

Position 152

Black has defended against the check with his bishop and White must decide with which piece to take the d5-pawn, his queen or the rook at e5. What is your opinion?

Position 153

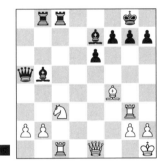

How would you reply to **1...♖b6** ?

Position 154

Position 155

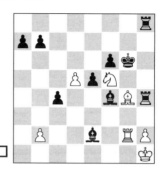

White has an extra rook, but it is under attack. At the same time, mate is threatened on h8. What should he do?

Black has a material advantage, but the bad position of his king allows White to save the game.

# Eliminating defenders

So far we have looked at the idea of taking defenders out by deflecting or luring them away from the defence. In combinations with elimination of defenders, we see the more basic method of the direct capture of the pieces or pawns which fulfil a valuable defensive function. This includes combinations designed to destroy the king's defensive pawn wall.

Position 156
**Petrosian**
**Ivkov**
Belgrade, 1979

The ex-world champion played **1.♖xd4!**, and Ivkov stopped the clocks; whichever way he takes back, he is mated (2.♖(x)e5+ ♔xg4 3.h3#).

Position 157
**Nezhmetdinov**
**A. Romanov**
USSR, 1950

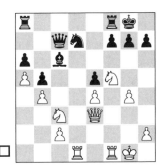

**1.♕g5 g6 2.♘e7+ ♔g7**
On 2...♔h8 there is 3.♖xd7 ♕xd7 4.♕f6#.
**3.♖xd7!**
Removing the defender of the f6-square.
**3...♗xd7**
Or 3...♕xd7.
**4.♕f6+ ♔h6 5.♖f5**
Threat: 6.♖h5#.
**5...♕a7+ 6.♔f1**
Black resigned.

## Position 158
**Auzins**
**Dudzinskis**

Correspondence game, 1985

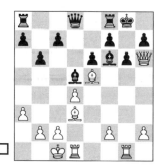

The sacrifice of bishop and rook destroys the pawn barrier: **1.♗xg6! fxg6 2.♖xg6+ hxg6 3.♕xg6+ ♔h8 4.♖g1** (or 4.♖d3). On 4...♕e7 there is 5.♕h6+ ♕h7 6.♗xf6+ and mate.

## Position 159
**Nowrouzi**
**Sakser**

Germany, 1996

**1.♗xh6 gxh6 2.♕xh6+ ♔g8 3.♗c2 ♖e8 4.♗h7+ ♔h8**. And now what? Answer: mate in four: **5.♘xf7+! ♗xf7 6.♗g6+ ♔g8 7.♕h7+** and **8.♕xf7#**.

## Position 160
**Fernandez**
**Santos**

Portugal, 1979

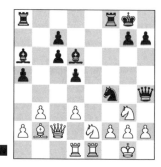

**1...♘xg2! 2.♔xg2 ♖xf2+ 3.♔xf2 ♕xh2+ 4.♔e3 ♖e8+ 5.♘e4** Fleeing was also unsuccessful: 5.♔f3 ♖f8+ 6.♔e3 (6.♔g4 ♗c8+) 6...♕f2+ 7.♔d2 ♗f4+ 8.♔c3 ♕c5# or 5.♔d2 ♕h6+ 6.♔c3 ♗b4+ mating. **5...♗f4+** Here there are already several winning continuations. **6.♔f3** 6.♘xf4 ♕xc2. **6...dxe4+ 7.dxe4 ♗xe2+** After any capture of the bishop there is 8...♕g3#.

## Position 161
**Krasenkow**
**Smagin**

Germany, 2003/04

By eliminating the defender of the d5-square, White creates mating threats: **1.♖xb6! axb6** After 1...♕xb6 the attack develops in the same way as in the game. **2.♕h5+ ♔f8** 2...g6 3.♗xd5+. **3.♗xd5 ♕c7.** On 3...♖c7 White wins with 4.♗f4 g6 (if 4...g5, then 5.♕h6+ ♖g7 6.♗c7!) 5.♗h6+ ♖g7 6.♕f3 ♗c8 (or else ♖e1-e6) 7.♗c6 ♔f7 8.♕b3+. **4.♗f4 g6** 4...♕e7 5.♗d6. **5.♗h6+ ♗g7 6.♕f3+**, and mate.

Position 162
**Bareev**
**Sakaev**

Moscow, 2001

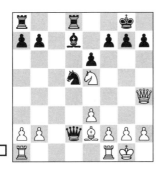

After **1.♗d3** Sakaev, not wishing to weaken the dark squares (1... h6 2.♕e4 f5 3.♕d4), defended

the h7-square with the move **1... g6**. In reply, by a knight sacrifice, Bareev destroyed the black king's pawn cover and drove it into the centre: **2.♘xf7! ♔xf7** Declining the sacrifice by 2...♖f8 3.♘g5 hardly requires any comment. **3.♕xh7+ ♔f6** After 3...♔f8 4.♗xg6 ♗e8 5.♕h8+ ♔e7 6.♕g7+ ♔d6 the black king also ends up in the centre, and White wins in the same way as in the game. **4.♕xg6+ ♔e7** Or 4...♔e5 5.♕g7+ ♔d6 6.♖fd1. For his knight, White gets three pawns and a decisive attack. **5.♕g7+ ♔d6 6.♖fd1 ♕b4 7.e4 ♗a4**

**8.♖ac1!** Black resigned. If the rook is taken, then 9.e5#, whilst after 8... e5 the simplest is 9.♗c2, although other continuations also win, e.g. 9.♕f7, 9.♕h6+ and 10.exd5 or 9.b3.

# Exercises

Position 163

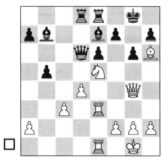

Position 164

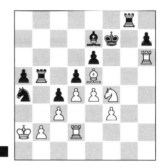

Position 165

Position 166

Position 167

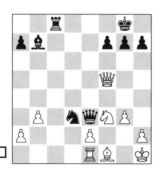

Position 168

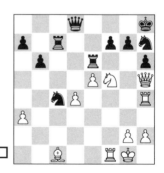

Position 169

White's superiority is evident, but how does he crown the attack?

Position 170

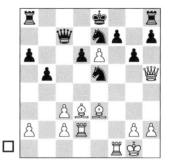

Black is attacking the queen, counting on being able to play ...f7-f5 after it retreats. How does he continue the attack?

Position 171

How should White's last move ♘f2-e4 be answered?

Position 172

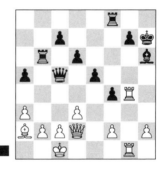

Can Black play **1...f3** ?

# Clearing squares and lines

Sometimes one's own pieces or pawns get in the way of a favourable manoeuvre or tactical blow. In such cases, we strive to free the relevant square or line which the piece is occupying, often being prepared to sacrifice in order to do so.

## Clearing squares

Position 173
**Ravinsky**
**Simagin**
Moscow, 1947

Position 174
**Ivkov**
**Portisch**
Bled, 1961

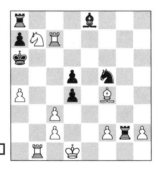

The knight prevents the bishop from landing the decisive blow, and therefore it is sacrificed: **1...♘g4+!** (or 1...♘f3+, with the same idea) No matter how White captures, there follows **2...♗e5+**.

There are various ways to win this position. Ivkov preferred to give a problem-like mate, by freeing the c7-square for his bishop:
**1.♖c6+! ♗xc6 2.♘c5+ ♔a5 3.♗c7#**

Position 175
**Hübner**
**Penrose**
Cheltenham, 1971

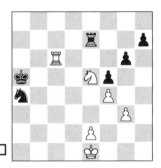

**1.♖xg6!**
By freeing the square c6, White wins a rook with the help of a fork, and obtains a winning endgame (1...hxg6 2.♘c6+, 3.♘xe7 and 4.♘xg6). Black cannot play 1...♖xe5 2.fxe5 hxg6, since after 3.e6 the pawn is unstoppable, whilst if he doesn't take either the rook or the knight, but just defends against the fork, he loses the f5-pawn as well.

Position 176
**Vaisman**
**Hoxha**
Tirana, 1954

White played **1.♕xg6**, and expected his opponent to resign; there are mates threatened on g7 and h7... However, there followed **1...♕e1+** (clearing the square for the knight fork) **2.♖xe1 ♘f2+ 3.♔g1 ♘xh3+ 4.gxh3 hxg6**. As a result, Black has the exchange for a pawn.

Position 177
**Shashin**
**Kolevit**
Moscow, 1974

The queen cannot be taken because of mate. On 1.♕e2? there follows 1...♕xe4, whilst if 1.h3, then simply 1...♕xg4 2.hxg4 ♖d1+ 3.♔h2 ♗e7. However, the insecure position of the black king allowed White with the single move **1.♗f4!** to liquidate the mate threat and at the same time create decisive threats himself, namely mate (2.♖c1+) and the capture of the black queen.
Black defended his queen with the move **1...♖d5**, freeing d8 for the king, but after **2.♖c1+ ♔d8 3.♗g5+ ♗e7** White ended the game with **4.♘d6!**.

## Clearing diagonals

Position 178
**Solmanis**
**Aravin**
Jurmala, 1981

After **1.♘d6+!** White, by clearing the bishop's path to a6, announced mate.

Position 179
**Karpov**
**Csom**
Bad Lauterberg, 1977

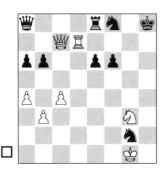

The rook is attacked and the h7-square defended – Black feels quite safe and is ready to realise his extra piece.

However, there followed, **1.♘f5!**, and he had to resign.

The knight has freed the way for the queen to reach h2. On 1...♘xd7 there follows 2.♕h2+! ♔g8 3.♕g3+ ♔h8 4.♕g7#. If 1...exf5, then again 2.♕h2+ with mate.

The deadly check on h2 can be prevented by the move 1...♕b8, but then White has another mate, by freeing the square g7 for the queen: 2.♖h7+.

Position 180
**Alekhine**
**Rubinstein**
Carlsbad, 1923

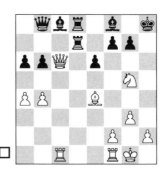

How can the queen be brought to the h-file? The move 1.♗b1 (freeing the long diagonal for the queen, in order to come via e4 or g2) is met by 1...♕e5 (not 1...♕b7 because of 2.♕c4).

Alekhine solved the dilemma by **1.♗g6!**, winning an important tempo by the attack on f7. The variation he had in mind was 1...fxg6 2.♕g2 ♗xb4 3.♕h3+ ♔g8 4.♕h7+ ♔f8 5.♕h8+ ♔e7 6.♕xg7+ ♔e8 (6...♔d6 7.♖fd1+) 7.♕g8+ ♗f8

(7...♔e7 8.♕f7+) 8.♕xg6+ ♔e7 9.♕xe6#.

Rubinstein declined the sacrifice by playing **1...♕e5**. After **2.♘xf7+ ♖xf7 3.♗xf7 ♕f5 4.♖fd1**

White had an extra exchange and pawn, and easily won the game.

## Clearing files

Position 181
**Westerinen**
**Larsen**
Havana, 1967

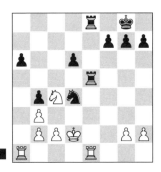

Expecting the exchange of rooks, White was ready to continue to resist in the knight endgame (1...♖xe1 2.♖xe1 ♖xe1 3.♔xe1 ♘xc2+ 4.♔d2 ♘d4 5.♘xd6 ♘xb3+ 6.♔d3).

However, he was disappointed. The move **1...♘f3+!** cleared the d-file. On **2.gxf3** there followed mate starting with **2...♖d5+**.

## Clearing ranks

Position 182
**Neishtadt**
**Baranov**
Moscow, 1949

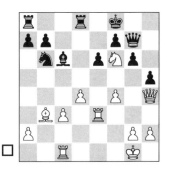

**1.f5!** Clearing the 4th rank. By sacrificing themselves, the f- and d-pawns open a path for the queen to get to the square b4.

**1...exf5**

If 1...gxf5, then 2.♖g3 ♕h8 (or 2...♕h6 3.♖g8+ ♔e7 4.♘d5+ with mate) 3.d5! with the terrible threat of ♕h4-b4+.

After 1...g5 White continues 2.♕xh5 and on 2...♕xf6 – 3.fxe6! (with the threats 4.e7+ and 4.♖f1) 3...♕f4 4.♖ce1.

There is also the intermediate move 1...♕h6. White replies 2.♘g4!, for example: 2...♕f4 3.fxe6 hxg4 4.♖ce1 ♔g7 5.exf7 ♖f8 6.♖h3!.

**2.d5**

The threat of 3.♕b4+ cannot be staved off without material loss.

After **2...♖d6** (or 2...♕h6 3.♕b4+ ♔g7 4.♕d4! ♔f8 5.♕c5+) **3.♘xh5 ♕h6** (3...g5 4.♕b4 ♕g6 would not have helped much either because of 5.♖e6!.) **4.♕e7+ ♔g8 5.dxc6 ♖f8 6.♖ce1** (sufficient for the win, but inserting 6.cxb7!, threatening a variety of things such as 7.♗xf7+ or 7.b8♕, would have been even better) **6...♖xc6 7.♘f6+ ♔g7 8.♖h3** Black resigned.

# Exercises

Position 183

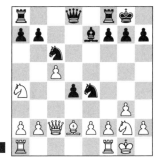

Position 184

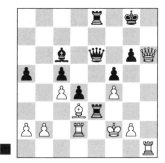

Position 185

Position 186

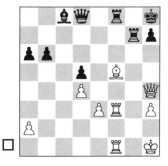

Position 187

Position 188

Position 189

On **1.f5** Black played **1...exf5**. How would you reply?

Position 190

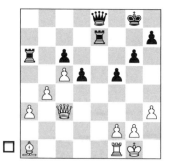

With complete control of the long diagonal, White can check on h8 and take the h7-pawn. But then the king hides on the other flank. Is there anything stronger?

Position 191

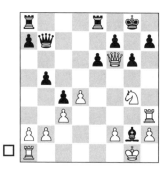

Finish off the attack.

Position 192

♖d1-d3 has just been played. What happens if the rook is taken?

# Pinning and unpinning

When pinned by a queen, rook or bishop, a piece (or pawn) is wholly or partly limited in its mobility, since it has to protect another piece, more valuable than itself, or just undefended, along the same line.

If it is the king that stands behind the pinned piece, then that piece's mobility is restricted to the maximum extent (it can only move up the same line).

If the pinned piece is protecting not the king, but another piece, then the pin may not be total, since the pinned piece may quit its post, 'in pursuit of a higher goal', leaving the more valuable or undefended piece behind it under attack.

Position 193

In the left half of the diagram, White wins by pinning the rook – **1.♗d4**, and then attacking it again (1...♚b6 2.b4).
In the right half of the diagram, after **1.♗e3** Black loses a knight, since if it moves away, it leaves the rook hanging.

However, not every pin allows one to derive the maximum advantage. For example, when a knight is pinned by a bishop, if the number of attackers and defenders is the same, the only advantage is the lack of mobility of the pinned knight. Pins may be made in pursuit of positional or tactical aims. We will look at some positions where a pin played the decisive role.

Position 194
**Samkov**
**Yablonsky**
Riga, 1978

After **1.♕c4!** Black has no defence against both ♖d1 and ♖c1. If 1...♚f7 the game is decided by 2.♖c1 ♕e6

3.♗xc5 ♖d1+ 4.♔g2, and after
1...♕d6, White wins by 2.♖d1 ♗d4
3.♗xd4.

**Position 195**
**Botsari**
**Kadimova**
Debrecen, 1992

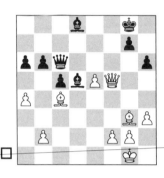

A double diagonal pin by **1.♕e4**
decided the game.

**Position 196**
**Polugaevsky**
**Hort**
Manila, 1976

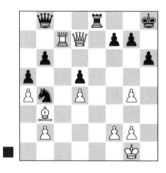

There followed **1...♖e1+ 2.♔h2**, and
the move **2...♖c1** left White a rook
down.

**Position 197**
**Bykov**
**Sinoviev**
Odessa, 1983

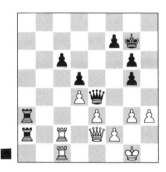

By playing **1...♖c3!**, Black pinned
the rook on c2 along the c-file and
the second rank. **2.♖xa2** (2.♖xc3
♖xe2) **2...♖xc1+** and **3...♖h1#**

In all these examples, a pin and
attack on the pinned piece led to
a decisive material advantage. In
combinations, the decisive pin and/
or its exploitation is achieved by
means of an initial sacrifice.

**Position 198**
**Pirc**
**Stoltz**
Prague ol, 1931

With the move **1...d4** Black wins a piece. The knight and the e3-pawn are both pinned. On 2.♕xd4 there follows 2...♕a1+ (3.♘d1 ♕xd4).

Position 199
**Dahl**
**Schultz**
Berlin, 1956

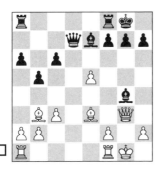

**1.e6! ♗xe6 2.♗d4 f6**
If instead 2...♗g4, then 3.h3 c5 4.♗e5 c4 5.♗d1.

After the introductory moves, a double diagonal pin on the bishop at e6 decides things:
**3.♕g4!**
On 3...♔f7 there follows 4.♖fe1. Black resigned.

Position 200
**Nimzowitsch**
**Rubinstein**
Berlin, 1928

White played **1.♕g6!**, leaving the rook attacked, which, moreover, can be taken with check. But Black resigned: the g7-pawn is pinned, and so 2.♕xh6# is threatened. If 1...♖xd1+, then 2.♔g2, and after 2...♖d2+ the king escapes the checks on h3.

The only possibility of defending the square h6 is to play 2...♖g1+ (instead of 2...♖d2+) and then transfer the bishop to e3 with tempo: 3.♔xg1 ♗c5+ 4.♔g2 ♗e3. But then g7 is left undefended. One small addendum should be made to this nice finish by the two great masters. Instead of the rook sacrifice, the game could have been ended by the simple move 1.♖d3. There is no defence against ♕e4-g6: 1...♖xd3 2.♕xd3, 3.♕g6 and 4.♕xh6# or 1...♖d5 2.♖xd5 exd5 3.♕g6 ♕h3 4.♕xg7+ ♗xg7 and 5.f8♕+.

As we have already said, sometimes a favourable tactical opportunity (or the lesser of two evils) provides that 'higher goal', in the cause of which the pinned piece may move away and expose a more valuable or undefended colleague to attack.

Position 201
**Alokhine**
**Tenner**
Cologne, 1911

In reply to the 'energetic' **1...♘e5?** there followed **2.♘xe5! ♗xd1** After 2...♕h4+ there could have followed 3.g3 ♘xg3 4.♗xf7+ ♔d8 5.♕xg4 ♕xg4 6.♘xg4 ♘xh1 7.♗f2, also winning. **3.♗xf7+ ♔e7** After 3...♔f8 4.♗xc5+ White keeps an extra piece. **4.♗xc5+**

**4...♔f6** Hopeless is 4...♕d6 5.♗xd6+ and 6.♖xd1. But now Black is mated: **5.0-0+ ♔xe5** After 5...♔g5 it is mate in a few moves after 6.♗e3+. **6.♖f5#**

Position 202
**Mondolfo**
**Kolisch**
Vienna, 1859

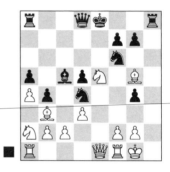

An old and classical example of unpinning.
White has an extra piece, and he threatens a discovered check. However, the semi-pinned knight on f6 lands the deadly blow **1...♘e4! 2.♗xd8.**
If White does not take the queen, but plays 2.dxe4, then 2...♕xg5, and after 3.exd5 – 3...0-0-0! with unstoppable mating threats.
The move 2.♘xf7 is refuted by 2...♕c7! (3.♘xh8 ♘f3+ 4.gxf3 ♕g3+ 5.♔h1 ♕h3+ 6.♔g1 gxf3 with mate; the same mechanism occurs in the variation 3.♕xe4+ dxe4 4.♘xh8 ♘f3+ etc.).
And if 2.♕xe4, then 2...dxe4 (3.♗xd8? ♘e2#).

Finally, after 2.♗xd5, 2...♘g3! wins – not one check helps White!

In the game, after the capture of the queen, there followed: **2...♘g3! 3.♘c6+ ♘de2+** Answering a check with a check. **4.♕xe2+ ♘xe2#**

Here the same operation takes place on the queen's flank.

Position 203
**Mayet**
**Harrwitz**
Berlin, 1847

A position from a game between two well-known masters of long ago, reached via a Queen's Gambit (1.d4 d5 2.c4 e6 3.♘c3 ♘f6 4.♗g5 ♘bd7). White naively took the pawn – **5.cxd5 exd5 6.♘xd5?**

Nowadays, almost every textbook warns for this trap. After **6...♘xd5 7.♗xd8 ♗b4+** White was a piece down.

Many different such tactical rebounds can occur with semi-pinned pieces.

Position 204

In this textbook position, Black lands a deadly blow with the queen sacrifice **1...♗xd3!**, and on **2.♕xd5** (2.♕g4+ ♗g6+) – **2...♗e2#**.

Position 205
**Parr**
**Wheatcroft**
London, 1938

In order to attack the square h6, the rook leaves the queen unguarded: **1.♖h5! ♛xd7 2.♘g5+ ♚h8** And now a different pin is exploited – **3.♖xh6#**

Position 206
**Von Popiel**
**Marco**
Monte Carlo, 1902

In playing **1.♖d1**, White attacked the bishop a third time and Marco resigned. However, he could have won with the move 1...♝g1!. A classical example of unpinning a partially-pinned piece.

Castling can also be used as a means of unpinning.

Position 207
**Silins**
**Tobak**
Polanica Zdroj, 1999

White thought he would win the game with **1.♘xe6**, since the knight is immune because of the pin. But Black took the knight – **1...♛xe6**, and after **2.♖e1** broke the pin by means of **2...♝xf2+ 3.♚xf2 0-0+**. After 4.♚g1 ♛f7 (or 4...♛d7 as in the game) Black has an extra pawn, with his development already complete.

# Exercises

Position 208

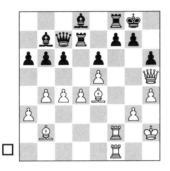

Position 209

Position 210

Position 211

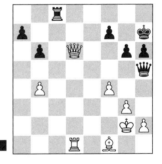

Position 212

Position 213

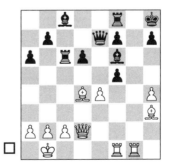

## Position 214

## Position 215

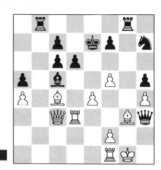

## Position 216

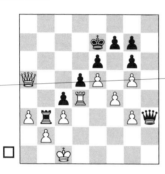

## Position 217

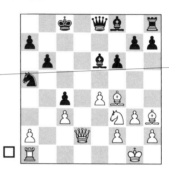

## Position 218

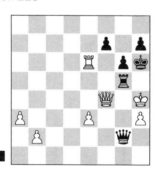

## Position 219

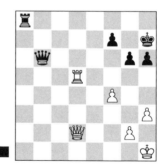

Position 220

Black is attacking the knight. How would you answer?

Position 221

White is a pawn down. Can he re-establish material equality?

Position 222

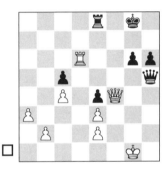

White has an extra pawn and excellently-placed heavy pieces. On **1.♕f6** Black replied **1...♕g4+**. Where should the king retreat to – f2 or f1?

Position 223

In playing **1...dxc4**, Black left his knight under attack. Can it be taken?

# Interference and shutting-off

In combinations using the theme of interference, we either see the connection between two long-range enemy pieces interrupted, or else the path of a long-range piece to a crucial square is shut off.

Position 224
**Kotloman**
**Zinman**
Leningrad, 1985

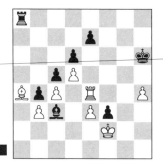

**1...♖xa4 2.bxa4 b3**
Black sacrificed the exchange to get the b-pawn going. After 3.♖xe7 (3.♔xf3 b2; 3.♖e6+ ♗f6) 3...b2 4.♖b7 the bishop shuts off the b-file by 4...♗b4, ensuring that the pawn promotes. **3.♖g4**

Trying to stop the pawn by bringing his rook back to the first rank.

But now the game was decided by another interference: after **3...♗e1+** the pawn promotes.

Position 225
**Neiman**
**Haase**
Correspondence game, 1968

White has already sacrificed a knight and two pawns and crowns his attack with **1.♖e7!**. The rook can be taken neither with the bishop (2.♕xh7#) nor with the rook (2.♕xf8#).

After **1...♕b7+ 2.♗e4 ♕xe4+ 3.♖gxe4 ♗xe7 4.♖xe7** mate still cannot be avoided.

Position 226
**Luchovsky**
**Gridnev**
Correspondence game, 1976

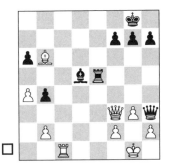

Black thought he was winning here. The queen has to move, and after 1.♖d1 ♕e6 White cannot avoid material loss.

One can easily imagine Black's reaction when he received the postcard bearing the move **1.g4!!**...

Position 227
**Fatalibekova**
**Baumstark**
Tbilisi, 1976

'g2 is attacked indirectly, so there is no threat of ♖h3', decided the German player. So she played **1...♞xe5**.

However, the shutting off of the long diagonal by means of **2.♗d5!** (2.♘d5 would have been even stronger) made the threat real. After 2...exd5 (or a queen retreat) the move 3.♖h3 decides. Black resigned. Instead of 1...♞xe5? the correct continuation was 1...♗c5. The shut-off then does not work, and the pressure on the g2-square neutralises White's threats along the h-file.

Position 228
**Sergeev**
**Panchenko**
USSR, 1984

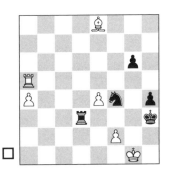

White is threatened with mate. But after **1.♖d5!** it is Black's king which turns out to be in danger. After 1...♘xd5 there follows 2.♗d7#, whilst after 1...♖xd5 2.exd5 White wins the endgame. Nor does 1...♔g4 help (2.♖xd3 ♘xd3 3.a5). The game went **1...♘e2+ 2.♔h1 ♖xd5 3.exd5 g5 4.♗d7+ g4 5.a5 ♘c3 6.a6 ♘xd5 7.a7 ♘b6 8.a8♕ ♘xa8 9.♗c6**. After a knight move, Black is mated on g2, and after a pawn move, on d7.

Position 229
**Réti**
**Bogoljubow**
New York, 1924

**9.♗e8!**, breaking the coordination between rook and bishop, forced capitulation.

For a shut-off in the endgame, here is another classic position.

Position 230
**Nenarokov**
**Grigoriev**
Moscow, 1923

White's position is markedly more active. The inevitable opening up of the position will bring him good attacking prospects.

In an attempt to change the picture, Bogoljubow played **1...exd4** and after **2.exf5 – 2...♖ad8**.

Here, one possible continuation was 3.♕c4+ ♔h8 4.♗xd4 ♗xf5 5.♗h5 and White retains the initiative.

But Réti calculated a variation, concluded by a hidden shut-off. There followed **3.♗h5 ♖e5 4.♗xd4 ♖xf5 5.♖xf5 ♗xf5 6.♕xf5 ♖xd4 7.♖f1 ♖d8**.

If 7...♕e7, then 8.♗f7+ ♔h8 9.♗d5!, shutting off the d-file and not allowing the rook to retreat to d8 and defend the bishop (9...♕f6 10.♕c8).

After the text, a different shut-off decides the game. But first the king must be deflected: **8.♗f7+ ♔h8**, leading to a classic position, which can be found in almost every textbook.

The rook holds up the d-pawn, the bishop the h-pawn. Nevertheless, Black wins:

**1...♗d6!!**

The bishop cannot take the bishop because the d-pawn queens, and after 2.♖xd6 White loses control of the diagonal b8-h2, and 2...h2 ends the game.

Position 231

**Simagin**

**Bronstein**

Moscow, 1947

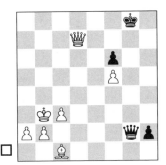

White has an extra bishop, but the black pawn is only one square from queening. What should we do?

**1.♗g5!**

Beautifully played! If 1...fxg5, then 2.f6, and mate is unavoidable. After 1...♕xg5 White takes the pawn on h2 and wins the queen ending: 2.♕d8+ ♔g7 3.♕c7+ ♔g8 4.♕xh2 ♕xf5 5.a4.

That just leaves what happened in the game:

**1...h1♕ 2.♕e8+ ♔g7 3.♕g6+ ♔f8 4.♕xf6+ ♔g8 5.♕d8+ ♔g7**

Or 5...♔f7 6.♕e7+ ♔g8 7.♕e8+.

**6.♕e7+** (6.♗f6+ mates one move faster) **6...♔g8 7.♕e8+**, and Black resigned because of the unavoidable mate (7...♔g7 8.f6+ ♔h7 9.♕f7+ and 10.♕g7#).

# Exercises

Position 232

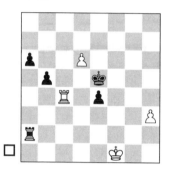

Position 233

Position 234

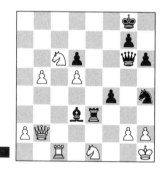

Position 235

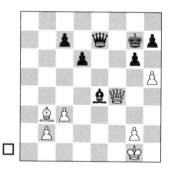

Position 236

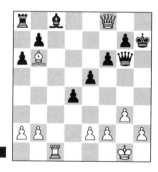

Position 237

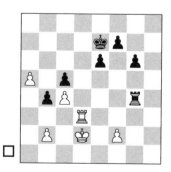

Position 238

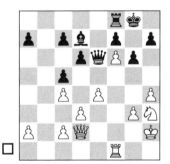

The black king has no cover, but how can we create decisive threats?

Position 239

The king's pawn cover is weakened, and all the white pieces are in the attack. All that remains is to finish the job.

Position 240

Continue the attack.

Position 241

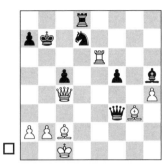

White played **1.♘e5**, after which there followed **1...♛xd4 2.♘xc6 ♛e4+ 3.♗e3 bxc6 4.♘c3 ♛xg2**. Black has won two pawns, but is behind in development. What happens now?

Position 242

Position 243

Black played **1...♘d3**, threatening mate on h2 and attacking the bishop on b2 at the same time. Assess the consequences of **2.♗xh7+**.

The g-pawn is ready to queen, and White cannot create a mate threat with 1.♔g6 because the pawn promotes with check. What can he do?

Position 244

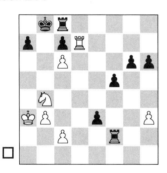

Position 245

How should the game end?

There are two tempting ways to pursue the attack: 1...♕c2 and 1...♗xc3. Which would you choose?

# Combining themes

We have looked so far at examples containing one particular theme, but very often, two or more themes are combined in one situation.

## Deflection and decoy

Position 246
**Smejkal**
**Adorjan**
Vrnjacka Banja, 1972

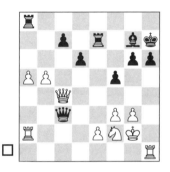

White met the offer of a queen exchange with **1.♖xh6+!**, after which Black had to resign. He cannot take the rook with the bishop because his queen will be undefended, and if 1...♔xh6, then 2.♕h4#.

The rook sacrifice on h6 realises the ideas of deflection (the bishop on g7) and decoy (the king is brought to h6) in one move.

Position 247
**Alekhine**
**Freeman**
Simultaneous display, New York 1924

**1.♖e8+ ♘f8 2.♘h6+** Deflecting the queen opens a path to the square d8. **2...♕xh6 3.♖xf8+** Decoying the king to f8. **3...♔xf8 4.♕d8#**
Here the ideas of deflection and decoy are realised by separate successive sacrifices.
It is not hard to see that 1.♘h6+ would have been a mistake because of 1...♔f8.

And now deflection and decoy in reverse order.

Position 248
**Schmid**
**Rossolimo**
Heidelberg, 1949

Here Rossolimo crowned his attack by sacrificing both rooks:
**1...♖xg2+! 2.♔xg2 ♖xf2+! 3.♗xf2 e3+ 0-1**
The first sacrifice drew the king onto the diagonal of the bishop at b7, and the second deflected the enemy bishop.

Position 249
**Polees**
**Kremenietsky**
Moscow, 1973

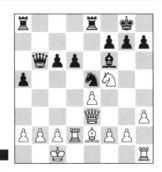

**1...♕xb2+!**
A deflection, after which a discovered check follows.

**2.♔xb2 ♘d3+ 3.♔a3**
Or 3.♔b3 (3.♔b1 ♖ab8+) 3...♖eb8+ 4.♔a4 (4.♔c4 ♘b2#) 4...♖b4+ 5.♔a3 ♗b2#.
**3...♗b2+ 4.♔a4**

**4...♖xe4+!**
Now the rook deflects the queen – 5.♕xe4 ♘c5#. Without this second sacrifice, the combination would not work.
**5.c4**
5.♔b3 a4#.
**5...♖xc4+ 6.♔b3 ♖c3+ 7.♔a4 ♖a3#**

## Deflection and line clearance

Position 250
**Makogonov**
**Flohr**
Tbilisi, 1942

There followed **1.♗b8!** (deflecting the queen and at the same time clearing the d-file ) and Black resigned: 1...♕xb8 2.♕d7+ ♚f8 3.♕d8+ mating.
Other bishop moves also work: 1.♗c5 and after 1...♕c7 – 2.♗b6, and also 1.♗xe5 (1...♘d5 2.♗xg7 ♖xg7 3.♕xf5).

## Deflection and pinning

Position 251
**Pidorich**
**Chernousov**
Tyumen, 1981

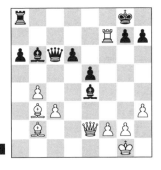

Defending against the discovered check (♖f7-c7+), Black closed the bishop's diagonal with **1...♗d5**. Even so, there followed **2.♖c7!** A deflection (2...♕xc7 3.♗xd5+) and a pin (2...♗xc7 3.♕e4). Material loss is inevitable, and Black resigned.
Instead of 1...♗d5?, the move 1...♔h8 was obligatory, and after 2.♕g4 not 2...♖g8? because of 3.♕xg7+ and 4.♖f8+, but 2...♗g6.

Position 252
**Wolf**
**Burn**
Ostend, 1905

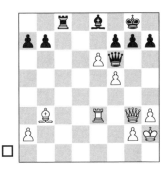

**1.♕c7! ♖xc7** 1...♖a8 2.♕xb7 ♖d8 3.♕c7 only postpones defeat.
**2.exf7+**, and thanks to the pin, there is mate on e8 after any capture.

## Deflection and interference

Position 253
**Hallbauer**
**Mandel**
Berlin, 1952

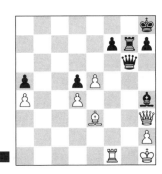

**1...♗f2!**
A deflection after 2.♖xf2 ♕g1# and a shut-off of the f-file after 2.♗xf2 ♕e4+.

White's only way out is **2.♕c8+ ♖g8 3.♕xg8+ ♔xg8 4.♖xf2** (4.♗xf2 ♕c2). However, after **4...♕e4+ 5.♖g2+ ♔f8 6.♗g1 ♕f3** Black won the a-pawn and, easily, the game.

Position 254
**Finn**
**Nugent**
New York, 1900

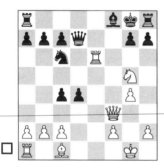

This is a combination from an old line of the Two Knights Defence, best known from the games Maroczy-Vidmar, Ljubljana 1922, and Sämisch-Reiman, Bremen 1927: 1.e4 e5 2.♘f3 ♘c6 3.♗c4 ♘f6 4.d4 exd4 5.0-0 ♗c5 6.e5 d5 7.exf6 dxc4 8.♖e1+ ♗e6 9.♘g5 ♕d5 10.♘c3 ♕f5 11.♘ce4 ♗f8?! (theory considers 11...0-0-0 strongest; 11...gxf6? loses after 12.g4! ♕e5 13.♘f3) 12.♘xf7! ♔xf7 13.♘g5+ ♔g8 (13...♔g6) 14.g4 ♕xf6? (14...♔g6) 15.♖xe6 ♕d8 16.♕f3 ♕d7.
With **1.♖e7!** White placed the rook under attack, forcing his opponent to resign. After 1...♕xe7 (deflection) there follows 2.♕d5+, whilst after 1...♗xe7 or 1...♘xe7 (shut-off) – 2.♕f7#.

Position 255
**Eliskases**
**Hölzl**
Austria, 1931

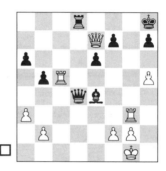

The stunning **1.♖d5!** ended the game. The rook can be taken in several ways, but all lead to mate: 1...♖xd5 2.♕f8# or 1...♕xd5 2.♕f6# (deflection); 1...♗xd5 or 1...exd5 – 2.♕xd8# (shut-off).
That said, 1.♕xf7, 1.♖cg5 or 1.♖e5 would also have been winning.

## Deflection and clearing squares/lines

Position 256
**Daly**
**Rochev**
Bunratty 1999

After **1...♗h4**, White resigned.
Black could also have used deflection and square clearance to give
mate with two knights: **1...♘g3+
2.♔g1 ♕g2+! 3.♖xg2 ♘h3#**

Position 257
**Baburin**
**Adianto**

Liechtenstein, 1993

A typical sacrifice to lure the king
to h1 and free h8 for the queen:
**1...♖h1+! 2.♔xh1 ♖h8+ 3.♔g1 ♖h1+
4.♔xh1** Now the queen comes to h2
with tempo: **4...♕h8+**, and mate.

Position 258
**Richter**
**NN**

Berlin, 1930

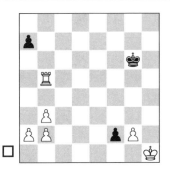

How can the pawn be prevented
from promoting?
**1.♖f5! ♔xf5 2.g4+!**
The black king, which has been
lured to f5, must now provide the
tempo White needs to free g2 for
his king.
After **2...♔xg4 3.♔g2** Black
resigned.

Position 259
**Varavin**
**Zavarnitsky**

USSR, 1991

**1.♕xf7+!**
White has already sacrificed the
rook on a1, and now he sacrifices
the queen, to force the enemy king
to remain in the centre.
**1...♔xf7 2.♗e6+ ♔f6 3.e5+!**
Drawing the king onto the open
file and freeing the e4-square for
the knight (after 3...♘xe5 or 3...dxe5
there is 4.♘e4#).
**3...♔xe5**
The bridges are burned – White has
to checkmate his opponent.

In order to deprive the king of an escape to the d-file, White played a 'quiet' move:

**4.Rd1!**

Creating the deadly threat of 5.f4+ and 6.♘e4#.

**4...♔f6**

If 4...Rf8, then 5.f4+ Rxf4 6.gxf4+ and 7.♘e4#.

**5.♘e4+ ♔e5 6.♗f4+ ♔xe4 7.f3#**

Let us return to the position after Black's second move:

If, instead of 3.e5+, White had chased the king by means of 3.♗g5+, he would have achieved nothing. The black king retreats: 3...♔g7 (not 3...♔xg5? 4.e5! and ♘c3-e4# and not 3...♔e5? 4.Rd1! and 5.f4#) and after 4.♗h6+ ♔f6 (4...♔h7? 5.♗f8#) the position is repeated.

However, after 3.f4!, as after the move played in the game, mate cannot be avoided. The threat is 4.e5+ and after any capture: 5.♘e4#. And if the e4 pawn is blockaded by 3...♘e5, then 4.♗g5+ ♔g7 5.fxe5 dxe5 6.♗h6+ ♔f6 7.Rf1#.

Position 260

**Herrmann**

**Hussong**

Frankfurt am Main, 1930

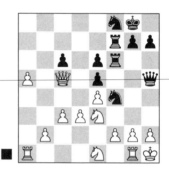

**1...♕xh2+! 2.♔xh2 Rh6+ 3.♔g3 ♘e2+ 4.♔g4 Rf4+ 5.♔g5**

All that remains is to give mate, and with

**5...Rh2**

Black freed the square h6 for the fatal check:

**6.♕xf8+**

Else mate.

**6...♔xf8 7.♘f3**

It seems that when playing 5...♖h2, Black had not calculated all of the variations out fully – 'with such a king, it has to be mate!', he no doubt thought).

But his instinct did not deceive him. As the analysis shows, after both 7.♘f5 ♘xg1 (even stronger is 7...♔f7), and 7.♘g4 h6+ White cannot save himself.

**7...h6+ 8.♔g6 ♔g8 9.♘xh2**

**9...♖f5!** Elegantly freeing the square.

**10.♘xf5** (or 10.exf5) **10...♘f4#**

A striking combination, with quite complicated lines. However, it could have been made rather easier, had Black played 5...♖ff6, 5...♖fh4, or 5...♖g6+, mating quicker than 5...♖h2.

And finally, in the initial position, instead of sacrificing the queen, Black could have played 1...♘d7, in order after 2.♕xc6 (or 2.♕d6, or any other retreat) to give mate without the need for any quiet moves: 2...♕xh2+ 3.♔xh2 ♖h6+ 4.♔g3 ♘e2+ 5.♔g4 ♖f4+ 6.♔g5 ♖g6+ 7.♔h5 ♘f6#.

Position 261
**Kislov**
**Beribesov**
Voronezh, 1971

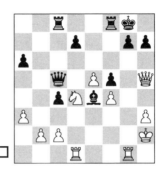

**1.♖xg7+!** Drawing the king onto the seventh rank. **1...♔xg7 2.♘e6+!** Freeing the rook's path to the seventh rank. After 2...dxe6 there follows 3.♖d7+ and mate. Black resigned.

Position 262
**Klaus**
**Wetzel**
GDR, 1970

How can White exploit the open h-file?

There followed 1.♘xh6 ♔xh6 2.♔g2 g5, and the black king

escaped to freedom (in the variation 3.♖e5 ♔g6 4.♗e7 f6 5.♖xe6 ♖f7 Black has three pawns for the piece).

The correct path is the immediate line clearance **1.♔g2!**. On 1...♘xg4 there would follow 2.♖h1+ ♘h6 3.♖xh6+! (decoy) 3...♔xh6 4.♖h1#. Mate occurs slightly later after 1...g5 (instead of 1...♘xg4) 2.♖h1 ♔g6 3.♖xh6+ ♔f5 4.♖e1 ♔xg4 5.f3+ ♔f5 6.♔g3.

## Position 263
### M. Gasparian
### P. Ornstein
Yerevan, 1999

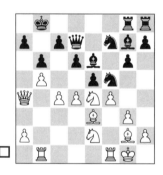

After **1.♖b3** the Swedish girl answered **1...exd4**, preparing to meet an attack on a7 (2.♖a3) with 2...a5.

However, White did not play the move ♖b3-a3 immediately, but only after clearing the long diagonal by means of **2.♘f6!** (2.♘c5! was equally effective).

The stunned Black player stopped the clocks, since after 2...♗xf6 she is mated: 3.♕xa7+ (decoy) 3...♔xa7 4.♖a3+ and 5.♖a8#.

## Decoy and pinning

## Position 264
### Mädler
### Uhlmann
Aschersleben, 1963

By luring the king to h1, Black exploits the diagonal pin: **1...♖e1+ 2.♔h2 ♖h1+! 3.♔xh1 ♕h3+**, and mate next move.

## Position 265
### Ragozin
### Boleslavsky
Moscow, 1945

The pawn can be stopped by 1...♖b8 or 1...♔f7. Out of general considerations, Boleslavsky preferred **1...♔f7** (the king attacks the pawn and also covers the promotion square, whilst the rook is kept for other, more active tasks). However, after **2.e8♕+! ♔xe8 3.♗a4** he had to resign; he loses a rook to the pin.

## Decoy and interference

Position 266
**Koblents**
**Moiseev**
Riga, 1955

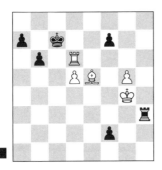

The pawn cannot promote because of the discovered check ♖f6+, whilst after a king retreat, the same rook move stops the pawn, and White remains with an extra piece. True, it is possible to play 1...♖e3, taking the bishop, but giving both f-pawns, which leads to a very sharp situation.

Moiseev found a striking combinative solution. With **1...f5+!** he invites the white king onto the f-file (2.♔xf5 f1♕+). If 2.gxf6, then after 2...f1♕ White doesn't have a good discovered check, as the line has been shut off. Nor does 2.♔xh3 (2...f1♕+ 3.♔h4 ♕e1+ 4.♗g3 ♕h1+) work, so White resigned.

Position 267
**Stolberg**
**Zak**
Gorky, 1938

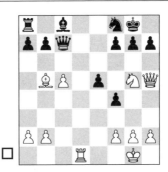

By cutting the queen off from f7, White crowns his attack: **1.♖d7!** **♗xd7** After 1...g6 2.♖xc7 gxh5 3.♘xf7 ♘e6 (3...♗e6 4.♘xe5) 4.♘h6+ ♔h8 5.♖e7 ♘xc5 6.♘f7+ ♔g7 7.♘d6+ ♔f6 8.♖c7 Black's position is hopeless. **2.♕xf7+ ♔h8 3.♗c4 ♘g6** And now the well-known 'smothered mate' – **4.♕g8+ ♖xg8 5.♘f7#**

## Eliminating defenders and deflection

Position 268
**Zheliandinov**
**Mikhalchishin**
Lviv, 1995

Black has two powerful bishops, the pawn on e3 is weak, and he could increase the pressure with 1...♖d6 (2.♗f3 ♗xf3 3.♕xf3 ♖d3). However, the game was decided by a tactic: **1...♖xd2!** Eliminating the defender of the e3-pawn. **2.♖xd2 ♗xe3** Deflecting the queen from the defence of g2. White resigned.

Position 269
**Lilienthal**
**Johannessen**
Oslo, 1976

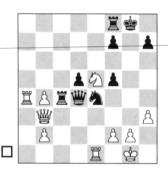

So as to give check with the queen from g3, White eliminates the enemy knight: **1.♖xe4! ♕xe4**
The same combination follows after the capture by the pawn, whilst on 1...♖c1+ 2.♔h2 ♕xf2, 3.♕e3 wins.
**2.♕g3+ ♔h8**

Now the deflection of the rook from the eighth rank decides: **3.♘xf7+** (3...♖xf7 4.♖a8+). Black resigned.

## Eliminating defenders and decoying

Position 270
**Zarovniatov**
**Pankratov**
Correspondence game, 1990

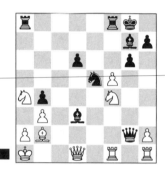

**1...♖xa4!**
Removing the defender of the bishop on b2.
**2.bxa4**
After the queen capture, there follows 2...♖xa2+ 3.♔xa2 ♖a8+ 4.♗a3 ♖xa3+ 5.♔b2 ♘c4+ 6.♔c1 ♖a1#. If 2.♕xd3, then 2...♖xa2+ 3.♔xa2 ♕a8+, whilst after 2.♘xd3 simply 2...♘xd3.
**2...♕xb2+!**
Decoying the king, which is then hunted down.
**3.♔xb2 ♘c4+ 4.♔b3**
4.♔c1 ♗b2#.
**4...♘a5+ 5.♔xb4 ♖b8+ 6.♔xa5 ♗c3#**
The final position deserves a diagram:

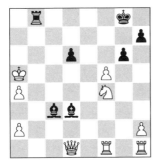

## Eliminating defenders and clearing lines

**Position 271**
**Rubinstein**
**Hirschbein**

Lodz, 1927

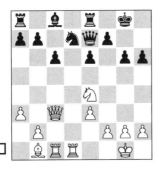

**1.♖xd7!** Eliminating the defender of f6. **1...♗xd7 2.♘f6+ ♚f8**

**3.♘d5!** Clearing the long diagonal, with an attack on the queen. Black resigned.

**Position 272**
**Levenfish**
**Freiman**

Leningrad, 1925

The queen sacrifice on h6 leaps to the eye: **1.♗xh6 gxh6 2.♖xh6+** (2.♕d2 is even stronger) **2...♚g7,** but what next?

Answer: **3.♗b7!**
By attacking the queen, the bishop clears the diagonal with tempo. Mate is threatened on g6, so the queen must be surrendered: **3...♚xh6 4.♗xa6** and Black's position is lost.

## Eliminating defenders and interference

Position 273
**Bologan**
**Movsesian**
Sarajevo, 2005

White sacrificed his central pawn:
**1.d5 exd5 2.cxd5 ♘xd5 3.♗c4**,
intending after 3...♘5f6 or 3...♘f4
to play 4.♘g3. Black, however,
preferred **3...♘b4**,

believing he had nothing to fear
from the opened diagonal.
After 4.♕c3, the reply 4...♘f6
is solid enough. But what if
this defender of the kingside is
eliminated?
There followed **4.♖xd7! ♕xd7**.

Understandably, not 4...♗xd7, since
after 5.♕c3 the game ends.
**5.♕c3 ♕g4**

The pawn on f7 is fixed because of
the pin, but Black believed that his
last move was perfectly good. And
he would have been right, had it not
been for the knight jump, shutting
off the queen from the attacked
square g7: after **6.♘fg5!** Black had
to give up the queen – **6...♕xg5
7.♘xg5 ♗f6 8.♕f3**, and White
easily realised his advantage.

## Deflection, decoy and interference

Position 274
**Karafiath**
**Neishtadt**
Correspondence game, 1965-66

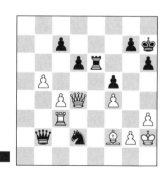

The game was ended by the tactical blow **1...♖e3!** which illustrates both deflection and decoying into a fork: 2.♗xe3 ♘f3+ 3.♔g3 ♘xd4 4.♗xd4 ♕d2; 2.♕xe3 ♘f1+, and also interference: the rook on c3 is attacked, and after 2.♖d3 the move 2...♘f3+ wins.

## Deflection, eliminating defenders and decoying

Position 275
**Skuja**
**Rozenberg**
Riga, 1962

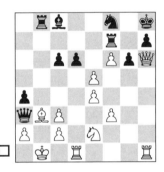

The bishop on b3 is pinned and attacked. However, it plays a key role.

There followed **1.♕xf8+!**.
Deflection (of the rook at f7) and at the same elimination of the defender of h7. **1...♖xf8 2.♖xh7+**
Decoying.
**2...♔xh7 3.♖h1+**
And Black resigned.

## Decoy, interference and clearing squares

Position 276
**Gershon**
**Zilberman**
Israel, 2000

A general glance reveals that the position is better for White, as confirmed by the tempting 1.♗xh5 gxh5 2.♘g3 ♗d4 3.♖g2 (3...fxe4 4.♘cxe4; 3...h4 4.♘xf5 ♗xf5 5.exf5 ♖xf5 6.♖e1 or 6.♘e2).
But drawing out the black king is much more decisive:
**1.♖xg6! ♔xg6 2.♗xh5+ ♔xh5**
Forced, since 2...♔h7 3.♗xf7 and 4.♘g3 does not need any assessment.
**3.♖g1!**

White has sacrificed a rook to reach this position. And not for nothing. One imagines that he had not calculated every variation to the end, only looking at the first 2-3 moves. For example, 3...♖g8 4.exf5 or 4.♕d1 ♗xc3 5.exf5; 3...♗f6 4.exf5; 3...fxe4 4.♕xe4 or 4.♘g3+.

**3...♗xc3**

This also loses.

**4.♕xc3**

There is no satisfactory defence against the threat of ♕h3+.

**4...fxe4 5.f5!**

Interference (after 5...♖xf5, 6.♕h3+) and at the same time freeing the square for the knight.

**5...♕h4**

Mate also follows after other replies.

**6.♕h3**

Pretty, but not forced. Any of 6.♘g3+, 6.♘f4+, and 6.♕e3 were also possible.

**6...♕xh3 7.♘f4+ ♔h4 8.♗e1+ ♕g3 9.♖xg3**

Black resigned.

# Eliminating defenders, decoy and clearing lines

Position 277
**Rossolimo**
**NN**
Paris, 1944

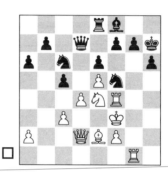

**1.♖xf5!**

Eliminating the defender of h6.

**1...exf5 2.♕xh6+!** Decoying.

**2...♔xh6** If 2...gxh6, then 3.♘f6+ and 4.♖g8#. **3.♖h1+ ♔g6**

But where is the mate? After all, White is a queen down...

**4.♔f4!**

Clearing the diagonal for the bishop; the threat is 5.♗h5+ and 6.♗xf7#.

**4...♕e6 5.♖h8!**

The final subtlety. After 5.♗h5+ ♔h7 6.♗xf7+ there follows 6...♕h6+. Now there is no defence to mate on h5, so Black resigned.

## Eliminating defenders, clearing lines and deflection

Position 278
**Bulach**
**Petrov**
Moscow, 1951

The white king is clearly uncomfortable, the squares d2 and c1 being his Achilles Heel. First the knight, which is defending d2, is eliminated.
**1...♖xf3! 2.gxf3**
Then the d-file is cleared.
**2...♗xb3+** Or 2...♗e4+. **3.axb3**

With the move **3...♕c1+!** Black deflects the rook from the d-file and mates: **4.♖xc1 ♖d2#**

## Clearing squares, decoy and deflection

Position 279
**Kristanov**
**Nikolov**
Sofia, 1979

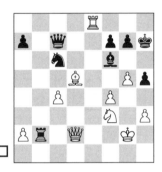

In reply to g4-g5, Black pinned the queen, expecting to win it for rook and a minor piece.
However, there followed **1.g6+!**. The combination begins with the clearing of the g5-square for the knight, if Black takes on g6 with the pawn. After other captures, the king is drawn into a mating net (1...♔xg6 2.♗e4+ and 3.♖h8#). If 1...♔h6, then 2.♖h8+ and 3.♗e4#.
**1...fxg6 2.♕xb2!**
Deflection. The queen cannot be taken – 3.♘g5+ ♔h6 4.♖h8#. This means that White has a decisive material advantage.

## Clearing lines, eliminating defenders, deflection and pinning, decoy

Position 280
**Korchmar**
**Polyak**
USSR, 1938

If it were not for the knight on d6, White could win immediately with a rook check on e8, and therefore he played **1.♘b4!**, clearing the d-file. **1...axb4 2.♕xd6!** Eliminating a defender. The queen cannot be taken, but it seems that Black can defend against the threats by means of **2...♕d7.**

Now 3.♕xd7 ♖xd7 4.♖e8+ ♔f7 favours Black.

However, the combination is not finished. By using the ideas of deflection and pinning, White again puts his queen en prise:
**3.♕d5!!**
If it is taken, then 4.♖e8+ ♖f8 5.♖xg7+ and 6.♖xf8+. Meanwhile, there is a threat of 4.♖xg7+. After 3...g6 there follows 4.♖ge3 and Black is mated.
That leaves the move **3...♔f8**, unpinning the rook on f7.

**4.♖xg7!**
Now another pin decides. After 4...♖xg7 the queen is undefended. After **4...♕xd5** there follows **5.♖g8+!** (decoying) **5...♔xg8 6.♖e8+ ♖f8 7.♖xf8#.**

# Exercises

Position 281

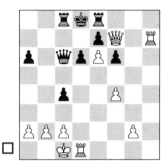

Position 282

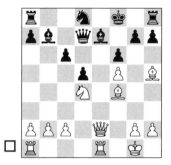

Position 283

Position 284

Position 285

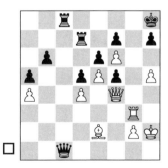

Position 286

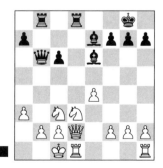

Position 287

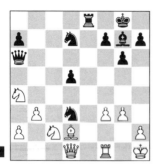

Position 288

Position 289

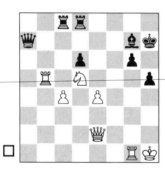

Position 290

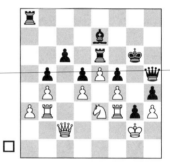

Position 291

Position 292

Position 293

Position 294

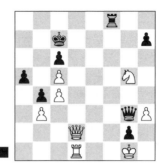

Position 295

Position 296

Position 297

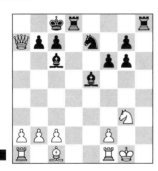

Position 298

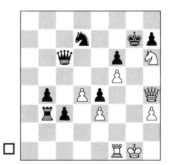

Position 299

**1...♜c2** was played. Can White take the pawn on d5?

Position 300

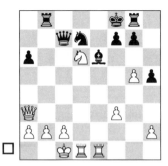

White has sacrificed a piece to prevent his opponent from castling. Discovered checks leap to the eye, but which one?

Position 301

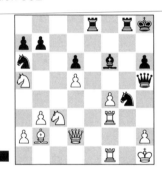

Finish off the attack.

Position 302

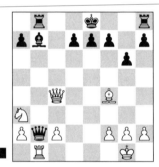

At the end of a complicated variation, White attacks the queen (♖a1-b1), assessing the position as roughly equal (1...♛xa3 2.♗xb8). Was he correct?

Position 303

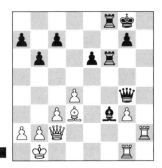

After **1...♗e4** with the threat of 2...♖f1+ (2.♗xe4 ♖f1+) White replied **2.♕d1**. Assess this move.

Position 304

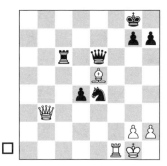

How should the game end?

Position 305

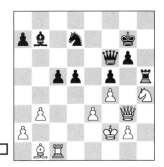

Is Black's kingside really well-defended?

Position 306

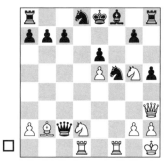

In the interest of rapid development, White has sacrificed two pawns. Now, by playing **1.♘de4**, he puts his bishop en prise. Is this sacrifice correct?

Position 307

White has sacrificed a piece to reach this position. The c2-square is attacked. What should White do?

Position 308

Black sacrificed a piece, ready to play a sharp endgame after **1...♘b3 2.♕f2 ♕xf2+ 3.♔xf2 ♘xc1 4.♗xc1 ♗xg2**. Check this variation.

Position 309

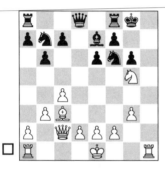

White has sacrificed a knight to open the h-file, and his pieces are aiming at the kingside. By playing **1.♕e4**, he threatens to bring the queen to h4. It cannot be taken because of mate on h8. How can Black defend?

Position 310

Black opens the a-file with **1...♘b3+ 2.axb3 axb3** and threatens the move 3...♖a1+. What can White do?

# Pawns on the brink

Thus far, we have looked at how combinations are found. In this and the subsequent sections, we will look at examples where the final outcome is the connecting factor.

It was allegedly Napoleon who said that 'Every soldier carries a marshal's baton in his knapsack'. Even so, neither in the wars of Napoleon's time nor in later ones do soldiers get to become marshals. But in the chessboard army, this fairytale transformation awaits any humble pawn which manages to reach the other end of the board.

When looking at combinations on the theme of deflection and other themes, we have already seen how a sacrifice can open up the possibility of a pawn promoting.

Position 311
**Sokolsky**
**Navrodsky**
Omsk, 1944

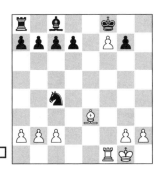

Black has an extra piece, and the bishop on e3 is attacked. But after **1.♗d4** there is no defence to ♗d4xg7+ and f7-f8♕.
The pawn promotion could also be assured by 1.♗g5 with the unstoppable threat of 2.♗e7+.

Position 312

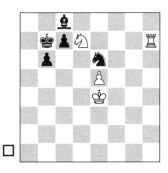

The move **1.♖e7** was played, and Black decided that his opponent had overlooked an elementary fork. There followed **1...♗xd7 2.♖xd7 ♘c5+ 3.♔f5! ♘xd7**. Black has achieved his aim, but his joy was short-lived. After **4.e6 ♔c8 5.e7** he had to resign.
(from a game between two amateurs, played in Belgium in 1968)

105

Position 313
**Kataev**
**Markov**
Bor, 1977

White threatens to take the pawn on f4, and Black can defend it by playing e.g. 1...♘d3, 1...♘g6 or 1...♗h6.

But in the game, he played **1...♖d1!**, and White resigned – he cannot prevent the pawn promoting.

Position 314
**Stoltz**
**Nimzowitsch**
Berlin, 1928

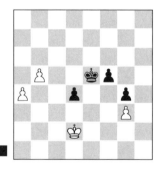

White has connected passed pawns. Black has not yet created a second passed pawn, but he still wins:

**1...f4 2.gxf4+**
After 2.a5 or 2.b6 – 2...♔d6.

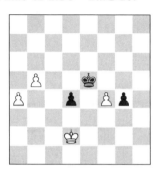

**2...♔d6!**
Now the king watches securely over the a- and b-pawns, while one of the black pawns reaches the first rank.

**3.a5 g3 4.a6 ♔c7 5.♔e2 d3+ 6.♔xd3 g2 0-1**

Position 315
**Medina Garcia**
**Tal**
Mallorca, 1979

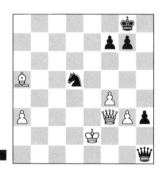

With his last move, White offered the exchange of queens.
Tal cheerfully accepted with **1...♕xf3+ 2.♔xf3**, and then played **2...♘e3!**. The pawn cannot be stopped, and White resigned.

Position 316
**Seipel**
**Arnegaard**
Correspondence game, 1902

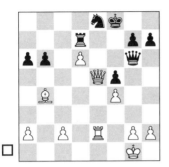

Black's position is very poor –
White only has to play 1.♕c3, 1.♕d4
or 1.♕d5. But a combination is the
quickest way to win:
**1.♕e7+! ♖xe7 2.d7!**
Do not take, but go past! The pawn
will queen, and Black resigned.

Position 317
**Dikchit**
**Kaliansundaram**
India, 1964

How can the pawn on e7 be given
wings? After 1.♗a4 Black replies
1...♗d6.

Instead, White decided things with
**1.♗c2+ ♔g8 2.♖f8+! ♖xf8**

**3.♗b3+!.**
Black resigned.

Position 318
**Engels**
**Maroczy**
Dresden, 1936

White has the advantage. He could
play 1.♕b4. If 1...♗d4, then 2.♗xe5
(2...♖c4 3.♕e1; 2...♗xe5 3.♕xb6),
and after 1...♘a4 – 2.d7 ♖d8 3.♕e7.
But there is a more effective
combinative route. By sacrificing
the exchange and then the queen,
White opens up the path for the
pawn to promote:
**1.♖xb2! ♕xb2 2.♕xc8+! ♘xc8 3.d7**
Black resigned.

107

Position 319
**Patience**
**Tilson**
England, 1964

There followed **1.♕xd4+! cxd4
2.♗g7+! ♔xg7** 2...♖xg7 3.♖xe8+.
**3.♖xe7+ ♖xe7.**
After 3...♔f6 4.♖xe8 ♕c2+ 5.♔g3 or
4...♕g5+ 5.♔f2 ♕d2+ 6.♖e2 White
gets a new queen, with two extra
rooks.
**4.h8♕+ ♔f7 5.♖h7+ ♔e6 6.♕c8+
♔f6** 6...♔d5 7.♕xf5+ and 8.♖xe7.
**7.♕f8+** Black resigned.

Position 320
**Chistiakov**
**Vakhsberg**
Moscow, 1938

White has an extra knight, whilst
Black's hopes are pinned on the

passed pawn. When playing **1.♘e3**,
White counted on 1...c3, when he
intended 2.♖d1. Then 2...♕f6? loses
at once to 3.♕xf6. 'If 2...♕xd1+
3.♘xd1 ♖xd1+ 4.♔g2,' – he thought,
'the pawn cannot advance because
of the threat 5.♕c8+'...
The moves **1...c3 2.♖d1? ♕xd1+
3.♘xd1** were indeed played, but
Vakhsberg did not take the knight.

There followed **3...c2!** instead of
3...♖xd1+?. **4.♘e3 c1♕+ 5.♔g2 ♕c8**.
Black has not only won back the
piece, but remains with an extra
exchange.

Position 321
**Veltmander**
**Polugaevsky**
Sochi, 1958

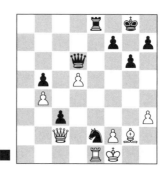

**1...♞g3+!** A sacrifice solely for the purpose of exchanging all the pieces and presenting the c-pawn with his marshal's baton.
**2.fxg3 ♛f6+ 3.♛f2 ♜xe1+ 4.♚xe1 ♛xf2+ 5.♚xf2 c2 0-1**

Position 322
**Ortueta**
**Sanz**
Madrid, 1933

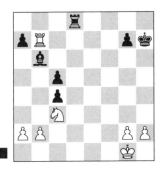

The finish to this seemingly simple ending was remarkable.
There followed **1...♜d2 2.♞a4**, and now Black suddenly sacrificed a rook – **2...♜xb2!! 3.♞xb2 c3.**

After 4.♞d3 there follows 4...c4+ 5.♚f1 cxd3, winning. If instead of 5.♚f1 White plays 5.♜xb6, then 5...cxd3 6.♚f2 c2 or 6.♜c6 d2.

But White can change the move-order, taking on b6 at once, and apparently refuting the combination: **4.♜xb6**
Now on 4...axb6 there follows 5.♞d3, when White stops the pawns and wins. What had Black planned?
**4...c4!!**
The pawns prove stronger than a rook and a knight. Now if 5.♞xc4, then 5...c2, and the pawn promotes. Also bad for White is 5.♜e6 cxb2 6.♜e1 c3.
That only leaves **5.♜b4.**

But then **5...a5!** – a third pawn comes into play, with decisive effect. **6.♞xc4 6.♜xc4 cxb2. 6...c2**
White resigned.

One of the most remarkable endgames in the history of chess. This bewitching finish was first published in the *Wiener Schachzeitung* (1934), and in Russia, in *Shakhmatny Ezhegodnik* (1937). With the above position (the preceding moves were not known), it appeared in my *Chess Practice* (1980). Since then I have found the full score of the game, and it appears that the crucial position requires some amendment.

Black had pawns on e6 and g5, whilst the white pawn stood not on h2, but h3.

The combination still works. The 'surgical operation' to remove the pawns on e6 and g5, in the popularly-quoted position, can be explained by the fact that they are superfluous, since they do not take part in the combination and simply clutter the position.

In addition, after **1...♖d2 2.♘a4** Black could realise his material advantage by playing, say, **2...e5**.

If **3.♘xb6** (on 3.♖e7 Black wins by 3...♖xb2 4.♘xb2 c3 5.♖xe5 cxb2 6.♖e1 c4+), then **3...♖xb2 4.♖xa7 c3**.

Even more remarkably, as Dutch author Tim Krabbé has found out,

the entire combination had been played before!

## Tylkowski
## Wojciechowski

Poznan, 1931

Black won with the same sequence of moves: 30...♖xb2 31.♘xb2 c3 32.♖xb6 c4 33.♖b4 (White could have gone for 33.♘xc4 c2 34.♖c6 c1♕+ 35.♔h2 with some chances of survival) 33...a5 34.♘xc4 c2 and with this pawn structure, Tylkowski could play on a little longer: 35.♘xa5 c1♕+ 36.♔h2 ♕c5 37.♖b2 ♕xa5 38.g4 ♕e1 39.g3 h5 40.gxh5 ♔h6 and fifteen moves later he resigned, as Krabbé wrote in his book *Nieuwe Schaakkuriosa* ('New Chess Curiosities').

More often, we see a pawn reach the promotion square in the endgame, when few pieces remain on the board. It is rarer in the middlegame, and rarest of all in the opening.
Let's have a look at the following opening position.

Position 323
**Kahn**
**NN**
Paris, 1929

Play continued **1.cxd5 ♕xb3 2.axb3**. Now, before retaking on d5, Black exchanged bishop for knight – **2...♗xb1**.
His opponent's reply **3.dxc6** he assumed to be a blunder, and he happily retreated the bishop, so as to defend b7 – **3...♗e4**.

Play lasted just two more moves: **4.♖xa7 ♖xa7 5.c7** and 'the soldier became a marshal.'
Doubtless the French master's anonymous opponent was unaware of the classic game Schlechter-Perlis, Vienna 1911, published in almost all textbooks: 1.d4 d5 2.c4

c6 3.♘f3 ♘f6 4.e3 ♗f5 5.♕b3 ♕b6 6.cxd5 ♕xb3 7.axb3 ♗xb1? 8.dxc6.

Perlis slightly belatedly realised his mistake and did not retreat the bishop to e4. instead, he continued 8...♘xc6 9.♖xb1 and remained a pawn down.

And finally, a pawn underpromotion to a knight.

Position 324
**Gulko**
**Grigorian**
Vilnius, 1971

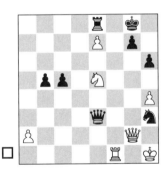

After **1.♖f8+! ♖xf8 2.♕d5+ ♔h7** Black is mated:
**3.exf8♘+! ♔h8 4.♘eg6#**, whereas the simple-minded 3.exf8♕? would allow 3...♕g1#.

# Exercises

Position 325

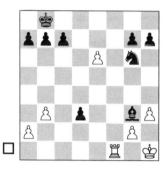

Position 326

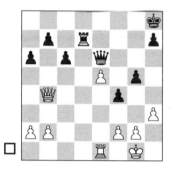

Position 327

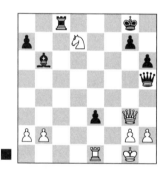

Position 328

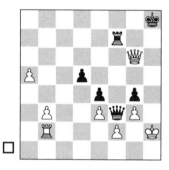

Position 329

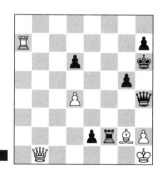

Position 330

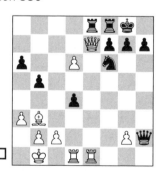

Position 331

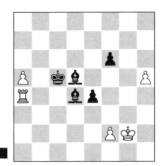

All hopes rest on the e-pawn...

Position 332

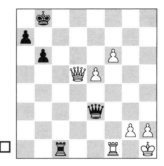

**1.♕b5? ♕f4! 2.♔g1 ♕e3+** was played, and the game ended in a draw. But in the initial position, White could have won. How?

Position 333

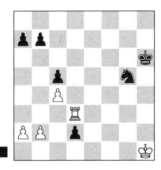

The pawn on d2 is attacked, and the promotion square is under control. Even so...

Position 334

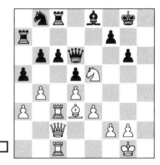

Exploiting the pin, White played **1.b5**, attacking the c6-pawn for a fifth time. Assess the position after the reply **1...c5**.

Position 335

Both 1...♖xg2+, and 1...♖xf3 are threatened. What is your reply?

Position 336

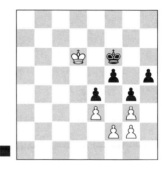

Whom does this ending favour?

Position 337

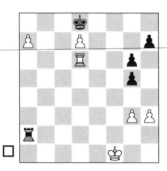

Analyse the position.

Position 338

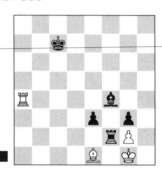

By attacking the rook, White breathed a sigh of relief. The worst is behind him... or is it?

# Miracle saves

Imagine we are at the cinema, watching a detective film. The hero is surrounded on all sides by enemies. His situation seems desperate, and a tragic end seems inevitable. But at the very last moment, when no hope seems to remain, our hero makes a miraculous escape and emerges intact from the danger. The author manages to create a scenario in which a most unlikely salvation comes to the hero, so beloved by the viewers, who do not want to believe in his final doom.

Such miracle escapes are described as 'like in a novel' or 'like in a film'. Chess players say 'like in an endgame study' to describe similar chessboard miracles.

Indeed, we will start with a study.

Position 339
**A. Troitzky**
1895

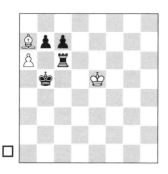

After **1.axb7** it is not obvious how a new queen can be prevented from appearing. But the black king can still move, and stalemate cannot be overlooked...
There is a way to save himself:
**1...♖e6+! 2.♔xe6**

**2...♔c6!!**
Now 3.b8♕(♖) leads to stalemate, after 3.b8♘+ there is 3...♔b7, and a piece is lost, whilst after 3.b8♗ ♔b7 the bishops have to defend one another; the black king moves between the squares b7 and a8, and the approach of the white king results in stalemate.

Many amazing occurrences are bound up with stalemate.

115

Position 340
**G. Jones**
**Asmundsson**
Internet, 2004

One does not usually see such positions played on, since White now queens with **1.b8♕**. Nonetheless, the game continued: **1...♘d3 2.♕g8+ ♔h5 3.♕xh7+ ♔g4** White can checkmate in various ways; for example, 4.♖c4+ ♘f4 5.♕h3#. However, he played **4.♖xf6?** (defending against mate from the knight at f2, and threatening 5.♕h3#).

And now: **4...♘f2+! 5.♖xf2 ♖xg1+**. After the rook is taken, it is stalemate.

Position 341
**Lipok**
**Gnegel**
Germany, 2002/03

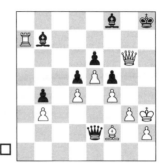

'Why not take the bishop? After **1.♖xb7 ♕f1+ 2.♔h4** Black's king has no moves, but the bishop does...' But after **2...♗e7+ 3.♖xe7** (3.♔h5? ♕h3#) **3...♕h3+ 4.♔g5 ♕h4+ 5.gxh4** led to stalemate.

Position 342
**Tornay Gomez**
**Cuero Reid**
Vitoria, 2003

White decided to finish things with **1.♖d7+ ♔h6 2.h4**, but ran into **2...♕h3+!**, and any capture is stalemate.

Position 343
**Fercec**
**Cvitan**
Croatia, 1996

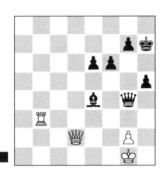

Of course, Black's position is winning. For example, he could play 1...h4 or 1...e5. But, after looking ahead a couple of moves, Black decided that the simplest thing to do was take the opponent's last pawn: **1...♗xg2**, expecting 2.♕xg2 ♕d1+ and 3...♕xb3... The stunning reply was **2.♖g3!** and after **2...♕xg3**

**3.♕h6+! ♚g8** (if the queen is taken it is stalemate) **4.♕h8+ ♚f7 5.♕e8+ ♚xe8** a draw resulted.

Even the strongest players are not immune to stalemate surprises.

Position 344
**Hübner**
**Adorjan**
Bad Lauterberg, 1980

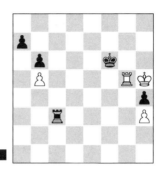

Instead of taking the h-pawn by 1...♖xh3 with a line such as 2.♖d5 ♚e6 3.♖d1 (3.♖g5 ♖g3) 3...♖b3 or 2.♖g6+ ♚e5 3.♖g7 ♚d6 4.♖xa7 ♚c5, Adorjan decided to win at once, by forcing the exchange of rooks: **1...♖c5?**
After the cold-blooded **2.♚xh4!** he had to agree a draw sincee taking the rook leads to stalemate, and otherwise the rook ending is a draw.

Position 345
**Browne**
**Planinc**
Wijk aan Zee, 1974

Black played **1...♗xe3**, and Browne, in time-trouble, automatically replied **2.fxe3?** (correct was 2.♕e8+ ♔h7 3.♕d7+ and only then 4.fxe3). White has three extra pawns, but the suicidal black queen saves the draw: **2...♕h2+** Or 2...♕f2+, 2...♕h1+, 2...♕h3+. **3.♔f3 ♕e2+ 4.♔g3 ♕g2+** (5.♔xg2 – stalemate).

Position 346
**Greco**
17th century

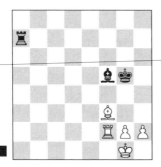

This example is taken from Greco's book *The Royall Game of Chesse-play*, written at the start of the 17th century.
Here there is no mate, but there is a draw:
**1...♖a1+ 2.♖f1 ♖xf1+ 3.♔xf1**

**3...♗h3! ½-½**
After 4.gxh3 (if White does not take the bishop, Black sacrifices it for the g-pawn anyway), we reach a theoretical ending, in which the king, bishop and rook's pawns cannot win against the lone king, if the bishop (in this case, a light-squared bishop) does not control the queening square of the pawn.

Stalemate combinations involving the forceful offloading of superfluous pieces are always entertaining.

Position 347
**Stolberg**
**Pimenov**
Rostov-on-Don 1941

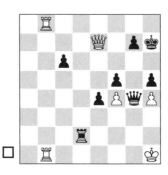

By a rook sacrifice, Black has stripped away the enemy king's pawn cover, and mate seems inevitable. However, White found a tactical resource in reply: by sacrificing all his remaining material, he saves himself:
**1.♖h8+! ♔xh8** 1...♔g6 2.♕e6#.
**2.♖b8+ ♔h7 3.♖h8+ ♔xh8 4.♕xg7+**
Whichever way Black takes the queen, White is stalemated.

Position 348
**Karacsony**
**Borbely**
Romania, 1948

White has four extra pawns and threatens ♕d5#. The game would be over if the black king had a square to move to. But because he does not, and the f6-pawn is blocked, Black can rid himself of his remaining pieces:
**1...♘f4+! 2.gxf4** 2.♔f3 ♕e2+ 3.♔xf4 ♕f3+ 4.♔xf3 also leads to stalemate. **2...♕xf2+ 3.♔h3 ♕xh2+ 4.♔g4 ♕h3+ 5.♔xh3** – stalemate.

Position 349
**Reefschläger**
**Seppeur**
West Germany 1982/83

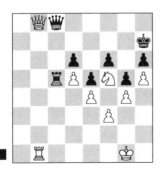

White has an extra (and very powerful) knight. Black's hopes are connected with the exposed position of the enemy king. There followed **1...♖c1+ 2.♔g2 ♕c2+ 3.♔h3**.

The rook cannot be taken because of the deadly check on a7. But bearing in mind that the black king has no moves, and all five of his pawns are blockaded, it is easy to see the saving combination: **3...♖h1+! 4.♖xh1 ♕g2+ 5.♔xg2** – stalemate. Another way for Black to draw was **1...♕xb8 2.♖xb8 ♖c2+** with perpetual check or stalemate.

Position 350
**Gogolev**
**Varshavsky**
Aluksne, 1967

With his last move White, who has an extra knight, offered the exchange of queens, and at the same time attacked the square h7. The variation **1...♖d1+ 2.♔h2 ♕g1+ 3.♔g3** suited him very well...

White had headed for this position, in the belief that his king was safe. However, there followed **3...♖d3+! 4.♕xd3 ♕e3+! 5.♕xe3** – stalemate. The unblocked pawn on g5 turns out to be pinned.

Position 351
**Rovner**
**Guldin**
Leningrad, 1939

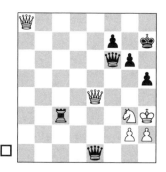

In this fantastic position with four queens on the board, which occurred in a real game, White is an exchange and a pawn down.
The queen on e1 cannot be taken because of 1...♕f5+ and 2...♕g4#. But White can save himself by giving away his queens:
**1.♕g8+! ♔xg8** After 1...♔h6 2.♕f8+ Black would have to return the king to h7, since it cannot go to g5 because of 3.♕h4#. However, the queen could also have been sacrificed – 2.♕f4+ ♕xf4 3.♕xg6+, which leads to stalemate immediately. **2.♕e8+** Preparing to immolate the other queen. **2...♔h7 3.♕g8+ ♔h6 4.♕h7+ ♔g5 5.♕h6+ ♔xh6** – stalemate.

No wonder Tartakower described stalemate as the tragicomedy of chess.

The following examples show stalemate in a prepared set-up with the help of a quiet move.

Position 352
**Zhdanov**
**Pigits**
Riga, 1953

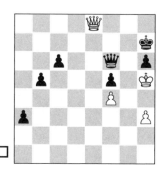

Black has too many pawns. After 1.♕d7+ ♔g8 2.♕e8+ ♔g7 White can resign, since after the next check 3.♕d7+ there follows 3...♕f7+. But with the quiet move **1.h4!!** (threatening stalemate after 2.♕g8+; if 1...♕d4, then 2.♕g6+ ♔h8 3.♕h7+) White saved half a point.

Position 353

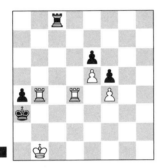

In this textbook position, Black is a rook down, but **1...♖b8!** draws.

Position 354
**Marshall**
**NN**
New York, 1923

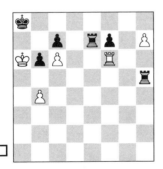

The h7 pawn is lost and White is a rook down. Is it time to resign?

But look: if the rook on f6 and the h-pawn are taken from the board, and we play b4-b5, White will have no moves. Therefore **1.♖h6! ♖xh6 2.h8♕+ ♖xh8 3.b5**.

Black can only release the stalemate by playing 3...♖d7, but after 4.cxd7 White will give the d-pawn on his next move, and it will still be stalemate, whilst after 4...c5? (or 4...c6?) White actually wins. There were also other solutions here, e.g. 1.♖xf7 ♖xf7 2.b5.
Now we will look at some miracle saves by means of perpetual check.

Position 355
**Kratkovsky**
**Lapsis**
USSR, 1982

In the previous play, White had lost a bishop. But after a mistaken queen move to b6, he has a happy chance to save himself: **1.♖xf8+ ♗xf8 2.♕g8+! ♔xg8 3.♘h6+ ♔h8 4.♘f7+** with perpetual check.

Position 356
**Neumann**
**NN**

East Germany, 1956

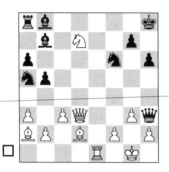

White drew by **1.♖e8+! ♘xe8 2.♕h7+! ♔xh7 3.♘f8+ ♔h8 4.♘g6+** with perpetual check.

A more complicated way was 1.♕h7+ ♘xh7 (on 1...♔xh7 there is 2.♘f8+ and 3.♘g6+) 2.♖e8+ ♘f8 3.♖xf8+ ♔h7 4.♗g8+ ♔g6 5.♗f7+

and after 5...♔f5 6.♗d5+ ♔g6 (6...♔g4? 7.f3+, mating) 7.♗f7+ it is again perpetual check.

Position 357
**Budovich**
**Kosikov**

Beltsı, 1979

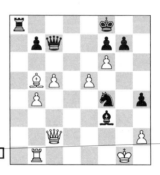

When playing **1.♕h7**, White was convinced that he was winning. After 1...gxf6 there comes 2.♕h8+ ♔e7 3.♕xf6+ ♔f8 4.♕h8+ ♔e7 5.♕xh4+.

But Black found the saving line: **1...♘h3+ 2.♔f1 ♗g2+! 3.♔xg2** The bishop must be taken, since if the king retreats, there is 3...♕xe5+.

**3...♖a2+ 4.♔h1** The knight is immune – 4.♔xh3? ♕c8+, and if 4.♔f3?, then 4...♘g5+. **4...♘f2+**

**5.♔g1** (or 5.♔g2) **5...♘h3+** and a draw, since the king cannot come to f1 because of 6...♖f2+ 7.♔e1 ♕xe5+.

## Position 358
**Brenninkmeijer**
**Van der Sterren**

Amsterdam, 1995

White has sacrificed two pawns for the attack, but the threats to his queenside are more important. A logical continuation was 1...♘c4, in order after 2.fxg7 to reply 2...♖fd8, with the advantage. For example: 3.♕f3 ♕d7 4.♖f2 d3 or 3.♗a1 ♕xa3 4.♕f3 ♕e7.

The attack 2.♕g3 (instead of 2.fxg7) 2...g6 3.♕g5 would be refuted by 3...♔h8 4.♕h6 ♖g8, and after 5.♖f3 (5.cxd4 g5 and ♖g8-g6) Black has 5...♖c5.

However, Black decided that the simple **1...dxc3** promised a safe advantage, and after **2.fxg7 ♖fd8 3.♖xc3 – 3...♘c4.**

However, he had overlooked the queen sacrifice **4.♕xh7+! ♔xh7 5.♖h3+.** After **5...♔g6** (or else it is mate) the game ended with a repetition of moves – **6.♖g3+ ♔h5 7.♖h3+** Draw.

# Exercises

Position 359

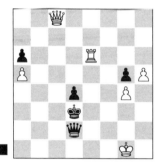

Position 360

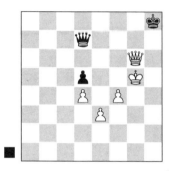

Position 361

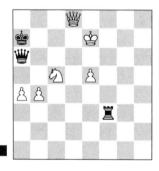

Position 362

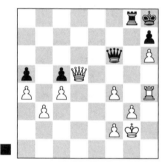

Position 363

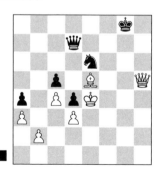

Position 364

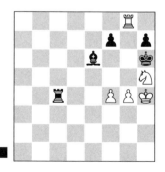

Position 365

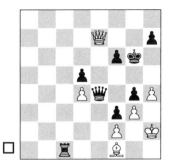

Position 366

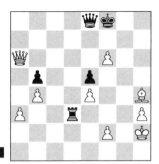

Position 367

Position 368

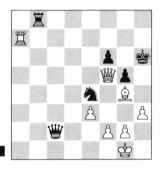

Position 369

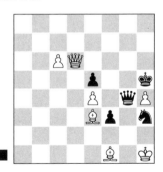

Position 370

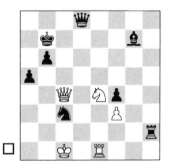

Position 371

Position 372

Position 373

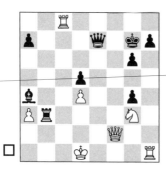

Position 374

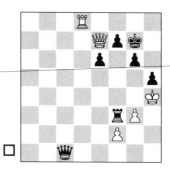

Position 375

Position 376

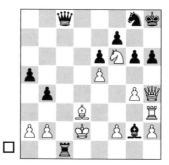

Position 377

Black has an overwhelming material advantage. Should he enter the pawn ending by means of a temporary queen sacrifice (**1...♕xf3+ 2.♕xf3 ♖a3**)?

Position 378

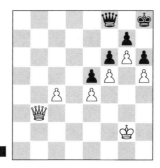

Black cannot fight against the passed pawn, supported by its queen, and at the same time protect his back rank. However, as they say, 'never stop trying'...

Position 379

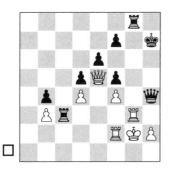

After **1.♖f3** there followed **1...♖c2+ 2.♔f1 ♖xh2**. How should the game end?

Position 380

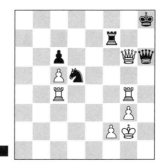

For Black, the exchange of queens is tantamount to resignation. Meanwhile, there are threats of ♕g8# and ♖h4. What should he do?

# Examination

'But almost the whole of this book is an examination in tactics,' the reader might object. 'So why is only this section called an examination?'

In all sections of the book, when trying to solve the positions presented, you know that there is some extraordinary tactical possibility in the position. But in the earlier sections, you have also had another very helpful clue, in the title of the section concerned. The previous sections are therefore more in the nature of a reinforcement of the topics discussed, rather than an examination.

In this examination, you will still have the general hint that the solutions are of a tactical character. The reader is offered the opportunity to judge for himself how well he has passed the test.

You have before you 356 test positions.

Position 381

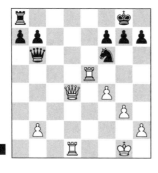

Position 382

Position 383

Position 384

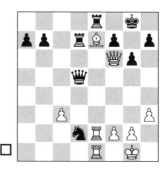

Position 385

Position 386

Position 387

Position 388

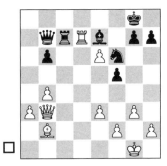

Position 389

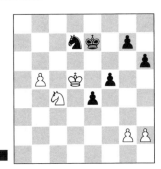

Position 390

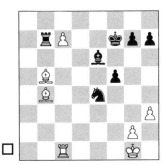

Position 391

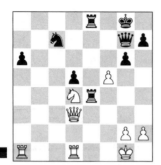

Position 392

Position 393

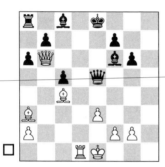

Position 394

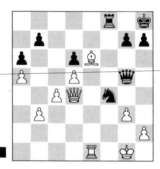

Position 395

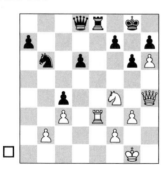

Position 396

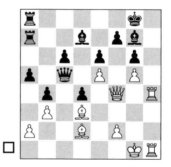

Position 397

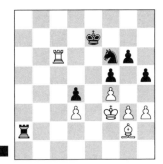

Position 398

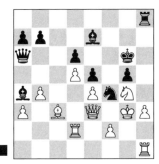

Position 399

Position 400

Position 401

Position 402

Position 403

Position 404

Position 405

Position 406

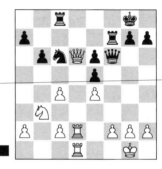

Position 407

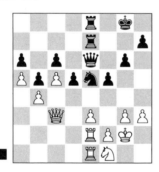

Position 408

Position 409

Position 410

Position 411

Position 412

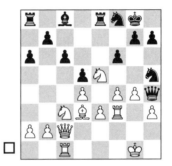

Find the most forcing win.

Position 413

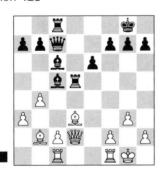

Position 414

## Position 415

## Position 416

## Position 417

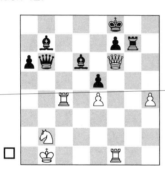

## Position 418

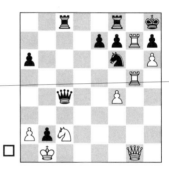

## Position 419

## Position 420

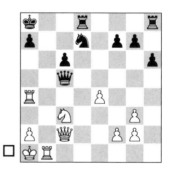

Position 421

Position 422

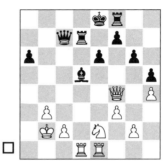

Position 423

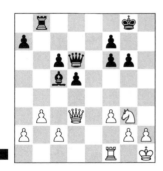

Position 424

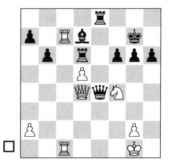

Position 425

Position 426

Position 427

Position 428

Position 429

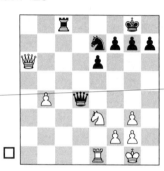

Position 430

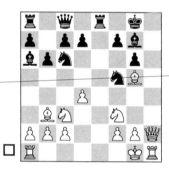

Position 431

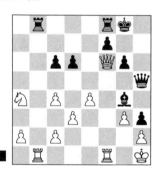

Position 432

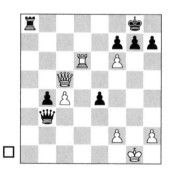

Position 433

Position 434

Position 435

Position 436

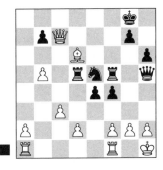

Position 437

Position 438

## Position 439

## Position 440

## Position 441

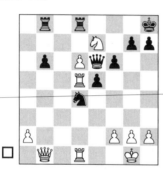

## Position 442

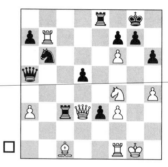

## Position 443

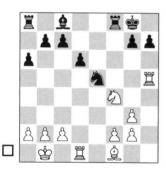

## Position 444

Position 445

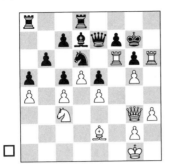

Position 446

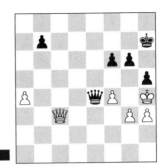

Position 447

Position 448

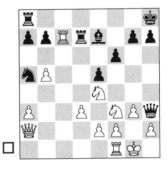

Position 449

Position 450

Position 451

Position 452

Position 453

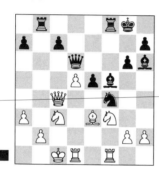

Position 454

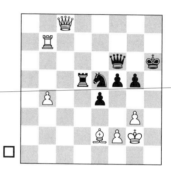

Position 455

Position 456

Position 457

Position 458

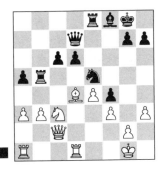

Position 459

Position 460

Position 461

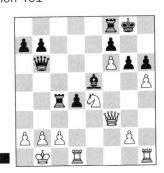

Position 462

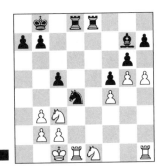

Position 463

Position 464

Position 465

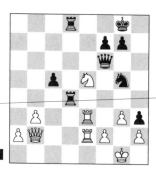

Position 466

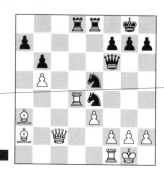

Position 467

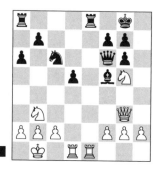

Position 468

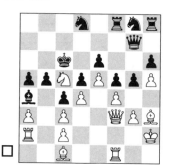

Position 469

Position 470

Position 471

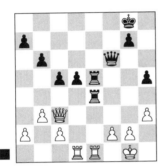

Position 472

Position 473

Position 474

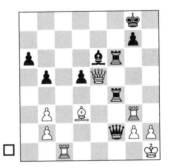

Position 475

Position 476

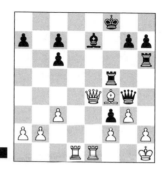

Position 477

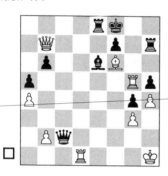

Position 478

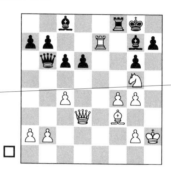

Position 479

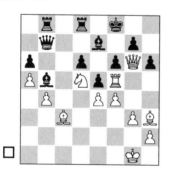

Position 480

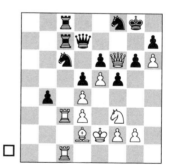

Position 481

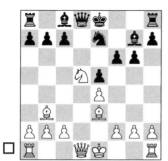

Position 482

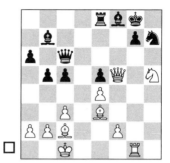

Position 483

Position 484

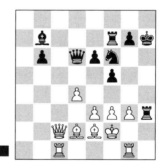

Position 485

Position 486

Position 487

Position 488

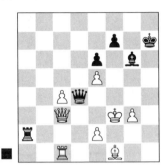

Position 489

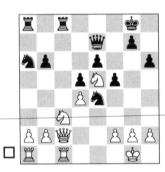

Position 490

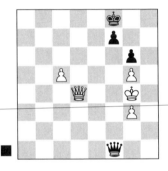

Position 491

Position 492

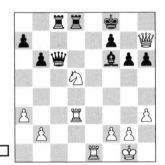

## Position 493

## Position 494

## Position 495

## Position 496

## Position 497

## Position 498

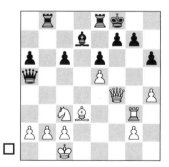

Position 499

Position 500

Position 501

Position 502

Position 503

Position 504

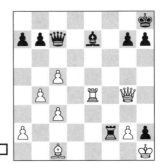

Position 505

Position 506

Position 507

Position 508

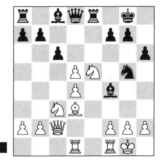

Position 509

Position 510

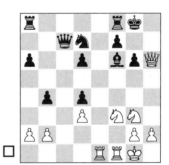

Position 511

Position 512

Position 513

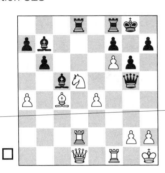

Position 514

Position 515

Position 516

Position 517

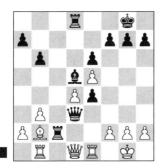

Position 518

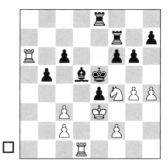

Position 519

Position 520

Position 521

Position 522

Position 523

Position 524

Position 525

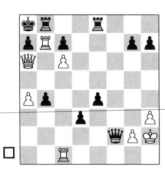

Position 526

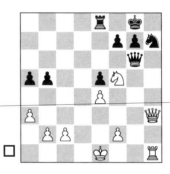

Position 527

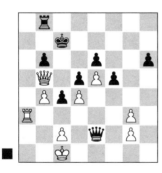

Position 528

Position 529

Position 530

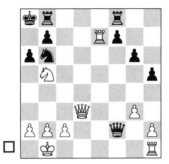

Position 531

Position 532

Position 533

Position 534

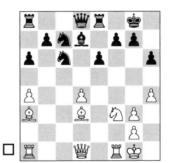

Position 535

Position 536

Position 537

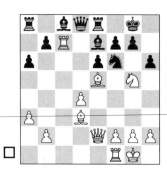

Position 538

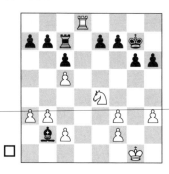

Position 539

Position 540

Position 541

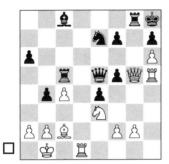

Position 542

Position 543

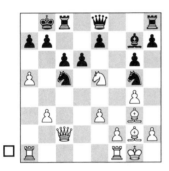

Position 544

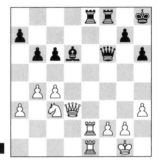

Position 545

Position 546

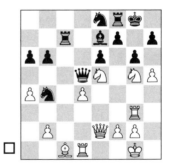

Position 547

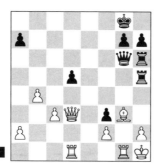

Position 548

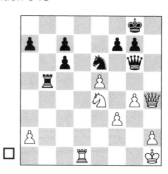

Position 549

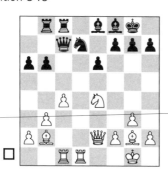

Position 550

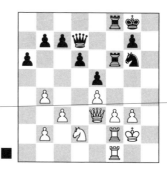

Position 551

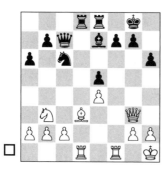

Position 552

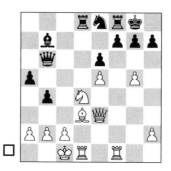

Position 553

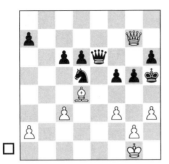

Position 554

Position 555

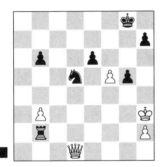

Position 556

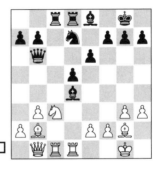

Position 557

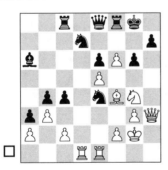

Position 558

Position 559

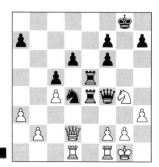

Position 560

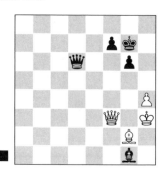

Position 561

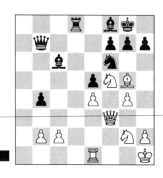

Position 562

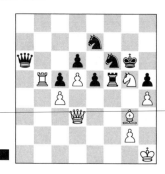

Position 563

Position 564

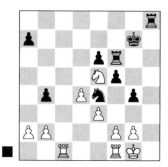

Position 565

Position 566

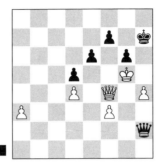

Position 567

Position 568

Position 569

Position 570

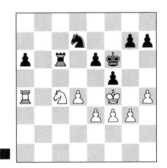

Position 571

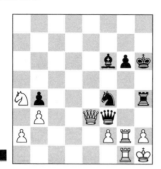

Position 572

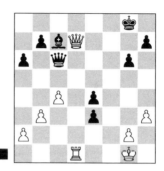

Position 573

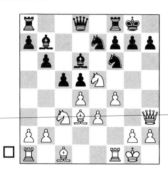

Position 574

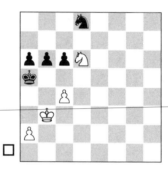

Position 575

Position 576

## Position 577

## Position 578

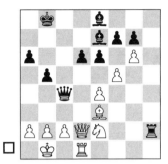

## Position 579

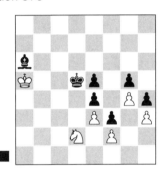

## Position 580

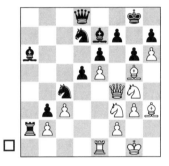

## Position 581

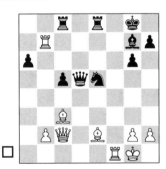

## Position 582

Position 583

Position 584

Position 585

Position 586

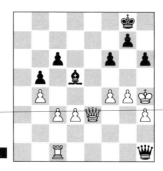

Position 587

Position 588

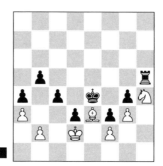

Position 589

Position 590

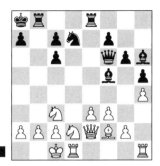

Position 591

Position 592

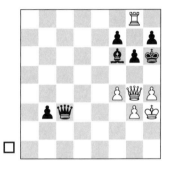

Position 593

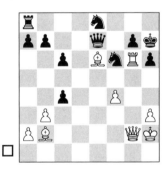

Position 594

Position 595

Position 596

Position 597

Position 598

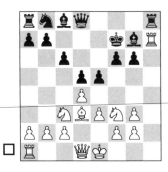

Position 599

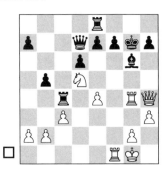

Position 600

Position 601

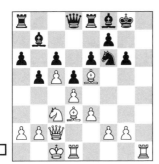

Position 602

Position 603

Position 604

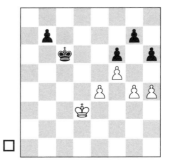

Position 605

Position 606

Position 607

Position 608

Position 609

Position 610

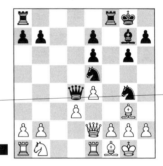

Position 611

Position 612

Position 613

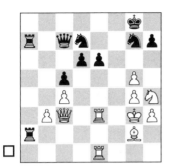

Position 614

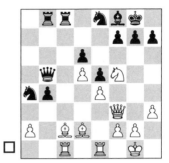

Position 615

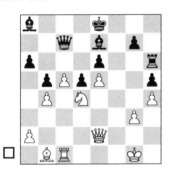

Position 616

Position 617

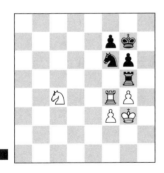

Position 618

Position 619

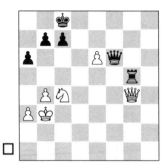

Position 620

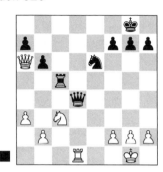

Position 621

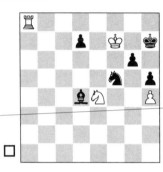

Position 622

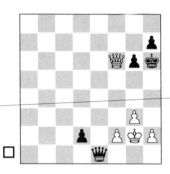

Position 623

Position 624

Position 625

Position 626

Position 627

Position 628

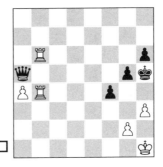

Position 629

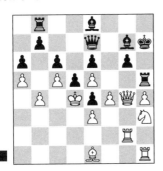

Position 630

Position 631

Position 632

Position 633

Position 634

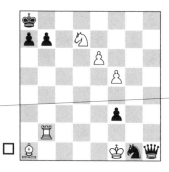

Position 635

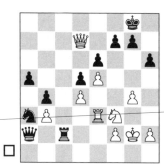

Position 636

Position 637

Position 638

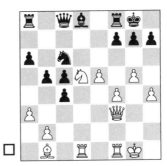

Position 639

Position 640

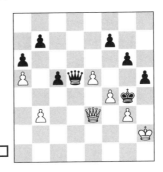

Position 641

Position 642

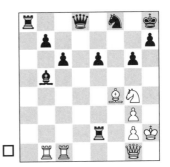

## Position 643

## Position 644

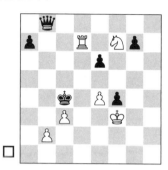

## Position 645

## Position 646

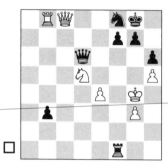

## Position 647

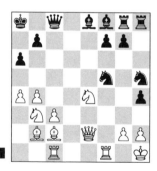

## Position 648

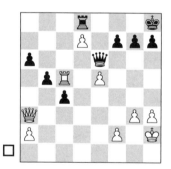

Position 649

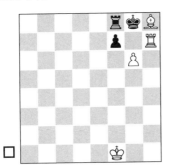

Position 650

Position 651

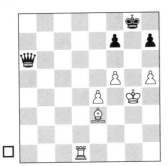

Position 652

How should **1...hxg5** be answered?

Position 653

**1.c5** was played. How would you reply?

Position 654

How should the game end after **1.♘f7+** ?

Position 655

Would you take the pawn on b7?

Position 656

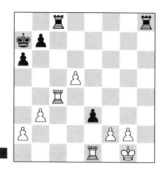

Black is two pawns down. What would you recommend?

Position 657

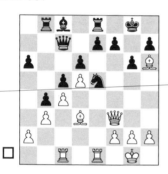

White played **1.♕f4**. What happens if the bishop is taken?

Position 658

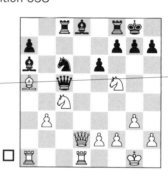

White played **1.♗c3**. What happens if Black replies **1...♗xc4** ?

Position 659

How would you answer **1...♘e5** ?

Position 660

How should White respond to **1...♗xf3** ?

Combinative themes – Examination

Position 661

**1.♖f3** was played. Hasn't White blundered a rook?

Position 662

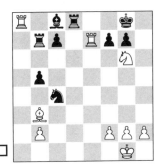

The knight on g6 is under attack. What should White do?

Position 663

Should Black castle queenside?

Position 664

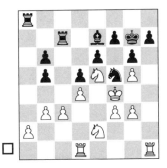

How should **1.g4** be answered?

Position 665

Black threatens mate in two. And what if we now pin the rook?

Position 666

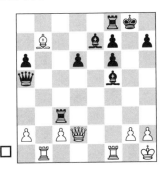

Can White take the bishop on f5, exploiting the queen's overloading?

175

Position 667

Where should the knight go?

Position 668

Can the position of the undefended knight on h5 be exploited?

Position 669

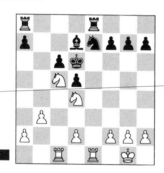

With the move **1...♞f5** Black offered an exchange. And White?

Position 670

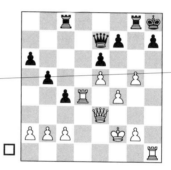

Realise White's advantage.

Position 671

Assess the continuation **1.♞f4**.

Position 672

Can White win a pawn?

Position 673

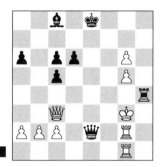

Black accepted the offered draw, believing that he had nothing more than perpetual check (1...♖g4+ 2.♔h2 ♖h4+). Was he right?

Position 674

White's last move was ♗d2-g5. What is your reply?

Position 675

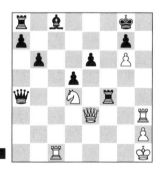

Your reply to **1...e5** ?

Position 676

Black moved the knight to e5, having calculated the variation **2.♘xe5 ♕h4+ 3.g3** (3.♔d2 ♕f4+ and 4...♕xe5) **3...♕xe4+** and **4...♕xh1**. Was he correct?

Position 677

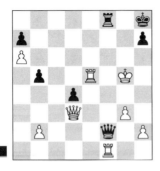

Black must decide whether to pursue the white king by 1...♖g8+ and 2...♛xh2+, or to satisfy himself with taking the rook on f1 and entering a rook ending.

Position 678

Can the bishop be taken?

Position 679

White has a piece less, and is threatened with ...♛d2-e1+ and then ...♛e1-f1. But the black king is also not totally safe...

Position 680

Exploiting Black's lag in development, White went over to active operations. He played **1.f5 exf5** (1...♗xf5 2.♘xf5 exf5 3.♘g5) **2.♘h4 ♗e7 3.♘gxf5 0-0 4.♛e2 ♖e8**. Continue the attack.

Position 681

Black is attacking b2, White is defending it. How can Black strengthen his position?

Position 682

How would you answer **1.♘c7** ?

Position 683

How should the queen exchange offer be met?

Position 684

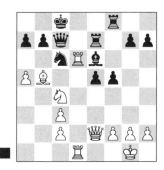

Should the pawn be taken: **1...♗xc4 2.♕xc4 ♘xa5** ?

Position 685

How should the game end?

Position 686

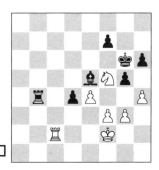

On **1.♘e7+**, where does the king go?

Position 687

**1...♘xe5** was played. What happens after **2.dxe5** ?

Position 688

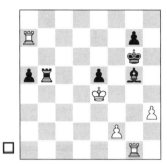

How can the pin on the bishop at g5 be exploited?

Position 689

What is your reply to **1...♖a8** ?

Position 690

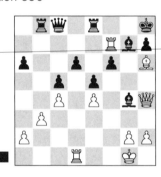

What happens if we take the rook?

Position 691

White's pieces are pointed at the kingside. How should he continue the attack?

Position 692

White played **1.g5**. What happens after **1...fxg5** ?

Position 693

White played **1.fxg4**. How should this be answered?

Position 694

Defending the mate, White played **1.♗f3**. Continue the attack.

Position 695

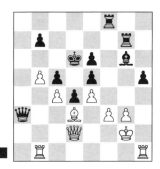

Realise the advantage.

Position 696

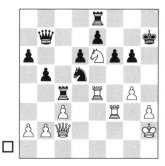

The black king has no defenders, but how do we get at it?

Position 697

White expected to win a piece here. What is your response?

Position 698

White played the interference move **1.♘d5**. How should the game end?

181

Position 699

Position 700

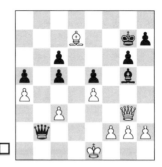

In order to create the threat of 2...♘d4, Black played **1...♚h8**. 'After **2.♗xe6 ♖xd1 3.♕xd1 ♕xe6** the game should be drawn,' he thought. Was he right?

Black has placed a bishop under attack, counting on exploiting the open position of the white king, to force either a repetition of moves or the regaining of the piece. Analyse the position.

Position 701

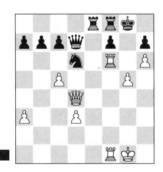

Position 702

How would you reply to **1...♖e4** ?

Continue the attack.

Position 703

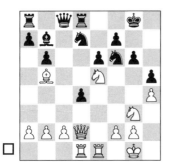

Black's pieces are all grouped on the queenside, whilst his kingside is weakened. Can this be exploited?

Position 704

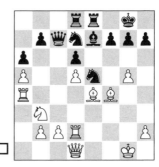

Would you sacrifice the bishop on h7?

Position 705

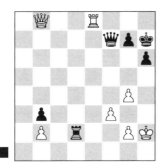

How should one reply to **1...♕xf3** ?

Position 706

Is the ...g6 weakening significant?

Position 707

Assess the consequences of the tactic **1...cxd4 2.cxd4 ♘xd4**.

Position 708

Black threatens 1...♕a3 and also 1...♗xb3. What should White do?

Position 709

White has sacrificed the exchange for an attack. What should he do now?

Position 710

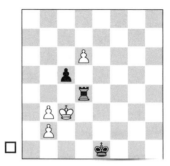

Black has an extra rook, and the pawn on d6 is doomed. However, do not hurry to resign – consider what you can come up with.

Position 711

White has several extra pawns, but he is significantly lagging in development. How should Black conduct the attack?

Position 712

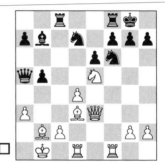

In order to create threats on the kingside, White deflected the knight from f6 – **1.♘xd7 ♞xd7**, and opened the long diagonal with **2.d5**. Analyse the position after **2...♝xd5**.

Position 713

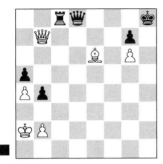

The rook is attacked, whilst mate is threatened on h1. What should Black do?

Position 714

Assess the sacrifice on h7.

Position 715

Both white bishops are pointing at the kingside, which makes one think about the typical sacrifice on h7 and g7. What is your decision?

Position 716

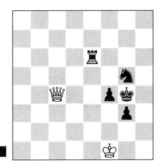

What happens after **1...♔h3** ?

Position 717

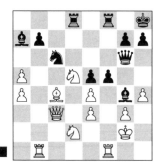

Black played **1...f4**, trying to open up the position of the enemy king. Consider the consequences of the combination **2.exf4 exf4 3.♘xf4 ♖xd2+ 4.♕xd2 ♕xe4+ 5.♔h2 ♕xc4**.

Position 718

Black has delayed castling. Can this be exploited?

Position 719

How should the attack be carried out?

Position 720

White thought about bringing his knight via c2 to d4, and so played **1.c3**. What happens if Black replies **1...♗xc3+** ?

Position 721

Can Black take the bishop?

Position 722

There followed **1.♞xd5 ♝xg5 2.h4 ♛a5+**. In giving this intermediate check, Black was not afraid of **3.b4** because of **3...cxb4**, and if **4.♞xg5** or **4.hxg5**, then **4...b3+**.
Was he correct?

Position 723

In order to realise his material advantage, Black decided to exchange the c- and d-pawns, and deprive the enemy bishop of the strong point d5. He played **1...♛a2+**, having in mind the variation **2.♔h3 ♛xc4 3.♛e7+ ♔g6 4.♛xd6 ♔f6** with a technically winning position. Check the correctness of this calculation.

Position 724

A natural development of the play in this typical Sicilian position would be 1.f5 or 1.♗e3.
White instead went over to the offensive with **1.g5 hxg5 2.fxg5**. Here, instead of counterattacking with 2...d5, Black played **2...♞g8**. There followed **3.g6 ♞gf6** (more tenacious was 3...♞e5) **4.gxf7+ ♔xf7**. After ...♞d7-e5 Black will consolidate his position. How can this be prevented?

Position 725

Assess the consequences of the queen sacrifice on h2 after **1...♛h3 2.♛f1**.

Position 726

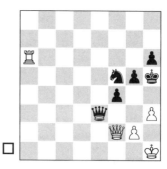

Black has offered the exchange of queens. Can White win?

Position 727

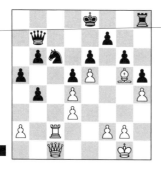

Would you take the pawn on d4?

Position 728

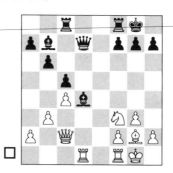

White played **1.♘xd4**, having in mind the sharp variation **1...♝xg2 2.♘f5 ♛b7 3.♘d6 ♛f3 4.♖d3 ♛a8 5.♘xc8 ♝xf1 6.♘e7+ ♚h8**. Assess the resulting position.

Position 729

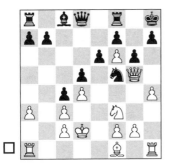

To develop his attack on the king-side, White played **1.g4** and after **1...♘d6 – 2.♖e1**. Now 2...♘e4+ is impossible because of 3.♖xe4 dxe4 4.♕h6 ♖g8 5.♘g5 with mate. But after **2...♘e8** Black wins the pawn on f6. How should we continue the attack?

Position 730

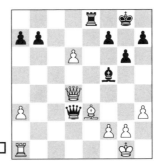

How should White meet the offer of a queen exchange?

Position 731

This position, typical for open games, arose from the Caro-Kann after 1.e4 c6 2.d4 d5 3.f3 dxe4 4.fxe4 e5 5.♘f3 exd4 6.♗c4 ♗b4+ 7.c3 dxc3. Consider the consequences of the move **8.♗xf7+**.

Position 732

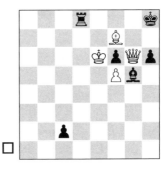

The c-pawn is one square from promoting. What should be done?

Position 733

Finish off the attack.

Position 734

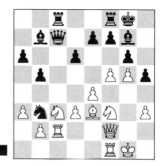

Despite the weakening of his king-side, Black decided to break up the enemy centre, playing **1...gxf5** and after **2.♕h4 – 2...fxe4**.
Assess the position and analyse the two sides' possibilities.

Position 735

White played **1.d7**. Assess the variation **1...♕xf1+ 2.♔xf1 d2**.

# SOLUTIONS

# Deflection (positions 35-86)

Position 35

There followed **1.♕xe5!**, and Black resigned. He cannot take the queen because of 2.♖d8#, nor can he retreat (Paramonov-Shekhtman, Moscow 1961).

Position 36

After **1...♕h4!** White resigned because of the inevitable mate after 2.♔g2 ♕g4+ in Farboud-Panno, Varna Olympiad 1962. Even faster, by the way, would have been 1...♕g5!.

Position 37

**1...♖e1!** Deflecting the rook – 2.♖xe1 ♕g2#, and the queen – 2.♕xe1 ♕h5#. **2.♕g4 ♕h1+! 3.♖xh1 ♖xh1#** (Belenky-Pirogov, Moscow 1975)

## Position 38

The knight on d4 is attacked and has no retreat. But if the queen did not control c2, White would be mated. Therefore the queen must somehow be deflected. This is achieved with the move **1...♕a5!**, after which White had to resign (Gliksman-Popovic, Wroclaw 1979).

## Position 39

Black has defended against the mate threatened on h7, offering the exchange of queens (the c8-square is covered by the knight). A bishop down, White needs to find an extreme tactical solution, as his rook and knight are attacked. **1.♖f4!**, deflecting the queen from the defence of either the square h7 (in the event of 1...♕xf4) or the 8th rank (in the event of 1...♕xd3), forced Black to resign (Belov-Ongemakh, Narva 1984).

## Position 40

**1...♕e2!**, and White resigned (Panno-Bravo, Brazil 1975).

## Position 41

The pin on the second rank prevents White mating by g2-g3, therefore **1.♕e1+!** (Stahlberg-Becker, Buenos Aires 1944).

## Position 42

**1.♕f7!** A deflection which forces resignation, since Black loses a knight: 1...♕c8 2.♕xc4; 1...♔b8 2.♖xd8+ ♕xd8 3.♕xc4 (Keres-Tröger, Hamburg 1960).

## Position 43

**1...♕b1! 2.♕e2 ♕e4** White resigned (Stefanova-Peptan, Moscow 1994).

## Position 44

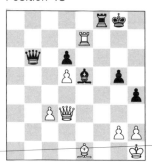

In reply to the offer of a queen exchange, Black deflected the bishop with the move **1...♗a6!**, after which White resigned (Uhlmann-Larsen, Las Palmas 1971).

## Position 45

1.♕c3 is strong, but mate is stronger: **1.♕xe5+! ♕e6** 1...♘xe5 2.♖d8#. **2.♘f6+! gxf6** 2...♘xf6 3.♖d8#. **3.♕xe6+ fxe6 4.♗h5#** (Zimmermann-W. Hübner, West Germany 1975/76)

Position 46

**1.♕g6!**, and Black resigned (1...♕xg6 2.♖h8+!).
(Katalymov-Kolpakov, Riga 1975).

Position 47

**1...♖d8! 2.♕e3 ♕xc2 3.♔f1 ♖d1+** and White
resigned in view of 4.♖xd1 ♕xd1+ 5.♕e1 ♕d3+
(Barcza-Tal, Tallinn 1971).

Position 48

**1...♕e5! 2.♕xe5 ♘d3+** and **3...♖xc1#**
(Demetriescu-Adam, correspondence game,
1934)

Position 49

There followed **1...♖xe1+** (but not 1...♘e2+?
because of 2.♖xe2 ♖xe2 3.♕h6, and Black is
mated) **2.♖xe1 ♘e2+!**, and White lost his queen,
because he cannot take the knight in view of
3...♕b1+ (Browne-Haik, Reykjavik 1986).

Position 50

This position arose in the game Alekhine-Mikenas from Kemeri, 1937. Mikenas played 1...♗xe4, and Alekhine could not refrain from exclaiming, 'Young man, you could have mated in three!' Indeed, **1...♖c2!** (we would point out that 1...♖c4 is also strong) and if White takes **2.♕xc2** it is mate in three after **2...♕xf3+ 3.♔g1 ♗h3**. 'Never mind', said Mikenas, overcoming his disappointment, 'I will win it over again.' After 2.♕xe4 ♕xe4 3.♖xe4 ♖c2 Black retained his advantage and eventually won.

Position 51

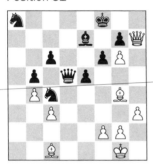

**1.♗h6! ♕g8** 1...gxh6 2.g7+. **2.♗e6!** After 2...♕xe6 there follows 3.♕h8+ ♕g8 4.♗xg7+. Black resigned (Shelochilin-P. Chernikov, Leningrad 1950).

Position 52

Black has an extra knight and some powerful passed pawns. However, his king lacks pawn protection and White easily crowned his attack: **1.♕g8+** On 1.♖exe7+ Black replies not 1...♖xe7 2.♕g8#, but 1...♕xe7. **1...♖f8 2.♕g6+!** Deflection. **2...♕xg6 3.♖exe7+ ♔d8 4.♖bd7#** (Hartston-Whiteley, England 1974)

Position 53

There followed **1...♛e1!**, and White resigned. After the capture of the queen, there follows 2...♞f3+ and 3...♜xh2#, whilst after 2.♔h1 there is 2...♛f2 (Ugoltsev-Ashin, USSR 1976).

Position 54

**1...♜xe3** Deflecting the pawn on f2, with the aim of opening the path of the f-pawn. **2.fxe3 ♝e4** The bishop sets up the ambush. **3.♜f2** 3.♛e5 f2+ 4.♛xe4 f1♛ loses. **3...♜xa2** Deflecting the rook from f2. **4.♜gf1** 4.♜xa2 f2+. **4...♛xf1+** Repeating the deflection of the rook leads to mate (Naumov-Petrushansky, USSR 1978).

Position 55

**1.e8♛+! ♞xe8 2.♞f5** The threat of 3.♛e7+ is unstoppable, Black resigned (Doroshkievich-Balitinov, Orel 1980).

Position 56

Black could take the e4-pawn, but giving mate is better: **1...♞f3!** (2.gxf3 ♜d2) (Stahlberg-Keres, Bad Nauheim 1936)

Position 57

**1.♕xf6! gxf6 2.♘ge4+ ♔h8** Or 2...♘g6 3.♘xf6+ and 4.♘xd7. **3.♘xf6** Both 4.♖g8# and the capture of the queen are threatened. Black resigned (Tolush-Mititelu, Warsaw 1961).

Position 58

**1.♖g5!** In defending the mate, White offers his opponent a choice of queen or rook. After either capture, there follows 2.♘xf7#. But Black can content himself with a pawn, at the same time defending f7: **1...♕xf6**. White has a rook and a knight attacked, and there is also a threat of 2...♕f2+, but after the problem-like move **2.♕d4!** Black has only **2...♖g6** and **3.♖xg6!** ends the game: **3...♕xd4 4.♘xf7#** (Suta-Suteu, Bucharest 1953).

Position 59

**1...♘f3+!** Deflection, with the aim of opening the g-file for the rook on c6. **2.gxf3** 2.♔h1 ♘xf2+. **2...♖g6+ 3.♔h1 ♘xf2+** Deflecting the rook from the first rank. **4.♖xf2 ♖d1+**, and mate next move (NN-Englisch, Vienna 1885).

Position 60

Without burdening himself with the calculation of the variation 1...♖c3 2.♗d3 ♘c7, Black deflected the enemy queen from the defence of the square f3: **1...♖xc2! 2.♕xc2 ♘f3+ 3.♔f2** If 3.♔h1, then 3...♕g3 with mate on h2 (or g1 if the knight moves). **3...♕g3+**. After 4.♔e2 there follows 4...♘ed4+. White resigned (Paoli-Smyslov, Venice 1950). Instead of 2.♕xc2 White could have given up the exchange by continuing 2.♖xe5, but after 2...♕xe5 3.♕xc2 ♕xa1 his position is bad.

## Position 61

By continuing 1.♖xe5, White can reach a rook ending with an extra pawn: 1...♖bxa6 2.♖xa6 ♖xa6 3.♔xb3. However, the move **1.♗d3!** immediately forced Black to resign. He cannot take the rook because of mate, whilst after 1...♖e8, White again deflects the rook from the back rank with the move 2.♖xe5 (Capablanca-Rossolimo, Paris 1938).

## Position 62

**1...♖e2! 2.♕xe2 ♖xb3+ 3.♔c1** If 3.axb3, then 3...♕a1+ 4.♔c2 ♕b2+ 5.♔d3 ♕c3#. **3...♕c3+** and then 4...♖b1+, mating (Pelaez-De Dovitiis, Havana 1993).

## Position 63

White wins by deflecting the queen from the defence of the rook at d8: **1.♕a7! ♕a5 2.♕xa6! ♕c7 3.♕a7!** The queen cannot retreat further, so Black resigned (Rovner-Kamishov, Moscow 1947).

The success of White's tactical operation was founded not only on the weakness of the back rank and the position of his heavy pieces. The bishop on f3 also played its role, by defending the rook on d1. If the bishop had been on b3, for example, the move 1.♕a7 would not have been possible, as Black could reply with the zwischenzug 1...♖xd2, and then take the queen.

**Position 64**

**1.♘e7+! ♛xe7** On 1...♖xe7 there follows 2.♖d8+ ♖e8 3.♖xe8+ (deflecting the queen from the defence of h7) 3...♛xe8 4.♛xh7+ ♚f8 5.♗c5+. But with his next move, White achieves his aim all the same: **2.♖xe6** and Black resigned (Pospisil-Keller, correspondence game, 1983-84).

**Position 65**

**1.♖e1! ♖d8** If 1...♖c8, then 2.♛b7, whilst after 1...♖f8 Black is mated: 2.♖xf8+ and 3.♛b8+. Now **2.♛b5** ends the game. After **2...♖xg2+ 3.♚h1** Black resigned in Wehnert-Leiss, East Germany 1962.

**Position 66**

**1.♛f6 ♛e5 2.♖xa5!**
A blow which deflects one of the pieces performing an extremely valuable defensive function: either the rook, which guards the 8th rank, or the queen, watching over g7. Black resigned in Zavialov-Apartsev, Moscow 1985. One should add that White needs to start with the move 1.♛f6, since after the immediate 1.♖xa5, Black can reply 1...♖xb2 or 1...♖c7.

**Position 67**

**1.♗xf6 gxf6 2.♛h6 f5** If 2...fxe5, then 3.♗xh7+ ♚h8 4.♗g6+, mating. **3.♘g4!** and Black resigned in Haik-Kiffmeyer, Stockholm 1974.

Position 68

In the game Hübner-Murey (Sukhumi 1972) White could have won by exploiting his powerful bishops and the open position of the enemy king: **1.g5! ♗xg5 2.♗d4+ ♗f6 3.♕b8!** Hübner missed the final deflection blow and instead played 1.♕f7.

Position 69

Firstly, 1.♖xe8 ♕xe8 2.♕a4! and Black cannot take the queen because of back-rank mate, whilst the counter-blow 2...♖c1+ fails to 3.♔f2 (Black can complicate matters with 2...♖c2+). The second method was 1.♕b5!. After 1...♖xb8 (or 1...♖c1+ 2.♔f2 ♖c2+ 3.♔e1 ♖c1+ 4.♔d2) 2.♕xb8 ♔g8 (there is nothing else) 3.♕b3+ White wins a rook. Neither of these tactical operations occurred in the game Capablanca-Thomas (Hastings 1929/30). Upon 1.♕a8, Thomas resigned, but wrongly! After the deflecting counterblow 1...♖xa2! White would have had to play a heavy-piece ending two pawns down, e.g. 2.♕xa2 ♖xb8; 2.♖xe8 ♖xa8! 3.♖xf8+ ♖xf8; 2.♕b7 c5 3.♕c7 ♖a8!.

Position 70

**1...♖f3!!** Neither the queen nor the rook can be taken because of mate (2.gxf3 ♕h2#; 2.♕xa2 ♖xf1#), whilst there is a threat of 2...♖xh3+. The move 2.♔g1 does not defend, because of 2...♕a7+ 3.♔h1 ♖xf1+ 4.♕xf1 ♕d7! 5.♕f6 ♗c7, and Black wins a knight because of the back-rank mate threat. **2.♘b7 ♖xh3+ 3.♔g1**. Here the game could have been ended by 3...♗h2+ 4.♔h1 ♗e5+ 5.♔g1 ♗d4+. Black chose **3...♕a7+ 4.♖f2 ♗g3**, after which White resigned (5.♕f1 ♗xf2+ 6.♕xf2 ♖h1+ and 7...♕xf2). This was the game Pogats-Hever (Hungary 1979).

In the initial position, there is also another winning move: **1...♕b3** with the threat of 2...♕g3 (2.♕e1 ♕g3).

Position 71

The move 1...♕d4? was a mistake in an equal position: **2.♖d1!** and Black resigned (2...♕xc3 3.♖xd7+ and 4.bxc3 in Stahlberg-Lundin, Stockholm 1937.

Position 72

After **1...♖c8?** White could have won by deflecting the queen from the defence of the back rank with **2.♖a7!**.

In the game Stephenson-Penrose from the British Championship, Bristol 1968, White failed to notice this possibility, played 2.♖c2, and eventually lost.

Position 73

The immediate 1.♕xd5+ (with the idea 2.♘e7+) fails, because the black queen takes with check. **1.♕d4!** wins. White not only defends against the threat of 1...♘f2+, but also threatens the queen, the knight, and to give mate. This manoeuvre (to be more exact: this triple attack), deflecting the queen from the defence of e7 (after 1...♕xd4 there follows the discovered attack 2.♘e7+ and 3.♖xf8#), leads to material gains.

Black's only chance is to give up the queen for rook and knight: **1...♖xf5 2.♕xc5 ♖xf1+ 3.♔g2 ♖f8 4.♕xd5+ ♔h8**, which, of course, does not save him from defeat (Jansson-Pytel, Stockholm 1975).

Position 74

1...cxb3? was the decisive mistake. After **2.♕a7!** Black had to resign in Minic-Honfi, Yugoslavia-Hungary match, 1966; for example, 2...♕c8 3.♕xa8!.

Position 75

**1...♖d3!** Deflecting the queen from the defence of g2. **2.♗xe5+ dxe5 3.♕b2** 3.♕c2 ♖xd1 4.♖xd1 ♕f3+. **3...♕f3+** (but not 3...♖xd1? because of 4.♕xe5+ ♔g7 5.♕e8+, drawing), and White is mated (Varjomaa-Lundqvist, Sweden 1980). Instead of 1.f2-f4? White should have continued 1.♗xe5+ dxe5 2.♕d5.

Position 76

The continuation **1.♖xg7? ♖xg7 2.♗xf6** loses after the deflection counterblow **2...♕g2+! 3.♖xg2 ♖e1+** mating (Uhlmann-P. Dely, Budapest 1962).

Position 77

The bishop does not have to retreat. There followed **3...♖g6! 4.gxh3?**. If White had seen his opponent's reply, he would have surrendered the exchange with 4.g3 ♗xf1 5.♗xe4 dxe4 6.♖xf1, although this would not have changed the result. **4...♕g1+ 5.♖xg1 ♘xf2#** (Balanel-Pytlakowski, Marianske Lazne 1952)

203

Position 78

No. Exploiting the insufficiently defended first rank, Black plays **1...♘f2+!** and after **2.♖xf2 – 2...♗d4!** with decisive material gains (Marciniak-Dobosz, Poland 1973).

Position 79

**1...♖xf2! 2.♖xe6**
The squares g2 and f1 are defended. White considered that his opponent had sacrificed the bishop for no good reason...
However, there followed **2...♕e2!**, and the game ended (V. Kahn-Bernstein, Paris 1926).

Position 80

No. After **1.♘xc3?** there follows **1...♘xc3 2.♖xc3 ♖xc3 3.♖xc3**. Now Black achieves nothing by 3...♕b1+ in view of 4.♕f1 (4...♖d1?? 5.♖c8+). But deflecting the queen from defending the first rank decides the game: **3...♕b2! 4.♖c2** 4.♕e1 ♕xc3!. **4...♕b1+**, and White loses a rook (Bernstein-Capablanca, Moscow 1914).

Position 81

In the final position, Black had missed the deflecting sacrifice **5.♕h4!**, forcing him to resign (5...♗xd4+ 6.♔h1 ♕g8 7.♖f8) (Ezersky-Lelchuk, Smolensk 1950).
In addition, instead of 3.♗xe8 White could have continued 3.♗xg5 ♕xg5 (3...♕xd4+ 4.♗e3) 4.♗xe8 and after 4...♗h3 – 5.♕g3, keeping a decisive material advantage.

Position 82

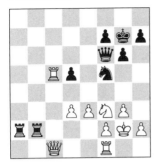

Black wins by a rook sacrifice, deflecting the queen from the defence of e3: **1...♖b1! 2.♕xb1 ♘xe3+ 3.♔g1** Or 3.♔h3 ♕f5+. **3...♕xf3**, and mate.

This interesting possibility was missed by Botvinnik in his game with Bouwmeester (Wageningen 1958). He played 1...d4 2.exd4 ♘xd4 3.♕e3 ♘e6 4.♖e5, and Bouwmeester, having an extra pawn, offered a draw.

Position 83

**1.♗f5!** The doomed bishop deflects its opposite number from the defence of e8. **1...♗xf5 2.♕c7!** Now the queen is deflected from defending e8. **2...♖xd1+ 3.♔xd1 ♗xc2+ 4.♔c1! ♗a4+** Because of the mate threat on the back rank, there is no other reply. **5.♕xc6 ♗xc6 6.♖e6 ♗b5 7.♖xb6 ♔g8 8.♖b7** with a technically winning endgame for White (Khalifman-Ehlvest, Lviv 1985).

Position 84

After 1.♖h8+ ♔d7, Black thought that he was safe. But there followed **2.♗c6+!**. The bishop, although attacked by three pieces, is immune. If 2...♘xc6, then the rook on f7 is taken with check, whilst after 2...♖xc6 there follows simply 3.♖xf7. And if 2...♔xc6, then 3.♖xc8+ ♘xc8 4.♖xf7.

**2...♔e6 3.♖h6+ ♖f6 4.♗d7+!** What a bishop! Black must capture, thereby losing the exchange. After **4...♔xd7 5.♖xf6 ♖e8 6.♖xg5 ♘g8 7.♖g7+ ♘e7 8.♔g3 ♖h8 9.♖ff7 ♖e8 10.♔g4** White won easily in Simagin-Zagoryansky, Ivanovo 1944.

Position 85

After White took on e5, Black replied **3...♖f5 4.♕e2**. On 4.♕e1, the reply 4...♖g5 creates unanswerable threats. **4...f3! 5.gxf3 ♖e8 6.♕d1** The same mating attack follows after 6.♕d3 ♖g5+ 7.♔h1 ♕h3. **6...♖g5+ 7.♔h1 ♕h3 8.♖g1 ♖e1!** A slightly later mate arises after 8...♖xg1+ 9.♔xg1 ♖e6.

The deflection of the two pieces defending the king, the queen (9.♕xe1 ♕xf3+) and the rook (9.♖xe1 ♕g2#) ends the game (Dille-Pigits, correspondence game, 1986).

Position 86

A) The tempting move 1.♖a3 loses to 1...♗xh2+ 2.♔h1 (2.♔f1 ♕e2#) 2...♗g3+ 3.♔g1 (3.♘h3 ♖d1+) 3...♖d1+ 4.♖xd1 ♕xd1+ 5.♘xd1 ♖e1#.

B) After **1.♖h3 ♕g5 2.♖a3** Black deflects the enemy queen with a sacrifice: **2...♕xc1+! 3.♕xc1** and now **3...♗xb2!**. The bishop cannot be taken because of mate, so Black wins a rook and so achieves a decisive advantage (Sznapik-Bronstein, Sandomierz 1976).

# Decoy (positions 120-155)

Position 120

**1.♕c4+! ♕xc4 2.g8♕+** and **3.♕xc4** (Pihajlic-Ivanka, Subotica 1976).

Position 121

**1.♖d8+ ♚e7** 1...♚xd8 2.♘xf7+ and 3.♘xe5.
**2.♖xh8 ♕xg5 3.♕d2**, winning. After 3...♘d5 there follows 4.c4 (Tal-Benko, Amsterdam 1964).

Position 122

**1.♗h7+ ♚xh7 2.♕xe6**. The square f7 is undefended, Black resigned in Kasparov-Browne, Banja Luka 1979.

Position 123

**1...♖xf1+! 2.♔xf1 ♗xg2+!** and White resigned in Van den Berg-Donner, Beverwijk 1963.

Position 124

**1.♕h8+! ♔xh8 2.♘g6+ ♔g8 3.♖h8#**
(Tikhonenkov-Kruchev, Moscow 1973)

Position 125

**1.♕xh7+! ♔xh7 2.♖h5+ ♔g7 3.♗h6+ ♔h7 4.♗f8#** (Santasiere-W. Adams, USA 1926)

Position 126

**1...♘e2+ 2.♔h1 ♕xh2+! 3.♔xh2 ♖h4#** (Meo-Giustolisi, Reggio Emilia 1959/60)

## Position 127

By sacrificing queen and rook, White lures the enemy king to h8, after which there follows a deadly discovered check: **1.♕xg8+! ♔xg8 2.♖h8+ ♔xh8 3.♗f7#** (Krylov-Tarasov, Leningrad 1961)

## Position 128

With the move **1.♘b6!** White won the exchange. The knight cannot be taken because of 2.♗a5, after which the queen is lost (Freiman-Rabinovich, Leningrad 1934).

## Position 129

**1.♕g7+! ♔xg7 2.♘f5+ ♔g8 3.♘h6#** (Mista-Kloza, Poland 1955)

## Position 130

After **1...♕xf3+!** White resigned. On 2.♔xf3 there follows 2...♗d5+ 3.♔f4 ♗h6#.
Other king retreats also lead to mate: 2.♔g1 ♗d5; 2.♔h3 ♗e6+ 3.♔h2 ♕xf2+ and 4...♗d5#; 2.♔h2 ♕xf2+ 3.♔h3 ♗e6+ (Stoltz-Orienter, Vienna 1976).

Position 131

**1...d4! 2.♘e4** After 2.♗xc6 ♖xc6 the knight cannot retreat, because c2 is undefended. **2...♕xc2+! 3.♔xc2 ♗xe4+** White resigned. After 4.♔d2 comes 4...♖c2#, whilst in the event of 4.♔b3 there is 4...♗c2# (Parma-Bielicki, Basle 1959).

Position 132

After **1.♘g5!** Black resigned in Yates-Réti, New York 1924. The knight cannot be taken because of 2.♖h8+ ♔xh8 3.♘xf7+ and 4.♘xg5. Meanwhile, both 2.♘gxf7 and 3.♖h8#, and also 2.♕g4 followed by 3.♕h4 are threatened. 1.♕e3 and 1.♕f3 would also win eventually, but the text is the most direct and the most elegant.

Position 133

**1...b5 2.♗d3** After 2.♗xb5, both 2...♖ab8 followed by ...a7-a6 and also 2...♗xb5 3.♕xb5 ♖ab8 and then ...♘d3+ win. **2...♕b4+!** Luring the king into a fork. Whether the queen is taken or the king retreats (3.♕xb4 ♘xd3+ and 4...♘xb4; 3.♔f1 ♕xb3 4.axb3 ♘xd3), White ends up a piece down (Naranja-Portisch, Siegen Olympiad 1970).

Position 134

A combination leads to favourable simplifications: **1.g5! fxg5 2.♕xh7+! ♔xh7 3.♘xg5+** and **4.♘xh3** with two extra pawns in a simple endgame (Maroczy-Rubinstein, Prague 1908).

## Position 135

**1.♗xf7+! ♔xf7 2.♖xc7+! ♕xc7** With the help of two sacrifices, White has lured the enemy king and queen onto the seventh rank and now gains a decisive material advantage: **3.♕h7+ ♔e6 4.♕xc7 ♖xd3 5.♕xa7** and Black resigned in Mecking-Tan, Petropolis 1974.

## Position 136

**1...♕xf4+! 2.♔xf4 g5+ 3.♔g4 ♘e3+** and **4...♘xc2**, remaining with an extra knight (Wittek-Meitner, Vienna 1882). Note that in this classical example, the win could also have been achieved with the quiet move 1...♕e1!, threatening the same fork plus mate on g3. For 1...♕g1! you would also get points.

## Position 137

**1.♕b8+ ♔e7 2.♗f6+! ♔xf6 3.♕d8+** and Black resigned, because he is mated: 3...♔g7 4.♖g3+; 3...♔g6 4.♕g5#; 3...♔f5 4.♕g5+ ♔e4 5.♕e5# (Bogdanovic-Suetin, Budva 1967).

## Position 138

By sacrificing themselves, the queen and bishop open the path for the g6-pawn to promote: **1.♕h8+! ♔xh8 2.g7+ ♔g8 3.♗h7+ ♔xh7 4.g8♕#** (Piotrowski-Tenenbaum, Lvov 1926)

**Position 139**

The queen sacrifice led to a forced perpetual check: **1.♕xh7+ ♔xh7 2.hxg6+ ♔xg6 3.♖h6+ ♔g5 4.♖h5+** (Von Scheve-Rubinstein, Ostend 1907).

**Position 140**

**1.♕h6 ♕f8 2.♕xh7+! ♔xh7 3.hxg6+ ♔xg6 4.♗e4#** (Fischer-Mjagmarsuren, Sousse 1967) Black is also mated after 1...c1♕+ (instead of 1...♕f8) 2.♖xc1 ♖xc1+ 3.♔h2.

**Position 141**

**1.♕xf5+!** A well-known motif: the black king is lured into the enemy camp. **1...♔xf5 2.♗e4+ ♔g4 3.h3+ ♔xg3** Mate results from 3...♔xh3 4.♗f5+ ♔xg3 5.♖e3+ ♔h4 6.♖h3#, and also 3...♔h5 4.g4+ ♔h4 5.♖e3 with the unstoppable threat of 6.♗e1#. **4.♖e3+ ♔h4 5.♗g6!** Cutting off the king's escape route and threatening 6.♗e1#. **5...♕g5+ 6.fxg5 ♗xe5 7.♖e4+ ♔xh3 8.♗f5+ ♔g3 9.♗e1#** (Zelinsky-Skotorenko, correspondence game, 1974).

**Position 142**

**1...♖xc4! 2.♕xc4 ♕xb2+ 3.♖xb2 ♘a3+ 4.♔a1 ♗xb2+ 5.♔xb2 ♘xc4+ 6.♔c3 ♖xe4** and Black has two extra pawns in the endgame (Honfi-Barczay, Kecskemet 1977).
A false trail is offered by 1...♖xe4 (instead of 1...♖xc4!) 2.♕xe4 ♕xb2+ 3.♖xb2 ♘c3+ 4.♔c1 ♘xe4 5.♖c2 with mutual chances.

**Position 143**

**1.♖xg6+! ♔xg6** 1...♘xg6 2.♘xf5+. **2.♖h6+! ♔xh6 3.♘xf5+ ♔g6 4.♘xe7+ ♔f6 5.♘g8+** and then **6.♗b3** with a material advantage sufficient for victory. This variation is from the game Lukin-Fedorov (Leningrad 1983). White did not see the combination and played 1.♖c5, after which the game later developed in Black's favour.

**Position 144**

After the queen exchange offer **1.♕b3**, the game Schulten-Horwitz (London 1846) continued **1...♕f1+ 2.♔xf1 ♗d3++ 3.♔e1 ♖f1#**.

**Position 145**

The queen cannot be taken. But with the help of checks, it is possible to reach a position where the e1-square is defended and then the queen can be taken: **1.♖xg7+! ♔xg7** Or 1...♔h8 2.♖g8+ ♖xg8 3.♕c3+; 1...♔f8 2.♖g8+ ♔xg8 and, as in the game, 3.♕g3+. **2.♕g3+** and **3.♖xd5** (Sandlik-Rybl, Prague 1937).

**Position 146**

After **1.♘fe5**, **1...♕xg2+!** was played and White resigned, not waiting for 2.♔xg2 ♘f4+ 3.♔g1 ♘h3# (Kärner-Mikkov, Tallinn 1954).

**Position 147**

**1.♖xg7+! ♔xg7 2.♕g4** There is no defence to the twin threat of mate and the discovered check 3.♘h6+, winning the queen. After **2...♕xf5 3.♕xf5** White's victory is only a matter of time (Keres-Gligoric, Yugoslavia 1959).

**Position 148**

On **1...♗xd3?** there follows **2.♕g8+!**, and Black is mated after 2...♔xg8 3.♗e6++ and 4.♖g8# (Nei-Petrosian, Moscow 1960).

**Position 149**

No. After **1.♕xc7?** there followed **1...♕h3+!**, and White stopped the clocks because mate is unavoidable: 2.♔xh3 ♗f1# or 2.♔h1 ♕f1+ 3.♗g1 ♕xf3#. This is how the game Andersson-Hartston (Hastings 1972/73) ended.

**Position 150**

After **1...♕xh2** White continues **2.♖b8+ ♔d7 3.♖d8+!**. If 3...♔xd8, then 4.♗b6+ and the queen is lost, whilst after 3...♔e6 Black is mated on d6 (Gudju-Wexler, Bucharest 1923).

**Position 151**

Black can boldly take the rook – **1...♘xd1**. After **2.♗xf6** he has the decoying queen sacrifice **2...♕h1+ 3.♔xh1 ♘xf2+** and **4...♘xg4**, ending up with an extra exchange and a pawn, with a winning position.

In the game Spiridonov-Estrin (Polanica Zdroj 1971) Black missed this possibility, and offered the exchange of queens with 1...♕e4.

**Position 152**

With the queen, of course. The tempting **1.♖exd5?** is refuted by **1...♕xg2+!** (luring White into a pin) **2.♔xg2 ♗xc6**, and White loses a rook (Olsen-Jakobsen, Aarhus 1953).

**Position 153**

The move **2.♗c7!** wins the exchange and the game. After **2...♖xc7 3.♕e5 g6** (Black can limit the damage with 3...♔f8! 4.♕xc7 ♗d6) **4.♕xc7** White realised his material advantage (Spassky-Averkin, Moscow 1973).

**Position 154**

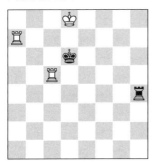

White wins by **1.♖h5! ♖xh5 2.♖a6+, 3.♖a5+** and **4.♖xh5**. This is a version of a position from the 15th century.

## Position 155

In the event of 1.♘xh4+ ♖xh4 2.♗xe2+ ♔f5 3.♗xc4 ♗xh2 or 2.♗e6+ (instead of 2.♗xe2+) 2...♗g5 3.♖xe2 ♖d4 White loses.

The correct decision is **1.♗h5+!** **♔xh5** (on 1...♔xf5? there follows 2.♗g6#!, whilst after 1...♔h7? there is 2.♖g7#) **2.♘g7+** with perpetual check on the squares f5 and g7. Black cannot avoid this by retreating the king to h7: 2...♔h6 3.♘f5+ ♔h7? 4.♖g7# (Tarasevich-Zlotnik, Moscow 1971).

# Eliminating defenders (positions 163-172)

Position 163

**1.♘xg6! hxg6 2.♖xe6 ♕d7** White is also better after 2...♗c8 3.♖xd6 ♗xg4 4.♖xd8 ♖xd8 5.♖xe7 or 2...♕d5 3.♖xe7 ♖xe7 4.♖xe7 ♕xa2. **3.♖xg6+ ♔h7 4.♖ee6!** with the threat of 5.♖g7+ ♔h8 6.♖h7+ and 7.♕g7#. On 4...♗f6, 5.♖gxf6 fxe6 6.♕g6+ (6.♕h4 is even more convincing) 6...♔h8 7.♖f7 wins (Mukhina-Pavlenko, Russia 1996).

Position 164

**1...♖xb2+! 2.♖xb2 ♘xc3+ 3.♔a1 ♖g1+** and mate next move (Rümmler-Mickeleit, Halle 1974).

Position 165

White has two ways to win, both connected with the weakness of the squares g6 and f5: **1.♗xd4 exd4 2.♘f4**, and if the rook retreats from f8, 3.♘g6+ and 4.♕f5.

The other is the more radical method of destroying the king's pawn cover:
**1.♗xh6! gxh6 2.♖xh6+ ♘xh6 3.♕xh6+ ♔g8 4.♗c4! ♘e6** If 4...♖f7, then 5.♘xe7+ ♕xe7 6.♖xf6. **5.♕g6+ ♔h8 6.♖f3 ♘g5 7.♖h3+** Black resigned because of 7...♘xh3 8.♕h6+ ♔g8 9.♘xe7# (Komliakov-Gadjily, Nikolaev 1993).

**Position 166**

**1...♘f3+ 2.♔h1 ♖xg3!** Eliminating the defender. **3.hxg3** 3.♘xg3 ♖xh2#. **3...♖g2!** and mate is unstoppable (Orlov-Chistiakov, USSR 1935). The combination also works in a different move-order: 1...♖g2+ 2.♔h1 ♖8xg3! and ...♘f3; but 2...♘f3? would be a mistake because of 3.♘d2! (3...♘xd2? 4.♖d8; 3...♖xd2 4.♖xd2 ♘xd2 5.♖d1 ♖xg3 6.hxg3 and ♖d1-d7; 3...♖8xg3! is best but only draws after 4.♘xf3 ♖xf3 5.♖c6).

**Position 167**

**1.♕xc8+!** But not 1.♕xd3? because of 1...♗xf3+ 2.♗g2 ♕f2!. **1...♗xc8 2.exd3 ♕xf3+ 3.♗g2** and White wins (Uhlmann-Pietzsch, Halle 1984).

**Position 168**

**1.♘xg7! ♔xg7 2.♗xh6+ ♔g8** Or 2...♔h8 3.♗g7+ ♔xg7 4.♕xh7+ ♔f8 5.♕h8+ ♔e7 6.♖xf7+ etc. **3.♖g4+ ♖g6 4.e6!** and Black resigned in Kotov-Unzicker, Stockholm 1952.

**Position 169**

Black is mated in two moves: **1.♕xg7+! ♘xg7 2.♘h6#** (Lechtynsky-Kubicek, Prague 1968)

## Position 170

**1.♕xe5! dxe5 2.exf7+** Black resigned. After 2...♔f8 there follows 3.♗h6#, whilst after 2...♔d8 there is 3.f8♕+. That leaves 2...♔d7, but then 3.♗f5+ ♔c6 4.♗e4+ ♘d5 5.♗xd5+ wins (Tal-Suetin, Tbilisi 1969).

## Position 171

The pawn can be taken: 1...cxd3 2.♘f6+ ♔e7. White cannot take the rook because of 3...♘g3+. After 3.h3 (defending against the mate) 3...♘g3+ 4.♔h2 ♖dd8 5.♕b7+ ♔f8 6.♕xa6 b4 or 6...♗e7 the black position is preferable, but play goes on. Instead, **1...♕xe4!** wins immediately. By eliminating the knight, Black sets up a standard (to the initiated!) mating combination: 2.dxe4 ♖xd1+ (2...♘g3+ mates one move quicker) 3.♕xd1 ♘g3+ 4.hxg3 hxg3+, and mate can only be delayed. Or 2.♕xe4 ♘g3+ 3.hxg3 hxg3+. White resigned in Wilhelm-Maier, Mulhouse 1977.

## Position 172

On **1...f3?** (much better is 1...♖fb8∓) there follows **2.♕xh6+!**. Also winning is 2.♖xg7+ ♗xg7 3.♖xg7+ ♔xg7 4.♕g5+ ♔h7 5.♕e7+ ♔g6 6.♕xf8 with a winning attack. 2.♗g8+ ♖xg8 3.♕xh6+ gxh6 4.♖xg8 h5 5.♖8g7+ ♔h8 6.♖7g5 e4 7.♖xc5 dxc5 8.dxe4 is another, less forceful win. **2...gxh6** 2...♔xh6 3.♖h4#. **3.♖g7+ ♔h8 4.♗g8!** ♖xg8 Or else mate on h7. **5.♖xg8+ ♔h7 6.♖1g7#** (Richter-NN, Germany 1939).

# Clearing squares and lines (positions 183-192)

### Position 183

After **1...d3!** White resigned due to inevitable material loss. If 2.exd3, then 2...♘d4 3.♕d1 ♘xd2 (4.♕xd2 ♘f3+) or 2.♕d1 (2.♕xd3 ♕xd3 and 3...♘xd2) 2...dxe2 3.♕xe2 ♘xd2 4.♖fd1 ♘d4 (Demetriescu-Nagy, correspondence game, 1936).

### Position 184

Black is threatened with mate, but by sacrificing a rook, he opens the queen's path to the key square e3 and mates first: **1...♖f3+! 2.gxf3** If 2.♔g1, then 2...♕e1+ 3.♔h2 ♕g3+ 4.♔g1 ♖e1+. **2...♕e3+ 3.♔g3 ♕xf3+** with mate (Kmoch-Rubinstein, Semmering 1926).

### Position 185

**1.♘d5+! cxd5 2.♕a3+** On 2...♔d8 the game is ended by 3.♕d6+ ♔c8 4.♖c1+ (Klavins-V. Zhuravlev, Riga 1968).

Position 186

The 'quiet' move **1.♗e6** (in freeing the f-file, the bishop attacks g8) forced Black to resign. He cannot take the queen because of mate, and after 1...♖gg8 2.♕xd8 and 3.♗xg8 White easily realises his material advantage (Pisarsky-Markushev, Novosibirsk 1983).

Position 187

**1.f5! ♗xf5 2.♕c7!!** and Black resigned because he loses a rook (Cramling-Martin, Barcelona 1985).

Position 188

With the move **1.♘d4!** White creates a deadly threat of 2.♕g4+. On 1...♘e5, 2.♘c6! wins (Csonkics-Porubszky, Budapest 1986).

Position 189

After 1.f5 exf5, by freeing the c4-square for his knight with **2.♗xf7+!**, White wins the queen: **2...♖xf7 3.♘c4** (Botvinnik-Stepanov, Leningrad 1931).

Position 190

**1.b5!** Clearing the sixth rank allows White to win a rook. **1...cxb5** If 1...♖a8, then 2.♕h8+ ♔f7 3.♕g7+ ♔e6 4.♕f6+. **2.♕h8+ ♔f7 3.♕g7+ ♔e6 4.♕f6+** This is why the move 1.b5 was played – the rook at a6 is undefended. **4...♔d7 5.♕xa6** and Black resigned in Malich-Bueno, Leipzig 1977.

Position 191

**1.♘h6+ ♔f8** Now, after moves like 2.♖h4 or 2.♕h8+ ♔e7 3.♕g7 ♖f8 4.♖g3 (4.♖e3, 4.♖h4) White keeps the attack. However, the striking **2.♘f5!** ends the game at once. After 2...exf5 (or 2...gxf5) there comes 3.♖xh7 with inevitable mate (Timman-Pomar, Las Palmas 1977).

Position 192

**1...exd4 2.♗d1** Threatening 3.g4 followed by a queen sacrifice on h7. If 2...♘xf6 3.♘xf6 ♖g7, then 4.♘xh7! ♔g8 (4...♖xh7 5.♕f8#) 5.♘f6+ ♔f8 6.♕h8+ ♔e7 7.♘d5+. After 2...♗e6 the attack breaks through by 3.g4 ♘g7 (3...♘xf6 4.♘xf6 ♖g7 5.♖h3) 4.fxg7+ ♖xg7 5.♘f6 and 6.♖h3. **2... g5 3.g4 ♖g6 4.♕f8+** 4.♕xg6! was both better and more spectacular. **4...♖g8 5.♕xf7 b5** 5...♗e6 was better. **6.♘e7 ♗e6 7.♕xh7+ ♔xh7 8.♖h3#** (Planinc-Matulovic, Novi Sad 1965).
But there was a defence after all! After 2...b5! 3.g4 ♘g7 the threats are parried, and 4.♘e7 ♗e6 5.♘xg8 ♖xg8 6.fxg7+ ♖xg7 7.♕f4 h5 leads to a position with roughly equal prospects.

# Pinning and unpinning (positions 208-223)

Position 208

**1.♕g6** wins. After 1...fxg6 there follows 2.♖xf8+ ♔h7 3.h5 and mate next move. **1...f5 2.exf6 ♗xf6 3.♖xf6** and Black resigned in Sajtar-Dietze, Prague 1943.

Position 209

After **1...♖e2!** White had to resign. After 2.♕xc5 there follows 2...♖gxg2+ 3.♔h1 ♖h2+ 4.♔g1 ♖eg2# (Bannik-Cherepkov, USSR 1961).

Position 210

**1.0-0-0!** wins, since after 1...♖xe3 White plays 2.♖xd6+ ♔e7 (or 2...♔c7) 3.♘d5+ (Pinkas-Fialkowski, Katowice 1977).

## Position 211

After **1...♖c2+ 2.♖d2**, a second attack on the rook decides: **2...♕d1!**, after which White must lose his queen (3.♖xc2 ♕xd6).

## Position 212

The rook on h8 is out of play, and White realises this advantage by means of a combinative blow: **1.♕a3+ ♕e7** 1...♔g8 2.♗xh7+. **2.♗c6!** and Black resigned in Evans-Bisguier, USA 1958/59.

## Position 213

White has a strong attack, a routine continuation of which would win: 1.♗xf6+ ♕xf6 2.♗xf5 ♖b6 3.b3 ♗xf5 4.♖xf5. But White found a shorter way, by exploiting the idea of a pin.
**1.♕g5! d5 2.♕g7+! ♗xg7 3.♗xg7+ ♔g8 4.♗f6#**
(G. Zhuravlev-A. Romanov, Kalinin 1952).

## Position 214

**1.♗xe7 ♖xe7** 1...♔xe7 2.♗xd5. **2.♖xe6!** A temporary exchange sacrifice, with the aid of which White obtains a winning pawn ending by force: **2...♖xe6 3.♗xd5 ♖e8 4.cxb6 axb6 5.♖e1 ♖e7 6.♖xe6 ♖xe6 7.♔b2 ♔e7 8.♗xe6 ♔xe6 9.♔b3**, and White won easily in Belov-Zhelnin, Narva 1986.

Position 215

**1...♖xg3+!** Also winning are 1...♖g4, 1...♖b4 and 1...♘f6. **2.♖xg3 ♖g8!** The triple pin (on the g-file, the third rank and the a7-g1 diagonal) forced resignation – White loses his queen (Gendel-Sushkevich, USSR 1956).
The quieter 1...♘f6 was also strong.

Position 216

White wins the queen, with the help of a pin:
**1.♕c7+ ♔e8 2.♕c8+.** Here Black resigned, since after 2...♔e7 there follows 3.♖xd5 ♕h1+ (or 3...♕f1+) 4.♖d1, attacking the queen and at the same time threatening 5.♕d8# (Kieninger-H. Herrmann, Bad Oeynhausen 1940).

Position 217

**1.♕d5! ♗xh3 2.♕a8+ ♔d7 3.♕xa7+ ♔c6**
3...♔e6 4.♘d4#. **4.♘d4+ ♔c5 5.♖b1 ♘b3** 5...♕d8 6.♖b5#; 5...♗d7 6.♕c7+. **6.♕a3#** (Tsvetkov-Arnaudov, Sofia 1956)

Position 218

The rook cannot be taken because of 2.♕f8#. The subtle move **1...f5!** decides the game. Black takes control of g4, after which White is defenceless against the threat of 2...♕g3+! (unpinning) 3.♕xg3 ♖h5#. This excellent tactical possibility was missed in Alekhine-Naegeli, Berne 1932. I should also point out another winning line, not mentioned by other commentators, starting with the move 1...♕g1, in order after 2.♖f6 (defending the mate on e1) to continue 2...♕e1+ 3.♕f2 ♕d1! 4.♖f3 (4.♕f3 ♖h5+) 4...♖g1!.

Position 219

First Black drove out the enemy king by means of **1...♖a1+ 2.♔h2 ♕g1+ 3.♔g3**, and then he played **3...♖a3+**.
If 4.♔g4 then 4...♕h2 wins (5.♕f2 f5+ and 6...♖xh3+ or immediately 5...♖xh3).
Therefore White blocked the check with **4.♖d3**.

*(see next diagram)*

We are following the game Bogatyrev-Zagoryansky, Moscow 1947. Black missed the chance to win the game, thanks to the pin, with the move **4...♕d4!**. He played 4...♖a7?, and the game eventually ended in a draw.

## Position 220

After **1.♕d3!** Black resigned. After 1...hxg5 there comes 2.♕g6!, mating (Bagirov-Machulsky, Chelyabinsk 1975).

## Position 221

No. The tactical operation **1.♘xe4? ♗xe4 2.♖e1** leads to defeat after **2...♗g5+ 3.♔d1 0-0!**, and White loses a piece (De Mey-O'Kelly de Galway, Brussels 1935).
The moves can also be inverted: 2...0-0! and if 3.♖xe4 ♗g5+.

## Position 222

Only to f1, which wins. In the event of **2.♔f2? ♖f8 3.♖d8 ♕h4+!** White loses his queen (Makogonov-Chekhover, Tbilisi 1937).

## Position 223

No. After 1...dxc4 2.♗xe4? Black, exploiting the pins on the bishop on e4 (diagonal and vertical) wins:
**2...♕f5! 3.♖e1 ♖ae8 4.♘c3 ♖xe4! 5.♘xe4 ♖e8** (Yuriev-Tishler, USSR 1927)

# Interference (positions 232-245)

Position 232

**1.罩d4!** An interference, allowing the d-pawn to promote. **1...♔xd4 2.d7** and Black resigned in Vatnikov-Vietal, Czechoslovakia 1973.

Position 233

**1.♗e8 ♕f5** Defending against the mate on d7. **2.罩e6!** By closing the c8-h3 diagonal, White wins (Augustin-Lanc, Brno 1975).

Position 234

There followed **1...♗c2**, and White stopped the clocks. The bishop shuts off the second rank, threatening 2...罩xe1+ and 3...♕xg2#. Neither the knight, nor the rook, nor the queen, can take the bishop (Ilyin-Genevsky-Kubbel, Leningrad 1925).

Position 235

**1.h6+ ♔h8 2.♗e6!**
Interfering between queen and bishop; White
wins. Taking on e6 is impossible because of
mate: 2...♕xe6 3.♕f8+ ♕g8 4.♕f6+. Meanwhile
the bishop on e4 is attacked. If 2...d5, then
3.♕e5+, and if the bishop retreats, it is mate after
3.♕d4+ (Ivanovic-Popovic, Yugoslavia 1973).

Position 236

The move **1...♗h3!** is the prelude to a deeply-
calculated combination. The rook cannot be
taken because of 2...♕e4 3.f3 ♕xe2 mating, so
White replied **2.♕a3**, defending against the
threats (2...♕e4 3.♕d3). There followed: **2...♖c8!**
Driving off the rook and preparing to shut off
the third rank. **3.♖e1** 3.♖xc8 ♕b1+. **3...♖c3!**
Interference. The queen is isolated from the
kingside, after which Black realises his original
threat. **4.bxc3 ♕e4 5.f3 ♕e3+ 6.♔h1 ♕f2 7.♖g1
♕xe2 8.cxd4**

(see next diagram)

Now what? The contact between the queen and
the kingside has been re-established... **8...e4!!**
A 'quiet' move, which had to be foreseen when
Black sacrificed the rook. The threat is both 9...
e3 and 9...exf3 followed by ...♗g2+. The e4-pawn
cannot be taken because of mate. **9.f4 e3** and
White resigned in Kitanov-Baum, Sterlitamak
1949.
If White had defended with the move 2.♕c5
(instead of 2.♕a3), there could have followed
2...♖c8 3.♗c7 ♕e4! 4.♕c2 (4.f3 ♕e3+) 4...f5!.
After the exchange of queens, the pin on the
c-file and the advance of the d-pawn decide the
outcome.

Position 237

**1.a6 ♖h4** If 1...♖g1, then 2.a7 ♖a1 3.♖a3 (interference) 3...bxa3 4.a8♕. **2.♖d8!** Shutting off the eighth rank prevents the rook stopping the pawn. **2...♔xd8 3.a7** Black resigned (from a simultaneous game by Alekhine, 1933).

Position 238

**1.♗e4+!**
Isolating the black king, after which it is defenceless. **1...fxe4 2.♕d5+ ♔c8 3.♕c6#** (Urzica-Honfi, Bucharest 1975)
A similar variation is **1.♕a6+ ♔a8**, and now the same move **2.♗e4+!** (2...fxe4 3.♕c6#), or 1.♕b5+ ♘b6 2.♖e7+ ♔a8 3.♗e4+.

Position 239

Shutting off the 6th rank with the move **1.♖1e6!** (or indeed 1.♖7e6) ends the game (1...♗xe6 2.♕xh6) (Suhle-Mayet, Berlin 1860).
Mate can be avoided by giving up the queen – 1...♕xe6 2.♖xe6 ♗xe6, but after 3.♕xh6 f6 4.♕g6+ the result is not changed.
White also had another option, forcing mate: **1.♖xf7! ♖xf7 2.♖e8+ ♖f8** (2...♕f8 3.♕g6+ ♖g7 4.♕xg7#), and now **3.♖e7!** followed by 3...♖f6 (or 3...♖f5, or 3...♖f4) 4.♕e8+ ♖f8 5.♖g7+ ♔h8 6.♖f7+ ♔g8 7.♖xf8+ ♕xf8 8.♕g6+ and mate. If 3...♕f6, then 4.♗xf6 ♖xf6 5.♕e8+ and 6.♕g6+.

Position 240

**1.♖f5!** Shutting off the diagonal c8-h3. **1...♔h8** 1...gxf5 2.♕g5+ and mate. **2.♕h6 ♖g8 3.♘g5** and Black resigned in Zinkl-Metger, Berlin 1897.

Position 241

White wins by exploiting the idea of interference: **5.♗d5!** Breaking the connection between the enemy queen and the c6-square. **5...exd5 6.♕xc6+ ♔d8** If 6...♔e7, then 7.♘xd5+. **7.♕xa8+ ♔d7 8.♕b7+ ♔e6 9.♕c6+ ♗d6 10.♗f4!** Black resigned. After 10...♕xh1+ 11.♔d2 ♕xa1 White mates with 12.♕xd6+ ♔f5 13.♕e5+ and 14.♕g5# (Janowski-Schallopp, Nuremberg 1896).

Position 242

After **1...♘d3 2.♗xh7+ ♔h8** Of course, not 2...♔xh7? 3.♕xd3+, when White defends the mate and has two extra pawns. **3.♕h5 ♘f4! 4.♕h4?** Losing at once. However, after 4.♘b5 ♘xh5 5.♘xd6 ♗xd6 or 4.c5 ♕f6 5.♕f3 ♔xh7 Black's material advantage would be enough to win. **4...♘h3+!** and White resigned in Shereshevsky-Kupreichik, Minsk 1976.

Position 243

The move ♔f5-g6 will become possible if we block the file with the preliminary bishop sacrifice **1.♗g5!**. After 1...fxg5, 2.♔g6 wins, whilst after 1...g1♕ there is 2.♗xf6+ and 3.h7+. Black resigned in Perenyi-Brandics, Budapest 1985.

Position 244

It is clear that White is not losing, just from the variation **1.♘a6+ ♚a8 2.♘xc7+**. Black cannot take the knight because of 3.♖d8+, mating, and therefore he should acquiesce in a repetition after **2...♚b8 3.♘a6+ ♚a8**

(see next diagram)

But is White forced to repeat? The study-like move **4.♖b7!** sets up a surprise mating net. The pawn cannot be taken because of 5.♖b8#, and meanwhile there is a threat of 5.♖b8+! ♖xb8 6.♘c7#. There is no defence, and Black resigned in Janowski-NN, Paris 1900.

Position 245

**1...♛c2** (or 1...♚h8 with the same point) wins by force after 2.♕xf7+ ♚h8 3.♖b1 ♛xb2+ 4.♖xb2 ♖e1+ mating, or 3.♖7d2 (instead of 3.♖b1) 3...♛xd2.
In the game Miles-Pritchett (London 1982) the apparently more energetic **1...♝xc3** was played, after which there followed **2.♕xf7+ ♚h8?**

(see next diagram)

**3.♝e5!!** Shutting off the long diagonal and the e-file changes the picture fundamentally – it is Black who has to resign. It is easy to see that after 3...♛xd7 or 3...♛xd1+ Black gets only a rook for the queen. 2...♚h7! would still have drawn, since after 3.♝e5 ♛xd7 4.♕xd7 ♝xe5, 5.♕xe8 is not with check!

# Combining themes (positions 281-310)

Position 281

**1.♖xd6+!** Deflection after 1...exd6 (2.♕d7+ ♕xd7 3.♖xd7#) and decoying after 1...♕xd6 (2.♕xe8+! ♔xe8? 3.♖h8#) (Paeren-Jaworski, correspondence game, 1974-76).

Position 282

**1.♕xe7+! ♕xe7 2.♗d6 ♕xd6 3.♖e8#** (Gligoric-Rosenstein, Chicago 1963)

Position 283

Black has just played ...h7-h6, believing the knight will retreat. However, the deflecting move **1.♘d5!** forces him to resign in this textbook example. If 1...♘xd5, then mate on h7, whilst in the event of 1...exd5 White eliminates the defender of h7 by 2.♗xf6.

Position 284

A position from Torre-Ed. Lasker, Chicago 1926. The tactical blow **1...c3!** could have decided the game, whilst still in the opening. The theme is deflection (the bishop on b2 is deflected from the defence of the queen) or interference (the diagonal of the bishop on b2), as a result of which the knight on e5 is left undefended. The intermediate exchange 2.♕xd6 does not help, since after 2...cxd6 two white pieces are attacked. But Lasker instead kicked the knight with 1...f6...

Position 285

**1.♖g8+!** and Black resigned. If 1...♖xg8, then the queen is undefended, whilst after 1...♔xg8 there follows 2.♕g3+ ♔f8 3.♕g7+ ♔e8 4.♕g8# (Barczay-Erdelyi, Hungary 1975).

Position 286

**1...♖xd3 2.cxd3 ♗g5** and White could have resigned immediately here (Shamaev-Ufimtsev, Leningrad 1949).

Position 287

With the move **1...♖e1!**, Black wins. After 2.♗xe1 (or 2.♘xe1) 2...♘b2!, both the queen and the rook f1 (with mate) are attacked. Therefore, White is obliged to part with the queen (I. Jones-Dueball, Nice Olympiad 1974).

Position 288

**1.♕d8+!** The queen must give the check, as the rook is needed on the 6th rank. **1...♔h7** 1...♖xd8 2.♖xd8+ and 3.♖h8#. **2.♖xh5+ gxh5 3.♖h6+ ♔xh6 4.♕f6+** and Black is mated (Makov-Vazhenin, Novosibirsk 1976).

Position 289

**1.♕xh5+! gxh5** 1...♔g8 2.♕xg6 needs no assessing. **2.♘f6+** Clearing the fifth rank and deflecting the bishop at the same time. **2...♗xf6 3.♖xh5#** (Bologan-Van Haastert, St Vincent 2005)

Position 290

It only takes the single move **1.♘xf5!**, after which it becomes clear that the solid-looking black position is in ruins. By decoying the enemy queen to f5, White then wins it: 1...♕xf5 2.♖xg3+ hxg3 3.♖xg3+.
In the game Schulz-Kostic, Bardejov 1926. Black replied **1...♔f7** and after **2.♘xe7 ♔xe7 3.f5** he resigned.

Position 291

**1.♘e7+ ♛xe7 2.♕xh7+ ♚xh7 3.♖h5+ ♚g8**
**4.♖h8#** (Spielmann-Hönlinger, Vienna 1929)

Position 292

**1...♖xg2+! 2.♖xg2 ♘f3+ 3.♚f2**
**3...♕xg2+! 4.♚xg2 ♘xe1+** and White resigned in
Finotti-Reinhardt, Hamburg 1937.

Position 293

A positional advantage is realised by combinative
means: **1.b4!** Decoying the queen onto the open
file. **1...♕xb4 2.♖eb1 ♕xc4**

*(see next diagram)*

After 3.♖b8+ Black replies 3...♖c8. White,
however, went into this position deliberately,
and had prepared the deflecting sacrifice **3.♗e2!**,
after which Black cannot defend the eighth
rank. The bishop cannot be taken because of
mate and after 3...♕c3 there follows 4.♖b8+
♖c8 5.♕xc3, whilst in the event of 3...♕c2 the
bishop continues to chase the queen: 4.♗d3!,
which ends the game. Black resigned in Bukic-
Romanishin, Moscow 1977.

Position 294

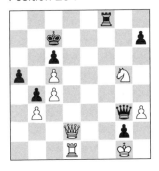

A composed illustration of a classical combination: **1...♖f1+! 2.♖xf1 ♕h2+! 3.♔xh2 gxf1♘+! 4.♔g2 ♘xd2** The endgame is hopeless for White (5.♘e6+ ♔d7 6.♘d4 a4 7.bxa4 b3 etc.).

Position 295

**1...♖c1+!** Deflection – either of the rook from the defence of the queen, or of the queen from the defence of the second rank, in particular the square a2. **2.♕xc1** 2.♖xc1 ♕xd2. **2...♖xa3+! 3.♔b1** 3.bxa3 ♕a2#. **3...♖a1+!** And now, decoying the king to a1, after which mate follows from a geometrical manoeuvre by the queen. **4.♔xa1 ♕a8+! 5.♔b1 ♕a2#** (Wheeler-Hall, England 1964).
The mating combination could also have been started with the move 1...♖xa3+.

Position 296

Were it not for the knight on e4, White could give mate. Therefore, the knight quits its post: **1.♘f6+!** Clearing lines, as a result of which the black king gets a square on g7. **1...gxf6 2.♕f8+!** Decoying, with the help of which the bolthole is closed. **2...♔xf8 3.♗h6+ ♔g8 4.♖e8#** (Richardson-Delmar, New York 1887)

Position 297

White is mated in five moves: **1...♖h1+!** Deflecting the knight. **2.♘xh1 ♗h2+!** Decoying the king. **3.♔xh2 ♖h8+ 4.♔g3 ♘f5+ 5.♔f4 ♖h4#** This is how the game Schiffers-Chigorin, St Petersburg 1897, could have ended.
Instead of 1...♖h1+ Chigorin isolated the enemy queen with 1...b6, after which there followed 2.♗e3. Now, too, the combination works. However, Chigorin continued the attack with 2...♘f5, and Schiffers managed to fight off the threats. The game was eventually drawn.

Position 298

**1.♕g3+** Even more accurate was 1.♕g4+, protecting f5. **1...♔xh6** Accepting the sacrifice is obligatory, since after 1...♔f8 2.♕g8+ a rook is lost. **2.♔h1!** Freeing the square g1 for the rook. **2...♕d5** 2...c2 loses to 3.♖g1 with the threat of 4.♕h4#. **3.♖g1 ♕xf5 4.♕h4+ ♕h5 5.♕f4+ ♕g5 6.♖xg5 fxg5 7.♕d6+** Black does not manage to play ...c3-c2, since the knight is taken with either check or a threat of mate. **7...♔h5 8.♕xd7** and White won in Pillsbury-Tarrasch, Hastings 1895.

Position 299

No. On **2.♕xd5** there follows **2...♖c1+!** (ideas: deflection – 3.♖xc1 ♕xd5 and interference – 3.♗xc1 ♕b1#). White resigned in Wisznewetzki-Auerbach, Lviv 1912.

Position 300

**1.♘c8+**, and Black resigned in Kupreichik-Tseshkovsky, Moscow 1976. After 1...♘c5 (if 1...♕c5, then 2.♕xc5+ ♘xc5 3.♖d8#) there follows the deflecting sacrifice 2.♕xc5+ ♕xc5 and 3.♖d8#. The discovered check has to be made with the move ♘d6-c8: the interference shuts out the rook on b8.

Position 301

**1...♘xh2!** After 2.♔xh2 there follows 2...♕xf3+! 3.♖xf3 ♖e1+ 4.♕g1 ♖exg1+ 5.♔h2 ♖1g2+ with a great material advantage (E. Polyak-Kofman, Kyiv 1941).

Position 302

The opponent's combination turns out to have a fatal hole at the end of the variation: **1...♕xb1+! 2.♘xb1 ♗a6!** – Black remains with an extra exchange (Johansen-Metzing, Berlin 1973).

Position 303

The move 2.♕d1? is mistaken. Black obtains a material advantage by force, by using the ideas of deflection and pinning:
**2...♕xd1+ 3.♖xd1 ♖f1! 4.♖d2** The realisation of Black's advantage is not made much more difficult by 4.♗xe4 ♖xd1+ 5.♔c2 ♖g1 6.d5 ♔f7.
**4...♖xd1+ 5.♖xd1 ♖f1 6.♗xe4 ♖xd1+**, and Black wins (Timofeev-Lobanov, Chita 1935).
Instead of 2.♕d1? White should have played 2.b3, 2.a3 or 2.♖c1.

239

Position 304

Black has to resign after the study-like move **1.♗d6!**. The ideas are interference (the knight cannot take the bishop because the queen on e6 is undefended) and deflection (after 1...♖xd6 there follows 2.♕b8+, mating – Black has lost control of c8). In the meantime, the queen on e6 is undefended, and 2.♖f8# is threatened (Berthold Lasker-Kagan, Berlin 1894). Emanuel Lasker's older brother was also not a bad chess player...

Position 305

No. After **1.♕xg6+! ♕xg6 2.♘xg6 ♔xg6** (more tenacious was 2...♔f6 3.♘e5 ♘xe5 4.fxe5+ ♔xe5 5.♖xc5±) **3.g4!** Black suffers material losses: **3...♖h2+ 4.♔g3 ♖d2 5.♗xf5+ ♔f6 6.♗xd7** (Spielmann-Hönlinger, Vienna 1936)

Position 306

The sacrifice 1.♘de4 is correct. After **1...♕xb2** in the game Krantz-Sellberg, played by correspondence (1975), there followed **2.♘xe6 ♕xe5** 2...♘xe6 3.♕xf5. **3.♖xf5 ♕xe6** Or 3...♕e2 4.♘xc7+ ♔e7 5.♕a3+ with mate.

*(see next diagram)*

**4.♖e5!** Black resigned.

## Position 307

There is a forced win by means of **1.♕xg7+!**, first decoying the king to g7, after which a discovered check follows. **1...♔xg7 2.♗d8+ ♔h8** If 2...♔f7, then 3.♗h5#; 2...♔h6 3.♖h3#. **3.♖g8+!** Deflecting the rook from f8. **3...♖xg8 4.♗f6+ ♖g7 5.♗xg7+ ♔g8** And now, the last discovered check. White not only regains the sacrificed material, but remains with an extra piece: **6.♗xd4+ ♔f7 7.♖f1+ ♔e7 8.♗xb2** and Black resigned in Westerinen-Sigurjonsson, New York 1978.

## Position 308

The ending finished in a draw. However, with the striking knight rebound **2.♘f5!** (instead of 2.♕f2) White could have won. After **2...♕g5** (if 2...♕xg2+ 3.♕xg2 ♗xg2, then 4.♗xg7+ ♔g8 5.♖c7, threatening ♘f5-h6#, 5...h5 6.♔xg2 – White has an extra piece) **3.♕xd8+! ♕xd8 4.♖c8! ♕xc8 5.♗xg7+ ♔g8 6.♗d5+** Black is mated, a chance missed in the game Yudovich-Ragozin, Tbilisi 1937.

## Position 309

On **1...♘d6?** there followed **2.♖h8+** (if 2.♕h4, then 2...♘h5) **2...♔g7** (2...♔xh8 3.♕h4 ♔g8 4.♗xf6) **3.♖h7+ ♔g8 4.♕h4** and Black resigned in Trockenheim-Wilczynski, Warsaw 1939. However, there was a saving line, and the move 1.♕e4 was not the best (the attack would have succeeded after 1.♖h6!).
Instead of 1...♘d6? Black should have played **1...♕xd2+!**, returning the sacrificed piece: 2.♗xd2 ♘xe4 3.♘xe4 ♖fd8=. After 2.♗xd2? ♘xe4+ 3.♘xe4 f5! 4.♖h8+ ♔f7 5.♖h7+ ♔e8 the knight has no retreat so White has to go for 6.♖xe7+ ♔xe7 7.♘g5∓.

Position 310

**3.♗a6!**
By closing the a-file for a moment, White invites his opponent to take the bishop with the rook, and create the threat of a deadly check on a1. But then, exploiting the fact that the rook has left the seventh rank, he is able to mate his opponent: 3...♖xa6 4.♖xh7+ ♔xh7 5.♘f6#.
In the meantime, after 3.♗a6 White threatens 4.♕g3, and also 4.♘f6. In the event of 3...♖xg7 4.♖xg7 ♗xa6 the same combination decides things: 5.♖xh7+, 6.♘f6+ and 7.♕h7#.
After 3...♕f2 White wins by 4.♖7g2 (4...♖xa6 5.♖xf2 ♖a1+ 6.♔d2 ♖xg1 7.♖f1), whilst after 3...♕a5, there is 4.♖xa7 ♕a1+ 5.♔d2 ♕xg1 6.♖xh7+.
In the game there followed **3...♗xa6**, and after **4.♕g3!** Black resigned (Richter-NN, Germany 1930).
Instead of the tempting 1...♘b3+ Black should have played 1...a3! with extremely strong threats.

# Pawns on the brink (positions 325-338)

Position 325

By decoying the knight to f8, White queens his pawn: **1.♖f8+! ♘xf8 2.e7**

Position 326

It may appear that this position has nothing to do with pawn promotion, but this is not so. After **1.♕f8+ ♕g8** the move **2.e6!** forced Black to resign. After **2...♕xf8** there follows **3.exd7** and the unavoidable 4.♖e8. The pawn reaches the coveted spot (Malysheva-Hjelm, Stockholm 2003/04).

Position 327

1...♗d4! is a strong positional continuation. But there is also a forcing decision: **1...♕d1! 2.♘xb6** If 2.♖xd1, then 2...e2+ and 3...exd1+. **2...♖c1!** After 3.♔f1 there follows 3...e2+. White resigned in Arnold-Duras, Prague 1920.

Position 328

**1.a6** Towards the queening square! **1...♖h7+ 2.♕xh7+ ♔xh7 3.a7 ♕f8 4.♖a2 ♕a8** The pawn is stopped, but only for a short time. After **5.b4** Black is defenceless. The further moves **5...d4 6.exd4 ♔g6 7.b5 e3 8.fxe3** were played, and then Black resigned in Lauberte-Semenova, Moscow 1945.

Position 329

**1...♖f1+! 2.♗xf1** Or 2.♕xf1 exf1♕+ 3.♗xf1 ♕e4+ 4.♔g1 ♕xd4+, winning another rook. **2...♕e4+! 3.♕xe4 exf1♕#** (Ruchieva-Eidelson, Tbilisi 1976) 1...♖f7 2.♖xf7 e1♕ 3.♕xe1 ♕xe1+ 4.♖f1 ♕e3 was also winning, but much more cumbersome.

Position 330

**1.♗xf7+! ♖xf7 2.♕xe8+ ♘xe8 3.♖xe8+ ♖f8 4.d7 ♕d6**

(see next diagram)

**5.♖f1!** and Black resigned in Velimirovic-Csom, Amsterdam 1974.

Position 331

**1...e3+ 2.♔f1**

*(see next diagram)*

Now after 2...♗c4+? there follows 3.♖xc4+, and White wins. However, the deflecting sacrifice **2...♗g2+!** ensures the promotion of the pawn: **3.♔xg2** 3.♔e2 exf2. **3...e2**, and Black won in Hradeczky-Hardicsay, Hungary 1980.

Position 332

White wins with **1.♕f3! ♕xf3 2.gxf3 ♖xf1+ 3.♔g2** (a variation from the game Zuidema-Bonne, Zurich 1962)
This is definitely the most elegant solution; 'unfortunately' White can also win more simply with 1.♕d8+, 2.♕d7 and 3.♕f5.

Position 333

Black wins with the move **1...♘f3!**.
The king cannot move (2.♔g2 ♘e1+), and if 2.♖d6+, then 2...♔g5 with the threat of 3...♘d4. In the event of 2.b4 the simplest is 2...b6 and then ...♔h6-g5-f4. However, the immediate 2...♔g5 (3.bxc5 ♔f4 4.♖d7 ♔e3 and ...♘d4) also decides things (Sternberg-Pawelczak, Berlin 1964).

Position 334

The move **1...c5** is well answered by 2.bxc5 bxc5 3.♖xc5, but also by **2.dxc5! ♕xe5**. Again, 2...bxc5 3.♖xc5. But the text is refuted by a nice combination: **3.cxb6! ♖xc3 4.bxa7! ♖xc2 5.♖xc2**, and the three black pieces are unable to prevent the pawn from queening (a variation from the game Kotov-Ragozin, Moscow 1949).

Position 335

**1.♕e8+! ♖xe8** Or 1...♗xe8 2.c7+ ♖xf3 3.c8♕#.
**2.♖xe8+ ♗xe8 3.c7+ ♖xf3 4.c8♕#** (Mieses-Von Bardeleben, Barmen 1905)
The aim can also be achieved by reversing the move-order (1.c7+ ♖xf3 2.♕e8+ etc.).

Position 336

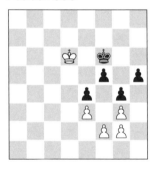

White's king has strayed too far from his forces and Black wins by a pawn breakthrough: **1...f4!** If 2.gxf4, then 2...h4, and the h-pawn promotes. After 2.exf4 there again follows 2...h4! (deflecting the g3 pawn) 3.gxh4 (otherwise 3...hxg3 and e4-e3) 3...g3 4.fxg3 e3. Nor does **2.♔d5** save White, because the fearless h-pawn again throws itself on the barricades: **2...h4 3.♔xe4** If 3.gxh4, then 3...g3!; 3.exf4 h3 or 3...hxg3.
(see next diagram)
**3...f3! 4.gxf3 h3**, and White had to resign in Pomar-Cuadras, Spain 1974.

## Position 337

The position may seem drawn, but by a study-like manoeuvre, White manages to instil some strength into his passed pawns:
**1.♖f6!** **♚xd7** The threat was 2.a8♕+ ♖xa8 3.♖f8+ or 2.♖f8+ and then 3.a8♕. If 1...♖xa7, then 2.♖f8+ ♚xd7 3.♖f7+. **2.♖f8!** After 2...♖xa7 there follows 3.♖f7+. Black resigned in Bukic-Marovic, Yugoslavia 1968.

## Position 338

White's joy was misplaced. There followed **1...e2!** **2.♗xf2**

*(see next diagram)*

**2...♗e3!!** A deflection sacrifice ensures the promotion of the pawn (Voitsekhovsky-Sandler, Riga 1982).

2.♖xf4 (instead of 2.♗xf2) 2...♖xf4 3.♗xg3 does not save White either. After 3...♚c6 4.♗f2 ♚d5 Black wins.

# Miracle saves (positions 359-380)

Position 359

White has an extra rook, but by putting his queen en prise with **1...♛c1+!** Black draws (Titenko-Murey, Moscow 1961).

Position 360

The black king has no moves and his only pawn is blocked, so by sacrificing the queen he saves the game: **1...♛g4+ 2.♔h6 ♛g5+** (after 2.♔f6 there would follow 2...♛e6+). This was the finish of the game Portisch-Lengyel (Malaga 1964).

Position 361

The black king has no retreat squares. By sacrificing the rook, and then the queen, Black reaches a stalemate: **1...♖f7+! 2.♔xf7** If White declines the rook with 2.♔e8, stalemate is reached after 2...♛c6+ 3.♔xf7 ♛g6+ 4.♔e7 ♛f7+ 5.♔d6 ♛d5+ 6.♔c7 ♛c6+. **2...♛g6+ 3.♔e7 ♛f7+**, and the rest is as in the variation after 2...♔e8 (this is a slightly amended position from the game Pribyl-Ornstein, Tallinn 1977).

## Position 362

**1...♖xg3+ 2.♔f1**
If 2.♔xg3, then 2...♕xh4+, whilst after 2.fxg3 a draw results from 2...♕b2+ followed by a queen sacrifice.
**2...♕a1+ 3.♔e2 ♖e3+ 4.♔xe3 ♕e1+ 5.♔f3 ♕e3+ 6.♔xe3** – stalemate (Danielsson-Lange, Helsinki Olympiad 1952)

## Position 363

After **1...♕c6+ 2.♔f5** Black saved himself by **2...♘g7+! 3.♗xg7 ♕g6+!** and any capture leads to stalemate (Pietzsch-Fuchs, Berlin 1963).

## Position 364

**1...♗xg4! 2.♖xg4** If 2.♔xg4, then 2...f5+ 3.♔h4 ♖xf4+ 4.♘xf4 – stalemate. **2...f5 3.♖g8 ♖xf4+ 4.♘xf4** – stalemate (Luik-Hindre, Tallinn 1955).

## Position 365

**1.♗d3! ♕xd3 2.♕e8+** with perpetual check, since after 2...♔h6 4.♕f8+ ♔h5 5.♕f7+ ♔g6, both 6.♕xg6+ and 6.♕xh7+ lead to stalemate. If Black does not take the bishop immediately, but first plays 1...♖h1+ 2.♔xh1 and only now 2...♕xd3, trying to exploit his extra pawn in the queen ending, then 3.♕e8+ ♔h6 4.♕f8+ ♔h5 5.♕f7+ at least draws by a repetition of moves, since 5...♕g6 6.♕xd5+ gives White winning chances.

Position 366

All attempts to create activity (for example, 1...♕d7 2.♗g3) are clearly in White's favour. The draw was forced by **1...♖xh3+! 2.♔xh3 ♕e6+! 3.♕xe6** – stalemate (Walter-Nagy, Györ 1924).

Position 367

**1...h3+! 2.♔xh3**

(see next diagram)

**2...♕f5+! 3.♕xf5 ♖xg3+! 4.♔h4 ♖g4+** It is only possible to avoid the checks on g3 and g4 by taking the rook, and then it is stalemate (Tieberger-Drelinkiewicz, Poland 1970).

Position 368

Black is threatened with mate, and he is two pawns down. However, after **1...♖b1+ 2.♔h2** the sacrifice of three pieces results in stalemate: **2...♖h1+! 3.♔xh1 ♘g3+! 4.fxg3** 4.♔h2? ♘xf5. **4...♕xg2+ 5.♔xg2** – stalemate (Ormos-Batoczky, Budapest 1951).

Position 369

**1...♘f2+! 2.♗xf2** But not 2.♔h2? ♕xh4+ 3.♔g1 ♕g3+. **2...♕h3+! 3.♔g1** 3.♗xh3 – stalemate. **3...♕g4+ 4.♔h2 ♕h3+** draw (Rodriguez-Vaisman, Bucharest 1974).

Position 370

**1.♘d6+! ♕xd6** 1...♔a7? 2.♕f7+. **2.♖e7+ ♕xe7 3.♕c7+** draw (Goldin-Ryabov, Novosibirsk 1982). In reply to 1.♘d6+ Black can also play 1...♔b8. There are no more checks, but 2.♕c6 forces Black to give perpetual check: 2...♘a2+ 3.♔d1 ♘c3+.

Position 371

**1.♖xg6+! hxg6** After a king move there follows 2.♕g4. **2.♖d8+! ♖xd8 3.♕b3+ ♔h7** The king cannot go to a dark square because a discovered check costs him his queen. **4.♕f7+ ♔h8 5.♕f6+** with good drawing chances (a variation from the game Panov-Abramov, Moscow 1949).

Position 372

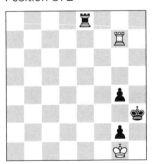

White saved his neck by **1.♖h7+ ♔g3 2.♖e7! ♖d8 3.♖d7** (from Salvio's 1634 book).

Position 373

**1.♘f5+! gxf5 2.♖xh7+! ♚xh7 3.♕xf5+ ♚g7**
He cannot flee to h6 because of 4.♖h8+ ♚g7
5.♖h7+ ♚g8 6.♕g6+ ♚f8 7.♖h8#.
**4.♕xg4+ ♚f6 5.♕f4+ ♚g7 6.♕g4+ ♚f6 7.♕f4+**
with perpetual check (Speelman-Ree, Lone Pine
1978).

Position 374

White is threatened with mate, and he has
nothing else to do except give checks.
**1.♕f8+ ♚f6 2.♕h8+ ♚f5**

(*see next diagram*)

And now what? Answer: **3.g4+! hxg4** (3...♚e4??
4.♖d4#). Now, with the white king stalemated,
the heavy pieces throw themselves on the fire:
**4.♖d5+! exd5 5.♕c8+ ♕xc8** – stalemate (Zazdis-
Zemitis, Riga 1936).

Position 375

After **1.♗xe4+ fxe4 2.♖e5+!** (2.♖xe4? ♖e2+)
**2...♚d6** (if the rook is taken, it will be stalemate)
**3.♖xe4**, play reaches a theoretical ending in
which the rook and knight cannot win against
the rook (Lisitsin-Bondarevsky, Leningrad 1950).

Position 376

White's attack has hit a dead end – the rook on h3 is attacked and Black threatens to bring his rook to c1, with extremely strong threats. After 1.♘xg8 ♚xg8 (but not 1...♗xh3? on account of 2.♘e7!) 2.♖g3 (and not 2.♕xh6!? ♗xh3 3.♗xg6 fxg6 4.♕xg6+ ♚f8 5.♕f6+ ♚e8 6.♕g6+ ♚d8 7.♕d3+ ♕d7 8.♕xd7+ ♚xd7 9.♗xc1 ♗xg4–+) 2...♖a1 or 2...♗f1 3.♖g1 ♖e1! White is in a bad way. However, by sacrificing the queen, he saved the game: **1.♕xh6+! ♘xh6 2.♖xh6+ ♚g7 3.♖h7+ ♚f8 4.♖h8+ ♚e7 5.♘g8+!** Black must acquiesce in a repetition of moves, since if his king retreats along the c-file, he loses a piece, whilst after 5...♕xg8 6.♖xg8 the threat of 7.♗b5 forces 6...♖c5, and after 7.f4 White reaches an endgame with an extra pawn. **5...♚f8 6.♘f6+** There is also no point in running to g7 (7.♖h7+), so the players agreed a draw in Ragozin-Levenfish, Moscow 1935.

Position 377

The queen sacrifice is incorrect. After **1...♕xf3+? 2.♕xf3 ♖a3** White saves himself in miraculous fashion:

(see next diagram)

**3.♚h4!!** The forced reply 3...♖xf3 leads to stalemate (Horowitz-Pavey, New York 1951).

Instead of 1...♕xf3+? it was simplest of all to play 1...♚d6.

## Position 378

If the black queen and the c-pawn are removed from the board, he will have no moves. Therefore **1...♕g8!**. Black temporarily pins the c4-pawn, and in reply to **2.♕b5** (or 2.♕f3) he parts with his queen: **2...♕xc4 3.♕xc4** – stalemate (Nesis-Kolker, correspondence game, 1979).

## Position 379

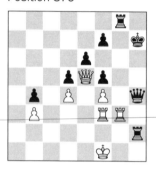

White draws by means of **3.♖xg8 ♔xg8** 3...♖h1+? 4.♖g1. **4.♖g3+! ♕xg3** 4...♔f8? 5.♕d6+ ♕e7 6.♕b8+ ♕e8 7.♕xb4+ ♕e7 8.♖g8+. **5.♕b8+ ♔h7 6.♕h8+ ♔xh8** – stalemate. This possibility was missed in the game Taimanov-Geller, Moscow 1951. Instead of 3.♖xg8 White played 3.♕e3, and after 3...♖a8 Black won.

White's drawing chance resulted from the hasty move 2...♖xh2. After 2...♖g4! his position would have been indefensible.

## Position 380

The draw is achieved by an introductory sacrifice of the rook: **1...♖xf2+ 2.♔xf2 ♕d2+ 3.♔g1 ♕e1+ 4.♔h2 ♕e2+ 5.♔h3**, and then of the knight: **5...♘f4+ 6.♖gxf4** Not 6.♔h4?? ♕e7!–+. **6...♕f1+ 7.♔g4 ♕xf4+ 8.♔h5 ♕h4+** (Shernetsky-Noordijk, Belgium 1953).

# Examination (positions 381-735)

## Position 381

After **1...♖d8!** White resigned (Letov-Khamatgaleev, Perm 1997).

## Position 382

**1.♖d7!** was played, and Black resigned because of the loss of the queen (2.♘f6+; Thelen-Chodera, Prague 1943).

## Position 383

**1.♕g8+** (1...♖xg8 2.♘f7#; Unzicker-Sarapu, 19th Olympiad, Siegen 1970).

Position 384

**1.♕h8+ ♔xh8 2.♗f6+ ♔g8 3.♖xe8#** (Butnorius-Gutman, Riga 1974)

Position 385

**1.♖xc6+ bxc6 2.♗a6#** (Karlsson-Rogard, Sweden 1978)

Position 386

**1...d5!** The introduction to a typical combination – the diagonal of the bishop on f8 must be opened. **2.♗xd5 ♕xc3+ 3.bxc3 ♗a3#** (NN-Boden, London 1860)

Position 387

**1.♖xe6+! fxe6 2.♗g6#** (Cody-Heaton, USA 1914)

**Position 388**

After **1.♖d8+!** Black resigned (1...♗xd8 2.e7+) in Kochiev-Maric, Kapfenberg 1976.

**Position 389**

The knight interferes with the march of the e-pawn, therefore it must be deflected: **1...♘b6+! 2.♘xb6** After 2.♔d4 ♘xc4 3.♔xc4 ♔d6 White loses the pawn endgame. **2...e3** White resigned in Goldenberg-Hug, Switzerland 1976.

**Position 390**

**1.♗c4!**, with the threat 2.c8♕, wins immediately (I. Kan-Chernov, Yaroslavl 1950).

**Position 391**

**1...♖xd4!** On 2.♕xd4 there follows 2...♖e1+ 3.♔f2 ♕xd4+ 4.♖xd4 ♖xa1. White resigned in Tunik-Veingold, Lviv 1984.

Position 392

**1.⌶c1!** wins (Shumov-Winawer, St Petersburg 1875).

Position 393

**1.♗b2! ♕xb2 2.⌶d8+** and Black resigned in Lerner-Sideif-Zade, Frunze 1979.
Black will have rook, bishop and pawn for his queen, but White wins easily.

Position 394

The game lasted one more move. After **1...♘e2+!** White resigned because he loses the queen (if the knight is taken, 2...♕c1+ and ♕f1#) in Costantini-Dziuba, Halkidiki 2000.

Position 395

After **1.♕f6!** Black resigned in Terpugov-I. Kan, Leningrad 1951.

Position 396

**1.♕f6!** and Black resigned.
The queen cannot be taken because of mate
(1...♗xf6 2.exf6 or 2.gxf6 and 3.♖h8#). On the
other hand, if it is not taken, then there is
no defence against the 'X-ray' 2.♖h8+ (Szabo-
Bakonyi, Hungary 1951).

Position 397

By continuing **1...♘g4!**, Black could have ended
the game. The threat is 2...♖f2#, and after the
sacrifice is accepted – **2.hxg4**, there follows **2...
hxg4#**.
In the game (Z. Nikolic-Miladinovic, Yugoslavia
1994) Black did not notice this possibility, and
played 1...♘d5.

Position 398

The 'long' move **1...♕f1!** deflects the rook from
the defence of the square h3. After the 'spite
check' **2.♘xe5+ dxe5**, White resigned in K.
Stein-Movsesian, Norilsk 2001.

Position 399

The move 1.♖d7 (or 1.♕xb7 ♖xb7 2.♘d6) 1...♕xc6
2.♘e7+ ♔g7 3.♘xc6 ♖e8 4.♖d5 is sufficient
for an advantage, as was played in the game V.
Zhuravlev-Semeniuk, Novosibirsk 1976.
However, play could have been ended
immediately with **1.♖d8+!**.

Position 400

**1.Ձe8+!**, and mate on the next move (1...♕xe8 2.♕xf6#; 1...♗xe8 2.♕f8#), Domuls-Skunda, USSR 1977.

Position 401

After **1.Ձd8!** all three of White's pieces are under attack, but not one of them can be taken (1...♕xc3 2.Ձxe8#; 1...♕xd8 2.♕g7#; 1...Ձxd8 2.♕xf6; 1...♕xf5 2.Ձxe8#), Durka-Jablonicky, Czechoslovakia 1977.

Position 402

After **1.Ձf8+!** Black resigned in view of 1...Ձxf8 (1...♗xf8 2.♕g8#) 2.♕g8+ Ձxg8 3.♞f7# (Nikolov-Slavchev, correspondence game, 1963).

Position 403

**1...axb4! 2.♕xa8 ♞b6**, and the white queen is trapped (Castaldi-Reshevsky, Dubrovnik Olympiad 1950).

Position 404

**1.♕xh7+!** and Black resigned because of the forced mate: 1...♔xh7 2.♖h3+ ♔g7 3.♗h6+ ♔h8 4.♗f8+ ♘h4 5.♖xh4# (Browne-Bellon Lopez, Las Palmas 1977).

Position 405

The move **1..♗g8!** forced Black to surrender in Trifunovic-Aaron, Beverwijk 1962.
This tactical blow became possible after Black played the move ...♖b8-b6, removing the second defence of the rook on d8.

Position 406

**1...♖cd8! 2.♕xc6 ♕xf2+!**, and mate after 3.♖xf2 ♖xd1+ or 3.♔h1 ♕f1+ (Nazarenus-Vologin, Budapest 1996).

Position 407

The move **1...♘f3!** wins the exchange, because after any move of the rook on e1, there follows 2...♕e4! with the threat of ...♘h4+ (or ...♘e1+) and ...♕g2#.
White gritted his teeth and played **2.♘d2.** But his losses are not limited to the exchange – after **2...d4** he had to resign: 3.exd4 ♘xe1+, whilst after 3.♕d3 or 3.♕b3 there is 3...♘xe1+ 4.♖xe1 ♕d5+ (Amarita-Olariu, Romania 2000).

Position 408

The calculation of the combination which occurred in the game Beletsky-Khasangatin (Sochi 2004) is fairly simple: **1...♗xg3 2.hxg3** 2.f4 would have avoided what comes next. **2...♕xg3+**, and after **3.♔f1** (or 3.♔h1), **3...♘g4!** with mate.

Position 409

The deflection of the rooks from the defence of the first rank by **1...♖xf7!** forced White to stop the clocks (Klimov-Evseev, St Petersburg 2004). After 2.♖xf7 there would follow 2...♖d1+ 3.♖f1 ♕xg2+ 4.♕xg2 ♖xf1# or first 2...♕xg2+ 3.♕xg2 and now 3...♖d1+.

Position 410

**1.♘f6+! gxf6 2.exf6 ♔h8** Or 2...♘e7 3.♕g5+ ♘g6 4.♕h6. **3.♗e4**, mating. From a simultaneous display by Garry Kasparov against computers (Hamburg 1985).

Position 411

**1.♗c4+! ♕xc4 2.♕e8+ ♘xe8 3.♖f8#** (Chigorin-NN, St Petersburg 1894) Among other moves, 1.♕d2 also wins.

## Position 412

The black queen has no retreat squares.
**1.♗xh7+!** The idea of the sacrifice is to remove the defender of the square g6. **1...♘xh7** 1...♔h8 2.♘f7#. **2.♘g6** and Black resigned in Rossolimo-Zuckerman, Paris 1937.

## Position 413

**1...♕xg3+! 2.hxg3 ♖h5** with mate (Shantharam-Murugan, Hyderabad 1994).

## Position 414

**1.♕g8+! ♔xg8 2.♘g6**. The f7-pawn is pinned, and the mate threat on h8 is unstoppable (Abrahams-Thynne, Liverpool 1932).
The retreat of the king by 1...♔e7 avoids the mate, but not the crushing attack after 2.♕xf7+ and 3.♖d1+.

## Position 415

White gave mate by means of **1.♕g8+ ♔e7** (on 1...♔xg8 there is 2.♘g6+) **2.♘g6+ ♖xg6** (or else mate on d8) **3.♕e8+** and Black resigned in view of 3...♔d6 4.♕d8# or 3...♔f6 4.♕f8# in Dobrev-Boichev, Bulgaria 2005.

Position 416

After **1.♘g5!** Black resigned. If the knight is taken, 2.♖h3 wins. The move 1...g6 does not save the game, because the pawn on f7 is pinned (Ivkov-Djuric, Yugoslavia 1983).

Position 417

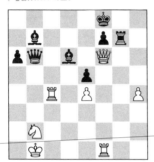

The move **1.♖b4!** was played, and Black stopped the clock. The rook cannot be taken by the queen because of mate on d8, and after 1...♕c7 there follows 2.♖xb7 (Sindik-Cebalo, Zagreb 1978).

Position 418

**1.♖c5!** Opening the queen's path to g7 and at the same time defending against the mate.
There is a threat of 2.♖xh7+ followed by 3.♕g7#, so Black resigned in Heemsoth-Heisenbüttel, West Germany 1958.
However, the computer finds an amazing resource: 1...♕e4! (or 1...♕d3), e.g. 2.f5 ♘h5! and there is no win for White. The immediate 2.♖xf7 ♕g6 3.♕xg6 hxg6 4.♖xc8 ♖xc8 also appears tenable.

Position 419

With **1...♕f3! 2.♗b1** (on 2.gxf3 there follows 2...♘xf3+ 3.♔f1 ♗h3#) **2...♕xg2 3.♔d2 ♕xf2** Black achieved an overwhelming superiority (Peev-Haik, Bucharest 1979).

Position 420

After **1.♘d5!** Black resigned the game. He cannot take the queen because of mate (2.♘c7#); after 1...cxd5 the rook sacrifice decides (2.♖xa7+! ♕xa7 3.♕c6+ or 2...♔xa7 3.♕a4+); whilst after 1...♖c8 there is 2.♕xc5 ♘xc5 3.♘b6+, 4.♘d7+ and 5.♘xc5 or 2.♕b2 ♕b5 3.♕a3 (Böök-Halfdanarson, Reykjavik 1966).

Position 421

**1.♖b3! cxb3** If 1...♕a5, then 2.♖b8+ ♔d7 3.♖d1+ and the black king cannot escape the chase.
**2.♕xb4** and Black resigned in Klaman-Lisitsin, Leningrad 1937.

Position 422

The advantage is realised by combinative means:
**1.♖xd5! exd5 2.♘d4+** and Black resigned in view of 2...♔d8 3.♘e6+ or 2...♖e7 3.♕xc7; Kasparov-Kramnik, Frankfurt am Main 1999.

Position 423

**1.♘h5! gxh5 2.♖g1** and Black resigned in Krutikhin-Chaplinsky, USSR 1950.

Position 424

After **1.♕xe4 ♖xe4 2.♖1c6!** Black resigned in Van Wijgerden-Donner, Leeuwarden 1976.

Position 425

1...♕xg3! 2.hxg3 ♔g7 and White resigned, because 3...♖h8 mate cannot be parried (Alapin-Schiffers, St Petersburg 1902).

Position 426

Black wins by means of the move **1...♕xf2+!** (2.♔xf2 ♗d4+ 3.♖e3 ♖xe3) – a tactical possibility missed in the game I. Farago-Hazai, Budapest 1976, where 1...♖ce8 was played.

Position 427

**1...♖xd5! 2.♖xd5 ♘f3** Mate can be prevented only by giving up the rook. After **3.♖5d2 ♖xd2 4.♖xd2 ♘xd2 5.b5 ♘c4** White resigned in Rayner-Kouatly, Groningen 1976/77.

Position 428

The rook's entry **1...♖e1!** decided the game. If it is taken, then 2...♗g3#, whilst in the event of 2.♗b3 there is 2...♖e2+ 3.♔f1 ♗g3, mating (Bialas-Mross, Berlin 1954).

Position 429

After **1.♘f5!** Black resigned. After 1...exf5 there follows 2.♕xc8+ (Khmelnitsky-Kabatianski, USSR 1989).

Position 430

The attack down the h-file is crowned by **1.♗f6!** (deflection – 1...♗xf6 2.♕h7+ and 3.♕xf7# plus the X-ray threat 2.♕h8+). Black resigned in Rytov-Malevinsky, Leningrad 1969.
The moves can also be switched round: 1.♕h7+ ♔f8 and now 2.♗f6.

Position 431

If the black queen ever gets to f3, the white king will be in serious danger. The motif is clear, but how can Black get rid of the opponent's heavy pieces and his own bishop? The first exchange deflects the rook from f1: **1...♖xb1 2.♖xb1**. Then the move **2...♗f5!** shuts off the f-file. Now the white queen is unable to come to the help of the king, and the threat is 3...♕f3+ and 4...♕g2#. After **3.♖f1** the game is decided by **3...♕e2** (V. Zhuravlev-Kapanadze, Tbilisi 1977).

Position 432

**1.♕a5! ♖f8** Or 1...♖e8. Including the moves
1...♕b1+ 2.♔g2 does not change anything.
**2.♕g5** and Black resigned in Shulman-Sandler,
Baldone 1977.

Position 433

On general considerations alone, the search for a
solution is bound up with attacks on the square
g2. Black has several combinative possibilities,
illustrating various themes: **1...♘xf2!** – freeing
the square e4, to attack g2 (2.♗xf2 ♕e4 mating).
This happened in the game E. Kahn-Banusz
(Budapest 2004). White resigned.
A slightly more complicated version of this
combination is 1...♖xg4 2.hxg4 ♘xf2 3.♗xf2
♕e4. Nor does the rook retreat save the game:
3.♖f1 ♘h3+ 4.♔h1 ♕h4 or 4.♔h2 ♕d6+. Also not
bad is the deflection of the bishop by 1...f5, and
then after 2.♗xf5 – 2...♖xg2+ (3.♔xg2 ♘xf2+;
3.♔f1 ♘g3+ with mate). And if 2.♗h5, then
2...♘xf2 (3.♗xf2 ♕e4; 3.♗xg6 ♘xd1), whilst after
2.♗f3 there is 2...♘xf2.
The positional solution was also sufficient for
victory – freeing the e4-square for the queen by
the simple move 1...♘f6 (2.♖d4 h5; 2.♖e1 ♘xg4
3.♗c5 ♕d7 4.♖xe8+ ♕xe8 5.hxg4 ♖xg4 6.g3 h5
with the irresistible threat of 7...♕e4 or 7...♕c6).

Position 434

**1...♕e2 2.♖f1 ♕xf3! 3.gxf3 ♖g6#** (Albin-Bernstein, Vienna 1904)

Position 435

The discovered attack **1.♘d5!** forced Black to resign. He cannot play 1...♕xd2 because of 2.♘e7#, and otherwise the queen is lost (Bonch Osmolovsky-Ragozin, Lviv 1951).

Position 436

After **1...♕xh2+!** White resigned, due to forced mate: 2.♔xh2 ♖h5+ 3.♔g1 ♘f3+ 4.gxf3 ♖dg5# (Prokopovic-Van der Mije, Belgrade 1979).

Position 437

**1...♖g3!** After 2.fxg3 (and also after a queen retreat) there follows 2...♕xh2+ 3.♔xh2 ♖h6+. White resigned in S. Pereira-R. Pereira, Portugal 1978.

Position 438

**1...♕xh2+! 2.♔xh2 ♖h4+ 3.♔g1 ♘g3** and mate next move (Reshevsky-Ivanovic, Skopje 1976).

Position 439

**1.♘xf7! ♔xf7 2.♕xe6+ ♔f8 3.♕e7+ ♔g8 4.♖g3 g5 5.♖xg5+ hxg5 6.♕xg5+** and Black is mated (Reis-Rodrigues, Lisbon 1996).

Position 440

**1...♗h2+ 2.♔f1 ♕b6! 3.♗f3** Other moves are no better. **3...♕xf2+ 4.♖xf2 ♘g3#** Tudrov-Khenkin, Moscow 1956.

Position 441

**1.♖1xd4!** Clearing a path to h5 for the other rook. **1...exd4 2.♕xh7+** Decoying. **2...♔xh7 3.♖h5#** (Abrosimov-Ambainis, Daugavpils 1975)

**Position 442**

**1.♕g6! fxg6 2.♖xg7+ ♔f8** Or 2...♔h8. **3.♘xg6#** (Bronstein-Geller, Moscow 1961)

**Position 443**

White wins by means of **1.♖xe5!**. After **1...dxe5** there follows **2.♗c4+ ♔h8** (2...♖f7 3.♖d8#) **3.♘g6+ hxg6 4.♖h1+** (Zaverniaev-Paromov, Arkhangelsk 1963).

**Position 444**

**1.e5!** wins a piece. After **1...♗xg2** (the preliminary exchange 1...dxe5 2.fxe5 does not change anything) **2.exf6**, the bishop cannot retreat because of the deadly blow on e6. The game Kramnik-NN (simultaneous display, Paris 1999) went **2...♗b7** (2...♗h3 3.♘xe6) **3.♖xe6+ fxe6 4.♕h5+** and mate.

**Position 445**

**1.♖e6!** Interference. **1...♗xe6** Or 1...fxe6 2.♕xe5+ ♔f7 3.♖h7+ ♔e8 4.♖xe7+ ♔xe7 5.♕f6+ etc. **2.♕xe5+ f6** Or else mate. **3.gxf6+ ♕xf6**, and finally a deflection: **4.♖h7+ ♔xh7 5.♕xf6** On 5...♗d7 there comes 6.e5, Black resigned in Khudyakov-Kovalev, Alushta 2005.

Position 446

**1...g5+! 2.♔xh5 ♛e2+ 3.g4 ♛e8#** (De Rooi-H. Kramer, Beverwijk 1962)

Position 447

**1...g5+ 2.♔xh5 ♛xg4+! 3.♛xg4 ♗f7#** (Lanni-Sarno, Italy 1993)

Position 448

White has an extra pawn. A logical continuation was 1.♖fc1. However, **1.♘eg5!** is significantly more active. After **1...fxg5 2.♖xd7 ♛xd7 3.♘xe5** the queen is attacked, and at the same time, the standard smothered mate with 4.♘f7+ is a threat (Bernstein-Metger, Ostend 1907).

Position 449

**1.f6! ♗xf6 2.♖xf6 ♛xf6 3.♗g5** and Black resigned in Najdorf-Bolbochan, Argentina 1965.

Position 450

**1.♖xf7! ♖xf7 2.♗xe6** and Black resigned.
If 2...♕xe6, then 3.♖d8+, whilst after 2...♕xf2+
3.♕xf2 ♖xf2 there is also 4.♖d8# (Tkhelidze-
Gutkin, Beltsi 1972).

Position 451

**1.♖xe6! fxe6 2.g4** The queen is trapped, Black
resigned in Smetankin-Vallejo Pons, Erevan
1999.

Position 452

Both sides' knights are attacked, but with the
move **1.b4!** White deflects the bishop to b4,
and after **1...♗xb4 2.♘c2** he wins a piece (Em.
Lasker-Euwe, Nottingham 1936).

Position 453

The double attack **1...♕b6!** decides the game.
Taking the queen is impossible because of
2...♘e2#!. Meanwhile, there is a threat of
2...♕xb2#, and also of taking the bishop on e3
(Shebarshin-Sozin, Novgorod 1923).

Position 454

With the move **1.♖b6!** White deflects the queen from the defence of the square h8. After **1...♛xb6** (the same happens after 1...♖d6 2.♖xd6 ♛xd6) there follows **2.♛h8+ ♚g6 3.♗h5#** (Mariotti-Panchenko, Las Palmas 1978).

Position 455

**1.♛f6+! ♞xf6 2.♗c5+!** (2...♗xc5 3.gxf6+ ♚f8 4.♖h8#) and Black resigned in Vladimirov-Kharitonov, Alma-Ata 1977. Mate can also be given via a different move-order: 1.♗c5+ ♗xc5 (1...♞xc5 2.♛f6+ and 3.♖h8#; 1...♚d8 2.♛xf7) 2.♛f6+ etc.

Position 456

**1.♗xh7+ ♚xh7 2.♛h5+ ♚g8 3.♖e4!** There is no satisfactory defence against the threat of 4.♖h4, so Black resigned in Skorpik-Vinklar, Czechoslovakia 1978.

Position 457

**1.♖xg7!**
By drawing the king into a pin, White sets up irresistible threats.
**1...♚xg7 2.♛g4+ ♚h8 3.♛h5** There is no defence to 4.♗xf6 and 5.♛xh7# (3...♚g8 4.♗xf6 ♖fe8 5.♛xh7+ and 6.♛h8#). Black resigned in Radulov-Söderborg, Helsinki 1961.

## Position 458

**1...♞xf3+! 2.gxf3 ♖g5+ 3.♔f1** 3.♔h2 ♕xh3+ mating. **3...♕xh3+ 4.♔e2 ♖g2+** After 5.♗f2 there follows 5...♖xf2+ 6.♔xf2 ♕h2+. White resigned in Quinteros-Kouatly, Lucerne 1985.

## Position 459

**1...♞xd4 2.♗xd4 ♞d3+! 3.exd3** If 3.♕xd3, then 3...♕c1+ 4.♕d1 ♕xd1+ 5.♔xd1 ♗xd4. **3...♗xd4** with a decisive material advantage (Pelts-Beloushkin, Chelyabinsk 1975).

## Position 460

**1.♗xf7+! ♔xf7 2.♕b3+** and Black resigned in Tal-Unzicker, Stockholm 1961. On 2...♔f8 (2...♞d5 3.exd5) there follows 3.♞g5, whilst in the event of 2...♔g6 White draws the enemy king into his own camp: 3.♞h4+ ♔h5 4.♕f3+ ♔xh4 5.♕g3+ ♔h5 6.♕g5#.

## Position 461

**1...d3 2.c3 ♖xe4! 3.♕xe4 ♗xc3** On 4.b3 there follows 4...♕f2. White resigned in Sax-Van der Wiel, Biel 1985.

Position 462

**1...♘e2+! 2.♘xe2 ♗xb2+! 3.♔xb2 ♖xd1** Black has given two minor pieces for a rook. However, the pin on the back rank and threats along the e-file make further losses inevitable. White resigned in Kamarainen-Svenn, Helsinki 1973.

Position 463

**1.♗a3!** The black bishop cannot leave the square e7 because of 2.♘f6+ ♘xf6 3.exf6 with inevitable mate. If **1...b6** (in order to control the square f6 after the exchange on e7), then **2.♘g5!** (2...♗xg5 3.♕xf8#), Sveshnikov-Gorchakov, Vilnius 1973.

Position 464

He wins by **1.♖xf7 ♖xf7 2.♕xc7!** (Ahues-Leopold, Dresden 1903).

Position 465

**1...♘f3+!** After 2.♘xf3 there follows 2...♕xf3! with unavoidable mate on g2 or the back rank. The move 2.♖xf3 also leaves the back rank undefended (2...♖d1+). White resigned in Petursson-Agdestein, Reykjavik 1985.
There was also another move-order: 1...♖d1+ 2.♖e1 ♘f3+.

**Position 466**

**1...♘f3+! 2.gxf3 ♕g6+ 3.♔h1 ♘g3+** and
**4...♕xc2** and White has no compensation for
the lost queen (Lyublinsky-Baturinsky, Moscow
1945).

**Position 467**

The threat is ♕g3-h4. However, Black does not
give his opponent time to execute the threat.
There followed **1...♗xc2+! 2.♔xc2 ♘b4+ 3.♔b1**
(3.♔d2 ♕xb2#) **3...♕f5+** and White resigned in
Dexter-Bles, Hungary 1985.

**Position 468**

The game was decided by **1.♘xe6!**. After
**1...♘xe6** there comes **2.♕xd5+!** (2...♔xd5
3.♗g2#), Firman-Gdanski, Cappelle-la-Grande
2006.

**Position 469**

After **1.♗xf7+!** (decoying the king) **1...♔xf7**
**2.♖xc8!** (decoying the queen) **2...♕xc8** (if
2...♕b6, then 3.♕b3+ ♕e6 4.♖c7+) Black's main
pieces are forked: **3.♘d6+** (Naipaver-Kishiniuk,
Uzhgorod 1984)

Position 470

Black wins by **1...♘xe4 2.♖xe4 ♕xb6!**. This possibility was missed in the game Lima-Segal, Brazil 1993.

Position 471

Black could just play 1...d4, when his position is the more active. But the outcome of the game was decided in a different way.
There followed **1...♖xe1+ 2.♖xe1**

*(see next diagram)*

**2...♖e2!!**, and White resigned in Bagirov-Kholmov, Baku ch-URS 1961.

Position 472

**1.♘xg7! ♗xc4** If 1...♔xg7, White wins by 2.♗f6+ ♔g6 (after 2...♔g8 there is 3.♕d2, mating) 3.♗xe6 fxe6 4.♕g4+. Relatively speaking, 1...♗e7 was Black's best defence. **2.♗f6! ♗e7** 2...♗xe2 3.♘f5+ and 4.♘h6#. **3.♕f3** This was the finish of the game Stein-Portisch, Stockholm 1962.

Position 473

**1...♗xf2+! 2.♕xf2** Or 2.♔xf2 ♖f5+. **2...♕xd1+**
An 'X-ray'. White resigned (3.♖xd1 ♖xd1+ 4.♕f1
♖ee1) in Novotelnov-Averbakh, Moscow 1951.

Position 474

Black threatens mate (1...♕f1+), but White
delivers it earlier: **1.♖c8+! ♗xc8** 1...♔f7 2.♕c7+.
**2.♕e8+ ♖f8 3.♖xg7+ ♔xg7 4.♕g6+** and **5.♕h7#**
(Horowitz-NN, USA 1941).

Position 475

White is mated: **1...♕g2+! 2.♖xg2 ♘f3+ 3.♔h1**
**♖d1+** and **4...♖xg1#** (Rodriguez Vargas-
Olafsson, Las Palmas 1978).

Position 476

**1...♖xh2+! 2.♔xh2 ♖h5+ 3.♔g1 ♖h1+ 4.♔xh1**
**♕h3+ 5.♔g1 ♕g2#** (Grabow-Kunde, East
Germany 1968)

Position 477

**1.♕e7+! ♖xe7 2.♖d8+ ♖e8 3.♖g8+ ♔xg8 4.♖xe8#** (Krause-NN, Leipzig, 1933). Admittedly, it was possible to manage without the queen sacrifice and give mate with her help: **1.♗e7+ ♖xe7 2.♖d8+ ♖e8 3.♖xe8+ ♔xe8 4.♖g8#**

Position 478

**1.♗d5+ ♔h8** Or 1...cxd5 2.♕xd5+ ♔h8 3.♘f7+. **2.♕c3!** Mate is unavoidable (Sgurev-Mechkarov, Sofia 1949).
Another combination is worth noting: 1.♘xh7 ♕f2 (after 1...♔xh7 there is 2.♕c3 and then as in the game) 2.♘xf8 ♕h4+ 3.♔g1 ♕xe7 4.♘xg6, but now White only has two extra pawns. But instead of 2.♘xf8, 2.♘g5! is best.

Position 479

**1.♖g5!** The bishop needs to come to e6. **1...fxg5 2.♗e6 ♗e8 3.♕h7**, and mate is unavoidable (Avirovic-Tagirov, Yugoslavia 1948).

Position 480

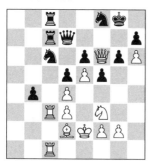

**1.♖xc6 ♖xc6 2.♖xc6 ♖xc6 3.♗xb4 ♕f7** After 3...♖c8 an interference decides matters: 4.♗e7. **4.♘g5! ♕xf6 5.exf6 ♖c7**
The threat was 6.f7+. If 5...♖c8 6.f7+ ♔h8, there is the variation 7.♗d6 ♘d7 8.♗e5+ ♘xe5 9.dxe5 ♖f8 10.d4 f4 11.♔f3, and zugzwang: after the rook moves there is 12.♘xe6. However, the simpler way 8.♘xe6 (instead of 8.♗e5+) is also possible. **6.♗e7** and Black resigned in Mnatsakanian-Prandstetter, Erevan 1984.

Position 481

**1.♗h6! ♔f8** 1...♗xh6 2.♘xf6+. **2.♘b6! ♕xd1+ 3.♖xd1 ♗g4 4.♘xa8 ♗xd1 5.♗e3! ♗g4 6.♘xc7** Realising the advantage does not pose particular difficulties (Kupreichik-Fritsche, Germany 1994/95).

Position 482

**1.♗xc5! ♕xc5 2.♗b3+ ♔h8 3.♕f7** and Black resigned in Titkos-Jompos, Hungary 1985.

Position 483

White was mated elegantly: **1...♕f2+ 2.♕xf2 ♖h5+! 3.♗xh5 g5#** (Georgadze-Kuindzhi, Tbilisi 1973)

Position 484

**1.♖a5+!** 1.♕c4+? ♔b6. **1...♗xa5 2.♕xc5+ dxc5 3.♘c4+ ♔b5 4.♖b6#** (from a book by Stamma, 1737).

Position 485

**1...♘g4+! 2.hxg4** After 2.♔g2 there comes 2...♗xd4 3.♕xd4 ♘e5. **2...hxg4 3.f3 ♗xd4 4.fxg4** 4.♕xd4 ♖e2+. **4...♘c3** winning (a variation from the game Egin-Guseinov, Tashkent 1985).

Position 486

**1...♘e4+! 2.fxe4 fxe4+ 3.♔e1 ♕xg3+!** and White resigned. After 4.♖xg3 there follows 4...♖h1+ 5.♗f1 ♖hxf1+ and 6...♖7f2# (Portisch-Hübner, Bugojno 1978).

Position 487

**1.♗xf7+! ♖xf7 2.♖d8+ ♖f8 3.♕b3+ ♕f7**
The mate threat on g1 has been eliminated, and the e-pawn now advances.
**4.e6 ♕e7 5.♖d7** Continuing 6.e7+, White wins (Apscheneek-Landau, Kemeri 1937).

Position 488

The obvious move is 1...♗e4+, but after 2.♔f4 the king escapes. The decisive move is **1...♖a3!**, deflecting the queen. After the forced **2.♕xa3** the queen and bishop easily cope with their task: **2...♗e4+ 3.♔f4 ♗g2+! 4.♔g5 ♕xe5+ 5.♔g4 ♕f5+ 6.♔h4 ♕h3+ 7.♔g5 ♕h6+ 8.♔g4 f5#** (Ivanov-Sveshnikov, Chelyabinsk 1973).

**Position 489**

**1.♘xd5! exd5** Declining the sacrifice and reconciling himself to the loss of a pawn does not not help Black: 1...♕b7 2.♘e7+ ♕xe7 3.♕xc8+, and the rest is as in the game. **2.♕xc8+ ♖xc8 3.♖xc8+ ♔h7** Or 3...♕f8 4.♖xf8+ ♔xf8 5.♘d7+ and 6.♘xb6. **4.♖h8+ ♔xh8 5.♘g6+** and **6.♘xe7**, winning easily (Volkevich-Liskov, Moscow 1952).

**Position 490**

**1...f5+! 2.gxf6** If 2.♔h4, then 2...♕h1#. **2...♕f5+** and 3...♕h5# (G. Borisenko-Simagin, Moscow 1955).

**Position 491**

**1.♖d7! ♘xd7 2.♗h6!** A beautiful move, leading by force to mate. **2...f6** 2...♘xe5 3.♗xg7+ and 4.♗xe5+. **3.♗xg7+ ♔g8 4.♗xf6+** Or 4.♕xe6+ ♖f7 5.♗h6+ ♔h8 6.♕xf7 with the same result. **4...♔f7 5.♖g7+ ♔e8 6.♖xe7+ ♔d8 7.♖e8+ ♔xe8 8.♕xe6#** (Korneev-Basos, Las Palmas 1999)

**Position 492**

After **1.♘e7!** Black resigned (1...♗xe7 2.♕h8#; and meanwhile there is a threat of 2.♕g8#) in Najdorf-Porat, Amsterdam Olympiad 1954.

## Position 493

The move **1...♘f5!** wins a piece. After 2.♖xd7 there is 2...♘xe3+ 3.♔e2 ♘xc4. If 2.♖e2, then 2...♕d1+ 3.♘xd1 (3.♖e1 ♘xe3+) 3...♖xd1+ 4.♖e1 ♘e3+ 5.♔e2 ♖xe1+ and 6...♘xc4 (Nikolaev-Karasik, Israel 2005).

## Position 494

There followed **1...♖f7!**, and White resigned. After 2.♕xf7 (and also any other queen move) there follows 2...♗d4+ and then 3...♕xg2# (Zinn-Sveshnikov, Decin 1974).

## Position 495

In order to give mate, Black needs to play ...♔g6 and ...♕h5#. But after 1...♔g6 there follows 2.♕xe6+. Therefore **1...♗f6+!** (interference). After **2.exf6** the move **2...♔g6** decides (3.g4 ♕e1+), Buksa-Kovacs, Hungary 1965.

## Position 496

**1...♘g4!** wins. After 2.♕xg4, 2...♕xg2+! decides: 3.♖xg2 ♖e1+ and 4...♖xf1#. And 2.♖d2 loses to both 2...♕xg2+ and 2...♘xh6 (Potze-Bitalzadeh, Hoogeveen 2005).

Position 497

**1.♘f6+! gxf6 2.♖xe8+** On 2...♕xe8 3.♗xf6 wins. If 2...♗xe8, then 3.♕h6 ♕d7 4.♕xf6 (4.♗xf6? ♕g4) 4...♔f8 5.♖e1 or 5.♕g7+ ♔e7 6.♕g5+ ♔f8 7.♗f6, mating (Tompa-Herrou, Val Thorens 1980).

Position 498

**1.♖xg7! ♔xg7 2.♕f6+ ♔f8** Or 2...♔g8 3.♕xh6 with the threat of 4.♗h7+ ♔h8 5.♗g6+, 6.♕h7+ and 7.♕xf7#. **3.♗g6!** and Black resigned in Keres-Szabo, Budapest 1955.

Position 499

**1.♘h5! gxh5 2.♘e6 fxe6 3.♖g5+ ♔f7 4.♕g6#** (Bjorkqvist-Tiemann, correspondence game, 1971/74)

Position 500

**1...e5! 2.♗xe5 ♗c3! 3.♕g1 ♗xe5** and White resigned in Tregubov-Emelin, Elista 1994.

285

Position 501

**1.♕xh7+! ♚xh7 2.g6+ ♚h8 3.♖g5!** Mate is threatened on h5, and after **3...fxg5** the other rook gives mate – **4.hxg5#** (V. Borisenko-Nakhimovskaya, Riga 1968).

Position 502

**1.♖xh7!** If Black takes the rook, a knight sacrifice opens the queen's path to h5: **1...♚xh7 2.♘g5+!** **fxg5 3.♕h5+** and **4.♕xg6+** with mate. Therefore, Black had to reply **1...f5**, but this only prolongs resistance (Seirawan-Wiedenkeller, Skien 1979).

Position 503

**1.♖c1+ ♚b8 2.♕b4+ ♚a8** Now that the king is cut off, two deflective sacrifices follow: **3.♗f3+!** **♖xf3 4.♕e4+!** Taking the queen leads to mate (5.♖c8#), Black resigned in Duras-NN, Prague 1910.

Position 504

**1.♗f4** White liquidates the mate threat, attacks the queen and at the same time closes the f-file, preventing the enemy rook coming to the defence – not bad for one move! After **1...♕d8** the game is decided by **2.♖xe7!** (deflecting the queen from the back rank) **2...♕f8** (2...♕xe7 3.♕c8+) **3.♕xg7+!** (3...♕xg7 4.♖e8+ ♕g8 5.♗e5+), Capablanca-Spielmann, San Sebastian 1911.

**Position 505**

With the move **1.♖b6!** White obtained a decisive material advantage. Black must surrender the queen, since after 1...axb6 there is 2.♘e7+ ♔h8 3.♕xh7+ and 4.♖h5#. Without the shutting off of the sixth rank, the combination would not work, since then after ♖h5+ Black could defend with ...♕h6. **1...♗xd5** Or 1...♕xb6 2.♘xb6 axb6 3.♕xc4 with the same result. **2.♖xa6 bxa6 3.♖xd5** (Ukhimura-Shain, USA 1980)

**Position 506**

**1.e5! dxe5** 1...♘e8 2.exd6+ ♘xd6 3.♕xg7 ♘f5 4.♖xf5 ♗xf5 5.♗c4+−. **2.♕c5+ ♔e8 3.♖xf6!** After 3...gxf6, 4.♘e4 decides (4...♕e7 5.♕xc6+). Black resigned in Nezhmetdinov-Sergievsky, Saratov 1966.

**Position 507**

**1.♖h8+! ♘xh8 2.♕h7+! ♔xh7 3.♖h5+ ♔g8 4.♗h7#** (Chudinovskykh-Muraviov, USSR 1990)

**Position 508**

**1...♖xe5! 2.dxe5 ♘f3+ 3.♔h1** If 3.gxf3, then 3...♕g5+ and 4...♕h4. **3...♕h4 4.h3 ♗xh3 5.g3 ♕h5** and White resigned in Lee-Ribeiro, Siegen Olympiad 1970.

Position 509

With his last move, Black gave check with the bishop, intending to answer 1.♘xd4 with 1...♖xd5. However, White played **1.♖xd4! cxd4.** Not 1...♖xd5 2.♖xd5 (2...♕xd5 3.♘h6+), but 1...♔h8!± would have made the win more difficult. **2.♘f6+ ♔f8** Taking the knight leads to mate after 3.♕h6. **3.♕xh7 gxf6 4.♖e1** and Black resigned in Duz-Khotimirsky-Bannik, Vilnius 1949.

Position 510

**1.♘h5! gxh5** After 1...♗h8, 2.♘g5 decides. **2.♘g5 ♗xg5 3.♕xg5+ ♔h7 4.♕xh5+ ♔g7 5.♕g5+** After 5...♔h7 6.♖f3 Black is mated (Pinter-Hardicsay, Hungary 1974).

Position 511

**1.♘xg6! ♘xg6** After 1...♔xg6, 2.♕e4+ ♖f5 3.♖xh5 decides. **2.♖xh5+ ♔g8** Or 2...♔g7 3.♗h6+ ♔g8 4.♗xf8 ♔xf8 5.♕e4. **3.♕e4 ♖f6 4.♖dh1** Threatening 5.♖h8+ ♘xh8 6.♕h7+. Black resigned in Bebchuk-Tomson, Moscow 1963.

Position 512

**1.♘d5! exd5 2.♕xd5+** Now Black noticed that he was being mated (2...♔h8 3.♖xh6+! gxh6 4.g7+ and 5.g8♕+), and he resigned. This was the game Cheparinov-Cortes, Spain 2003. However, even if he had seen the end and parted with the exchange, Black would not have lasted long. For example, after 1...♕d7 2.♘xf6+ ♗xf6 3.f5 ♘d8 4.♕xb4 or 3...♘d4 (instead of 3...♘d8) 4.♗xd4 ♖xc4 5.♗xf6 gxf6 6.♕xh6.

Position 513

**1.♘e7+! ♗xe7 2.fxe7 ♕xe7** The intermediate capture of the rook does not help Black: 2...♖xd2 3.♗xf7+! ♔g7 4.♕a1+. **3.♖xf7!** and Black resigned in Savon-Litvinov, Minsk 1975.

Position 514

By temporarily sacrificing the exchange, White wins queen and pawn for rook and bishop: **1.♖xf6! gxf6 2.♕g4+ ♔h8 3.♕h4 f5 4.♗xf5! exf5 5.♕f6+ ♔g8 6.♘d5 ♕d8 7.♘e7+ ♕xe7 8.♕xe7**, and White converted his advantage in A. Ornstein-L.A. Schneider, Sweden 1975.

Position 515

Black wins by **1...♕e1+ 2.♕g1 ♖xh2+! 3.♔xh2 ♕h4+**, forcing a won pawn ending after 4.♔g2 ♕xg5+ 5.♔f1 ♕xg1+ 6.♔xg1 ♘xd5 7.cxd5 ♔d6 (Ramirez-Miranda, Roque Saenz Pena 1997).

Position 516

The opposite-coloured bishops strengthen the white attack. Tempting is 1.♖fd3, but White preferred the decisive **1.♗f7!**. There followed: **1...♔xf7** After 1...♖xd2 there follows, of course, 2.♕xg6+. And if 1...♕xf7, then 2.♖xd8. **2.♖xd8 ♕xd8 3.♕b7+ ♔g8 4.♕xa6**, and White realised his advantage in Stahlberg-Najdorf, Buenos Aires 1947.

## Position 517

**1...e3! 2.♕xd3** After 2.f3, 2...♖d2 3.♕c1 ♕g6 wins. This same queen manoeuvre follows after 2.♖f1. And if 2.♖xe3, then simply 2...♕xd1+ and 3...♖xb2. **2...exf2+ 3.♔f1 ♗xg2+ 4.♔xg2 fxe1♘+** and **5...♘xd3** (Picco-Omar Garcia Martinez, Cuba 1997).

## Position 518

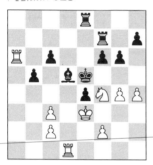

Black was mated in three moves: **1.♖xd5+! cxd5 2.♘d3+! exd3 3.f4#** (Opocensky-Hromadka, Kosice 1931)

## Position 519

**1...♖d3! 2.♕xb6** The rook cannot be captured by either the bishop (because of mate on g2) or the queen (because of 2...♗h2+ 3.♔h1 ♘xf2+ and 4...♘xd3). **2...♖xh3!** The rook is immune because of 3...♗h2 mate. If 3.♕xc6, then 3...♗h2+ 4.♔h1 ♘xf2#. The f2-square can be defended by **3.♗d4**. Then **3...♗h2+ 4.♔h1 ♗xe5+**, and White resigned, without waiting for the loss of his queen: 5.♔g1 ♗h2+ 6.♔h1 ♗c7+ (Gerasimov-Smyslov, Moscow 1935).

## Position 520

**1...♘xb2! 2.♔xb2 ♕a3+ 3.♔a1** Or 3.♔b1 ♘a4 and mate on b2. **3...b3! 4.cxb3 ♘xd3 5.♘c3 ♘xf2 6.♗xf2 ♕b4** and White resigned in Mihevc-Agababian, Moscow Olympiad 1994.

Position 521

**1...♖c1! 2.♕xc1 ♘e2+ 3.♖xe2 ♕xc1+ 4.♔f2 ♗a6!** White does not even get rook and minor piece for his queen. After the forced **5.♗d3** (5.♖c2 ♕d1!) **5...♕xa1 6.♗xa6 ♕d1** the game ended (Horberg-Averbakh, Stockholm 1954).

Position 522

**1...♕xh2+! 2.♔xh2 ♘g4+ 3.♔g1 ♘h3+ 4.♔f1 ♘h2#** (Emmerich-Moritz, Germany 1922)

Position 523

**1.♕xe4! fxe4** After 1...♗xf1 2.♖xf1 the same follows as in the game. **2.♗xe4+ ♔h8 3.♘g6+ ♔h7 4.♘xf8+ ♔h8 5.♘g6+ ♔h7** And now what? Answer: a change of route: **6.♘e5+! ♔h8 7.♘f7#** (Alekhine-Fletcher, simultaneous display, London 1928).

Position 524

By sacrificing the knight, then the queen, White liquidates the enemy king's pawn cover and gives mate: **1.♘c6+! bxc6 2.♕xa7+! ♔xa7 3.♖a1+ ♔b6 4.♖hb1+ ♔c5 5.♖a5#** (from a simultaneous display by Marco, 1898)

Position 525

Deflecting the queen from the defence of a7 via the 'diagonal of life' is impossible. But if White's second rook reaches a5, Black cannot avoid mate. This aim is achieved by **1.♖f1! ♕d4 2.♖f5!**. There is no defence to the threat 3.♖xa7+! ♕xa7 4.♖a5 (Capablanca-Raubitschek, New York 1906). On 1...♕e3, 2.♖f5! also wins, but it needs more work: 2...♖bc8 3.♖xb4! (3.♖a5? ♕f4+ with perpetual check) 3...♖b8 4.♖b7 ♖bc8 5.a5! d2 6.♖b1 ♖b8 7.♖fb5! ♕f4+ 8.♔h1.

Position 526

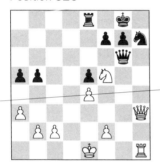

**1.♘e7+ ♖xe7 2.♕c8+ ♘f8 3.♕xf8+! ♔xf8 4.♖h8#** (Nikonov-Khardin, Kirov 1981)

Position 527

**1...♖a8! 2.♖xa8** After 2.♖c3 there follows 2...♕e1+ and 3...♕a1#, whilst in the event of 2.♖a6 there is 2...♖xa6 3.♕xa6 ♕f1+ and, as in the game, 4...c3+. **2...♕f1+ 3.♔b2 c3+**, winning the queen (Medina Garcia-Smederevac, Beverwijk 1965). Black could have inverted the moves, playing first **1...♕f1+** and then **2...♖a8**. Other variations: 2.♔d2 (2.♔b2 ♖a8 with the threat of ...♖a8xa3 and mate on a1; on 3.♖xa8 there is 3...c3+) 2...♖a8! 3.♖e3. Now the check with ...c3 cannot be given because the queen takes on c3 with check, but decisive is 3...♖a1 or 3...♕f2+ 4.♖e2 ♕xd4+.

Position 528

The 'quiet' move **1.♕c7!** forces capitulation. Black has no defence against the smothering sacrifice 2.♕b8+ ♖xb8 3.♘c7# (Zotov-Glebov, Moscow 1975).

There was also another, rather crude solution: 1.♘c7+ ♔b8 2.♘b5.

Position 529

**1...♖xe7!** Distracting the white queen from d7 where she controls the squares g4 (stopping the check ...♖g8+) and d3 (stopping the check ...♗a6+). **2.♕xe7 ♕xf3 3.gxf3 ♖g8+ 4.♔f1 ♗a6+ 5.♖e2 ♘d2+ 6.♔e1 ♘xf3+ 7.♔d1 ♖g1+** and mate next move (Stahlflinga-Gran, Denmark 1974).

Position 530

White mates: **1.♘c7+ ♔a7 2.♕xa6+! bxa6 3.♘b5+ ♔a8 4.♖a7#** (Munk-NN, Kassel 1914)

Position 531

**1.♗b7+!! ♗xb7 2.♘d7! ♕d8 3.♕b8+ ♕xb8 4.♘b6#** (the final part of a study by Seletsky, 1933)

293

Position 532

After **1...♗g4!** White resigned, since after 2.♖xg4 there follows 2...♕f1+ 3.♖g1 ♘g3+! 4.hxg3 ♕h3# (Pirrot-Hertneck, West Germany 1989/90).

Position 533

The move **1...♘e3!** assures Black a decisive advantage: **2.♕g3** After the capture of the queen there is 2...♘f3#, and after 2.♗xe3 ♕xe3 both 3...♘f3+ and 4...♕d2#, and also 3...♗xe4 are threatened. **2...♕xg3** (even better is 2...♘xc2+) **3.♘xg3 ♘xc2+ 4.♔d1 ♘xa1 5.♘xb7 b3 6.axb3 ♘xb3 7.♔c2 ♘c5**, and Black realised the extra exchange in Shirov-J.Polgar, Buenos Aires 1994).

Position 534

**1.♗h7+!** By comparison with the majority of similar combinations, here the black pawn stands on h6, not h7. **1...♔xh7** If 1...♔h8, then 2.♘g5!, and Black is defenceless. After 2...hxg5 there follows 3.♕h5. Nor does 2...♕b8 save Black because of 3.♘xf7+ ♔xh7 4.♕d3+ ♔g8 (or 4...g6 5.♘g5+ hxg5 6.♖f7+ ♔h6 7.hxg5+ ♔xg5 8.♗c1+ and 9.♕f3#) 5.♘xh6+ gxh6 (or 5...♔h8 6.♘f7+ ♔g8 7.♘g5) 6.♕g6+ ♔h8 7.♖f7, mating. **2.♘g5+ ♔g8** If the second sacrifice is accepted, White wins: 2...hxg5 3.♕h5+ ♔g8 4.♕xf7+ ♔h8 5.♕h5+ ♔g8 6.hxg5 with the threat of g5-g6 (on 6...♘e7, 7.♗xe7 decides). **3.♘xf7 ♕b8 4.♘xh6+ gxh6 5.♕g4+ ♔h8 6.♖f7** and Black resigned in Lisitsin-Ragozin, Leningrad 1934.

**Position 535**

First the rook is decoyed into a pin: **1.♖xc5!
♖xc5 2.♖c2 ♖fc8** And now **3.♕b5!** – this new
attack on the doubly pinned and twice-defended
rook leads to material gains. The additional
moves **3...♖xc2 4.♗xa7 ♖xa2 5.♗c5 h6 6.h4 ♔h7
7.h5** were played, whereupon Black resigned in
Kotov-Kholmov, Moscow 1971.

**Position 536**

**1...♗xd4** Only so. **2.♗xd4 ♕g5!** and White
resigned. There is a threat not only of mate on
g2, but also of 3...♘h3+ (Pacheco-Bachmann,
Turin Olympiad 2006).
After 1...♘xd4 the tactical blow does not work,
since White would take the knight on f4.

**Position 537**

**1.♘xf7! ♔xf7 2.♗xf6 ♕xc7** Neither pawn nor
king can take the bishop. On 2...gxf6 White
wins at once with 3.♕h5+. In the event of
2...♔xf6 White chases the king – 3.♕f3+ ♔g5
4.♕g3+ ♔h5 (4...♔f6 5.♕f4#) 5.♕g6#. **3.♕h5+
♔f8** 3...♔xf6 4.♕g6#. **4.♗xg7+ ♔xg7** 4...♔g8
5.♕g6. **5.♕g6+ ♔f8 6.♕xh6+ ♔f7** 6...♔g8 7.♗h7+
with mate. **7.♗g6+**, and Black is mated (Kallai-
Radulescu, Hungary 1980).

**Position 538**

The outcome of the game was decided by
the elegant move **1.♘d6!**, after which Black
loses a rook: 1...exd6 2.cxd6 or 1...♔h7 2.♘e8
(Peresipkin-Chekhov, Minsk 1976).

Position 539

**1...h3!** White had counted, after 1...hxg3 2.hxg3, on playing ♕e2, liquidating the attack. **2.♔f1 ♖c4!** On 2...♖g4 White defends by means of 3.♖ed1. **3.♕b2** If 3.♕xc4, then 3...♖d2. **3...♖g4!** The threat of 4...♖xg3 5.hxg3 h2 decides. On 4.♗e5 Black mates by 4...♖g1+. White resigned in Bielicki-Smyslov, Havana 1964.

Position 540

**1...♗a3+! 2.♔xa3 b4+ 3.♔a4** After 3.♗xb4 there follows 3...♕c1+ 4.♔a4 ♘b6#, but after 3.♔b2 bxc3+ 4.♔a3 ♕c1+ 5.♔a4 ♘b6+ 6.♔b4 a5+ 7.♔xc3 Black would have had to find 7...♖g3+! 8.♕xg3 ♕e1+!−+. **3...♘b6+ 4.♔xb4 ♖b5+ 5.♔a3 ♕c1+ 6.♗b2 ♘c4!** Mate is inevitable (Zinn-Minev, Halle 1967).

Position 541

The striking **1.♘g4!** ends the game (Kasparov-Lautier, Moscow Olympiad 1994). Variations which remained behind the scenes include 1...♖xg5 2.♘xe5 ♖xh5 3.♖d8+ ♔g8 4.♘xf7# and also the reply 1...♕e6. Then White has the move 2.♖d8!.

Position 542

It may appear that White has nothing more than perpetual check. But in reality, the pawn and bishop, which are included in the attack, create decisive threats: **1.h5! gxh5** Taking is obligatory: the threat is h5-h6, and then ♖g7-h7+, ♖b7-g7+ and ♖h7-h8#. If 1...♖ab8, then 2.♖h7+ ♔g8 3.♖bg7+ ♔f8 4.h6. **2.♗h4! e2 3.♗xf6** On 3...e1♕+ there follows 4.♖g1# (Perez-Lopez, Cuba 1995).

## Position 543

After **1.♕xc5!** Black resigned. On 1...dxc5 –
2.♘d7+ ♚a8 3.♘b6+ axb6 4.axb6+ ♗xa1 5.♖xa1#.
Tougher resistance is offered by 1...♗xe5 2.♗xe5
♚a8 3.♗xd6 ♘e6, but after 4.♕a3 exd6 5.a6 b6
6.♕xd6 the result is not in doubt (Golovnev-
Zorin, Dudinka 2000). A modern example of a
classical combination.

## Position 544

**1...♕xf2+! 2.♖xf2 ♖xe1+ 3.♖f1 ♖exf1+!** Not
3...♖fxf1+ 4.♕xf1 ♗h2+, after which 5.♔f2
♗g3+ 6.♔g1 leads only to a draw. **4.♕xf1 ♗h2+**
winning (Ge. Hernandez-An. Hernandez, Cuba
1997).

## Position 545

**1.♗xh6! gxh6 2.♘e7+ ♔h8 3.♖f8+ ♕xf8** 3...♘xf8
4.♕g8#. **4.♘g6+ ♔g7 5.♘xf8+ ♔xf8 6.♕g6** and
Black resigned in Blanc-Bar On, France 1979.

Position 546

With his previous moves, White prepared to shatter the enemy king's pawn cover. A possible continuation was 1.hxg6 hxg6 2.♘xg6 fxg6 3.♘xe6 (the position after 3.♕xe6+ ♔g7 4.♕xd5 ♘xd5 5.♘e6+ ♔f7 6.♘xc7 ♘exc7 or 3...♕xe6 4.♘xe6 ♔f7 5.♘xf8 ♗xf8 is unclear) and White's attack is very dangerous. Here is one variation: 3...♖c2 4.♖xg6+ ♔f7 5.♕g4 ♖h8. After 6.♖g7+! ♘xg7 7.♕xg7+ ♔xe6 8.♖e1+ White wins.

In practice, there is always the danger of a mistake in calculating such variations. White demonstrated a more exact course: **1.♘xh7! ♔xh7 2.hxg6+ fxg6 3.♕g4 ♖f6** On 3...g5 – 4.♕h5+ ♔g8 5.♕g6+ ♘g7 6.♖h3; or 3...♖g8 4.♖h3+ mating. **4.♕h4+ ♔g8 5.♖h3** and Black resigned in Naumkin-Michielsen, Hoogeveen 2005.

Position 547

**1...♕xg3!** This move, and the forced reply, are obvious. But how should Black continue after **2.♕xd5+ ♖xd5 3.fxg3** ?

*(see next diagram)*

**3...♖xh2+!** A move which had to be foreseen at the start of the combination. After 4.♔xh2 there follows 4...♖h5# (Isakov-Pitzhelauri, Syktyvkar 1978).

298

Position 548

**1.罝d8+! 勾xd8** 1...勾f8 2.罝xf8+ 勹xf8 3.豐d8#.
**2.豐xd8+ 勹h7 3.勾g5+ 勹h6 4.勾xf7+! 豐xf7**
4...勹h7 5.豐h8#. **5.豐h4+ 勹g6 6.豐h5#** (a
possibility missed in the game Kovacs-Beni,
Vienna 1950)

Position 549

**1.罝xd7! 奧xd7** After 1...豐xd7 2.勾f6+ Black
must take the knight, and then White wins
with 3.豐g4+. **2.勾f6+ 勹h8** As in the previous
variation, on 2...gxf6, 3.豐g4+ decides. **3.豐h5
h6** But now after 3...gxf6 there follows 4.奧e4.
**4.豐xf7** and Black resigned in Khalifman-Aseev,
Borzhomi 1984.

Position 550

**1...勾f4+! 2.gxf4 罝g6+ 3.勹h1 豐h3+ 4.罝h2**

(see next diagram)

**4...豐xh2+! 5.勹xh2 勹f7!** – White is mated
(Neiksans-H. Stefansson, Liepaja rapid 2004).A
similar mate arises after 3.勹h2 (instead of
3.勹h1): 3...豐h3+! 4.勹xh3 勹f7!.

Position 551

**1.♖xf7! ♔xf7** 1...g5 is more tenacious. **2.♗c4+ ♔f8 3.♖f1+ ♗f6 4.♖xf6+ gxf6 5.♕g8+ ♔e7 6.♕e6+ ♔f8 7.♕xf6+** and mate next move (Hartston-Penrose, London 1963).

Position 552

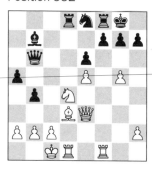

**1.♗xh7+! ♔xh7 2.g6+ ♔g8** After 2...♔xg6 there is 3.♕d3+ f5 (3...♔h6 4.♕h3+ and 5.♖g1+ with mate in a few moves) 4.exf6+ ♔h6 5.♕h3+ ♔g6 6.♕g4+ ♔h7 (6...♔f7 7.fxg7+) 7.♕h5+ ♔g8 8.f7+ ♖xf7 9.♕xf7+ and ♖f1-f4. **3.♕h3 ♘f6** 3...fxg6 4.♖xf8+ and 5.♘xe6+. **4.exf6 gxf6** Or 4...fxg6 5.fxg7 ♔xg7 6.♘xe6+; 5...♖xf1 6.♕h8+ ♔f7 7.♖xf1+. **5.g7** Instead of 5.♕h7#! Still Black resigned in Anand-Ninov, Baguio 1987.

Position 553

1.g4+ fxg4 2.hxg4+ ♔h4 3.♕xh6+!! ♕xh6 4.♔h2 and there is no defence against 5.♗f2 mate (Schlechter-Meitner, Vienna 1899).

Position 554

**1.♗xh7+! ♔xh7 2.♕h5+ ♔g8 3.♖xg7+! ♔xg7
4.♖g1+ ♔f6**

*(see next diagram)*

Now White gets nothing from 5.♕g5+ ♔e6
6.♕xe5+ ♔d7 7.♕xc3 ♕d6. The king chase
doesn't work either: 5.♕h6+ ♔f5 6.♖g5+ ♔e4
7.♖xe5+ ♔f3!! 8.♖xe7 ♖g8!. However, the 'quiet'
move **5.f5!** renders mate or the win of the queen
inevitable (Nedeljkovic-Matanovic, Belgrade
1950).

Position 555

After 1...♘f4+ 2.♔g4 ♖g2+ 3.♔f3 exf5 4.♕d8+
♔g7 5.♕e7+, the queen will chase the king. The
outcome of the game is decided by the striking
**1...♖g2!**. After the capture of the rook, there
follows 2...♘e3+. Meanwhile 2...♘f4# is a threat.
If 2.♕d4, then 2...♘f4+ 3.♕xf4 gxf4 4.♔xg2 e5,
with a winning pawn endgame (after Bellon
Lopez-Garcia, Cienfuegos 1976).

Position 556

**1.♖xd4!** Decoying into the subsequent discovered attack. **1...♕xd4 2.♘xd5 ♖xc1+** Otherwise the queen has no retreat. **3.♕xc1 ♕c5**

(*see next diagram*)

**4.♕g5!** This is the point of the combination. With the simultaneous attack White regains the sacrificed material and remains with three extra pawns. **4...f6 5.♗xf6** Also not bad was 5.♘xf6+ ♔h8 6.♕xg7+ ♔xg7 7.♘xd7+ and 8.♘xc5. **5...♗g6 6.♗xd8 exd5 7.♕xd5+ ♕xd5 8.♗xd5+ ♔f8 9.♗xb7**, and White easily realised his material advantage in Boneo-Roson, Buenos Aires 1924.

Position 557

White mates: **1.♕xh7+! ♔xh7 2.♖h1+ ♔g8 3.♘h6+ ♔h7**

(*see next diagram*)

**4.♘f7+ ♔g8 5.♖h8+! ♔xf7 6.♖h7+ ♔g8 7.♖g7+ ♔h8 8.♖h1#** (Platz-Just, East Germany 1972).

Position 558

**1.♗xf7+! ♔xf7 2.♖d6! ♗xd6** This removes
the defence from the square g7. However,
retreating the queen led to mate after 3.♘xh6+.
**3.♕xg7+ ♔e6 4.♘xd6 ♕d8** Black's position
is also hopeless after other moves. If 4...♕c7
(4...♖f8 5.♘xc8 ♖xc8 6.♕xh6+), then 5.♕f6+
♔d5 (5...♔d7 6.♘dxb5 with the threat of 7.♖d1+)
6.♖d1+. **5.♘xe8 ♕xe8 6.♕f6+ ♔d5 7.♕d6+ ♔e4
8.♖e1+ ♔f5 9.♕f6+ ♔g4 10.h3+ ♔h5 11.g4#**
This was the finish of a match game Lilienthal-
Landau, Amsterdam 1934.

Position 559

**1...♘e2+ 2.♔h1 ♕xg4! 3.hxg4 ♖h5+ 4.gxh5
♖h4#** (Gygli-Henneberger, Zurich 1941)

Position 560

**1...♕h2+ 2.♔g4 f5+ 3.♔g5 ♕xg2+! 4.♕xg2
♗e3#** (Zilberstein-Veresov, USSR 1969)

Position 561

**1...♗xe4! 2.♖xe4 ♖a8!**, and Black wins (Shofman-Ilivitsky, Sverdlovsk 1945).

Position 562

**1...♕a3! 2.♕xa3** If 2.♖b3, then 2...♕xb3 or 2...♕c1+ with mate. **2...♖f1+ 3.♔h2 ♘g4+ 4.♔h3 ♖h1+ 5.♗h2**

*(see next diagram)*

**5...♘f5!** After 6.♘f3 there follows 6...♘f2#, whilst after 6.♕g3 there is 6...♖xh2+ 7.♕xh2 ♘f2# (Kaabi-Lanka, Tunis 1988).

Position 563

**1...♘g3+** A means of opening the h-file which has been seen numerous times. **2.hxg3 hxg3+ 3.♔g1 ♘f2! 4.♖xf2.** Now what? Answer: deflection of the king, to allow the pawn to promote: **4...♖h1+ 5.♔xh1 gxf2** and White resigned in Mandel-Johner, Switzerland 1930.

Position 564

If Black manages to play ...Rf6-h6, White will be mated – but on one condition: if the c-file is closed. The fact is that the immediate 1...Rfh6 is met by 2.Rc7+ Kf6 (he cannot go to the back rank because of 3.Rc8 exchanging rooks, with a winning endgame for White) 3.Rf7+ Kg5 4.Rg7+ Kf6 (4...Kh5? 5.f3) 5.Rf7+, with a draw by repetition.

Therefore, with his first move, Black closes the c-file: **1...Nc3!** Now after 2.bxc3 the move 2...Rfh6 decides at once. In order to save himself from the threatened mate, White has to play **2.f4.** Then **2...g3**, forcing **3.Rxc3.** There was also a threat of 3...Ne2#. If 3.Rf3, then 3...Ne2+ 4.Kf1 Nxc1 5.Rxg3+ Kf8 6.Nd7+ Ke7 7.Nxf6 Kxf6, remaining with an extra piece. After **3...bxc3 4.Rf3** (it is still necessary to defend against 4...Rfh6) **4...cxb2 5.Rxg3+ Kf8 6.Nd7+ Ke7 7.Rg7+ Rf7** White resigned in Kreizahler-Leifold, West Germany 1973.

Looking at the initial position, it is hard to imagine that the outcome of the game will be decided by the promotion of the pawn on b4.

Position 565

**1.Rg8+ Kh7 2.Qe3!** This is markedly stronger than 2.Rxg6 – Black cannot take the rook because of discovered check, but after 2...Rd6 3.Rxd6 (3.Rg4 h5!) 3...Qxd6 White has only an extra pawn. Now, however, he threatens to take the rook, and also 3.Rh8+, so material losses are unavoidable.

This could have happened in the game Karpov-Hübner, Montreal 1979. In the game, the move 1.Qc4 was played, and the result was a draw.

Position 566

White has a distant passed pawn, and with his last move, he offered the exchange of queens. But there followed: **1...f6+! 2.♔g4** On 2.♕xf6 there is 2...♕g3#. **2...♕g2+ 3.♕g3 f5+ 4.♔f4**

(*see next diagram*)

**4...e5+!** Deflecting the king and at the same time a blockading sacrifice. **5.dxe5 ♕d2#** (Matokhin-Kuzmin, USSR 1970).

Position 567

Tempting (and strong) was 1...♖fe8, but Black decided the game with the striking **1...♘d3!**. After 2.♕xc7 there follows 2...♗xf2+ 3.♔h1 ♘xe1 with unstoppable mate on g2 (Oraevsky-Bubnov, correspondence game, 1926).

Position 568

**1.♘b5!** Clearing the queen's path to d5. **1...♕c6** On 1...axb5 there follows 2.♗xf7+ ♔xf7 3.♕d5+ ♔e8 4.♕e6+ mating. **2.♘c7+!** Deflecting the queen from the defence of this same key square. 2.♕d5, winning the queen, was also convincing: 2...♘xg5 (2...♕xd5 3.♘c7#) 3.♕xc6. **2...♕xc7 3.♗xf7+** Black resigned on account of 3...♔xf7 4.♕d5+ ♔e8 5.♕e6+, mating (Wilson-Diez Del Corral, Spain 1995).

Position 569

Mate is threatened on g1. After **1.g4+ ♔h4** the checks come to an end, so White forced a draw by perpetual check with **1.♕g4+ ♔h6 2.♕g7+ ♔h5 3.♕g4+**. This was the finish of the game Gaprindashvili-Veröci, Belgrade 1974. However, White could have given mate: **1.♖xe5+!** Freeing the square e7. **1...fxe5 2.g4+ ♔h4 3.♕e7+** Deflection and blockading. **3...♕g5 4.g3#**

Position 570

The decisive factor is the tactically unfortunate position of the white king. If the black knight could get to d5, it would be mate. He wins with **1...♖xc4! 2.♖xc4** and now: **2...♘b6 3.♖c5** Forced. **3...♘d5+.** After **4.♖xd5 exd5** the pawn ending with the distant passed pawn is hopeless for White: **5.e4 fxe4 6.fxe4 dxe4 7.♔xe4 ♔e6**, and Black wins (Dartov-B. Kogan, Riga 1977). Another, equally nice win would have been **2... e5+!** (instead of 2...♘b6) **3.dxe5+ ♘xe5–+.**

Position 571

**1...♖xh2+! 2.♔xh2 ♕h5+ 3.♔g3 ♗h4+ 4.♔xf4** Or 4.♔h2 ♗xf2+. **4...♕f5#** (Smirnov-Shubin, Petropavlovsk-Kamchatka 1977)

Position 572

**1...♗h2+! 2.♔xh2** If 2.♔f1, then 2...♕f6+ with mate. **2...♕xd7 3.♖xd7 e2** The pawn promotes by force, so White resigned in NN-Richter, Berlin 1931.

Position 573

**1.♞d7!** The knight cannot be taken because of the loss of the queen (1...♛xd7 2.♝xh7+ ♚h8 3.♝f5+). Meanwhile, 2.♞xf6+ is threatened. Black has to defend the square h7 with **1...♞g6** (or 1...♞e4) and part with the exchange (Simagin-Razuvaev, Moscow 1967).

Position 574

After **1.c5!** Black cannot avoid mate. If 1...bxc5, then 2.♞c4+ ♚b5 3.a4#. The same construction appears after 1...♞e6 2.♞b7+ ♚b5 3.a4#. But what if we reply **1...b5**, taking control of the two critical squares c4 and b7? Then comes the 'quiet' **2.a3!**, and Black is in zugzwang – any move leads to mate (Bernstein-NN, St Petersburg 1909).

Position 575

**1.♝xc5 ♛xc5 2.♝e6** First White deflects the queen, with the help of an exchange. Now he attacks the rook, which defends the square g8. **2...♜e7?** If Black had foreseen his opponent's reply, he would have given up the exchange with 2...♜af8.

*(see next diagram)*

**3.♛h6!** Black resigned. After 3...gxh6 there follows 4.♜g8+, mating, if 3...g6, then 4.♜xg6. Meanwhile, there is a threat of 4.♛xh7+ ♚xh7 5.♜h3# (Krämer-Rüster, Altheide 1926).

**Position 576**

**1.♖h8+ ♔g6 2.f5+! exf5 3.♕xh6+ gxh6 4.♖ag8#**
(Bernstein-Kotov, Groningen 1946)

**Position 577**

White wins with the help of a deflection and interference: **1.c6! bxc6** Several rook checks do not change anything. **2.♖b5!** and then 3.b7 (Eberle-Navarovszky, Budapest 1959).

**Position 578**

**1.f6!** The bishop cannot take the pawn, nor retreat to f8, because of the loss of a rook, whilst 1...gxf6 fails to 2.g7 ♖g2 3.♖g1.
That only leaves **1...♖xe2**, after which there follows **2.fxg7 ♖xd2 3.♗xd2** and, regaining a new queen, White easily converts his extra exchange: 3...fxg6 (3...♕e2? 4.♔c1) 4.g8♕ ♕c8 5.♗b4 (Tal-Koblents, Yurmala 1976).

**Position 579**

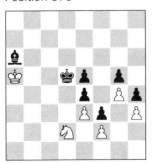

The move **1...♗f1** decided the outcome – White resigned. He has to take the bishop (else the pawns on h3 and g4 are lost), but then the black king can get to the square c4, and he enters via c4-d3-e2 to take the white pawns (Nikolac-Timman, Wijk aan Zee 1979).

Position 580

**1.♗xe7 ♕xe7 2.♘f6+ ♘xf6 3.exf6 ♕d6** If 3...♕d8 or 3...♕f8, then 4.♗xe6 (4...fxe6 5.♘g5).

*(see next diagram)*

**4.♖xe6! ♕d8** After 4...fxe6 White wins with 5.f7+ ♚f8 6.♕f6. **5.♕c7 ♕f8 6.♖e7** There is a threat of 7.♖xf7 ♕xf7 8.♗e6. Black resigned in P. Nikolic-Hartmann, West Germany 1979.

Position 581

**1.♗c4! ♕xc4 2.♖xg7+ ♚h8** 2...♚xg7 3.♗xe5+. **3.♗xe5** (also good are 3.♖b7, 3.♖a7, 3.♖d7, 3.♖ff7, and even 3.♖xg6) **3...♕xc2 4.♖f8+ ♖xf8 5.♖xg6+**, and mate next move (Taimanov-NN, simultaneous display, 1964).

Position 582

**1.♖xb6! axb6 2.♗c4 ♗e6 3.♖xe6! fxe6** If 3...♖xe6, then 4.♘xe6 fxe6 5.♕e3 ♚f7 6.♕f3+ ♚g8 (6...♗f6 7.♗g5 ♕d8 8.♕xb7+) 7.♕e4 ♚f7 8.♗xe6+ ♕xe6 9.♕xb7+ ♚f6 10.♕xa8 with an easy win. **4.♕f4 ♕d7 5.♗b5** and Black resigned in Chiburdanidze-Malaniuk, Odessa 1982.

Position 583

**1.♘f6+! gxf6** In the event of 1...♗xf6 2.exf6 ♕xf6 White wins a bishop with the move 3.♗g5. **2.exf6 ♗xf6 3.♗e4 ♖e8 4.♕xh7+ ♔f8 5.♗g6!** Ending the fight. The bishop cannot be taken because of 6.♗h6+. If 5...♗g7, then 6.♗h6 ♕f6 7.♖xd7 ♘e7 (7...fxg6 8.♕h8#) 8.♕h8+ ♘g8 9.♕xg7+ ♕xg7 10.♖xf7# (Reshevsky-Matsumoto, Siegen Olympiad 1970).

Position 584

**1.♖xe5! dxe5 2.f7+!** By clearing the long diagonal, White crowns his attack. **2...♖xf7** If 2...♗xf7, then 3.♕xe5 ♔f8 4.♕h8+ ♔e7 5.♗b4+ or 5.♖e1+ mating. **3.♕xe5 ♔f8 4.♕g7+ ♔e7** Or 4...♔e8 5.♕g8+ ♔e7 6.♗b4+. **5.♗b4+** and Black resigned in Panov-Makogonov, Tbilisi 1937.

Position 585

**1...♖xe4! 2.♕xe4 ♘g3! 3.♕xd4** 3.♕xh7 ♘de2#. **3...♘e2+ 4.♔h1 ♕xh2+ 5.♔xh2 ♖h8+**, mating (NN-Morphy, New York 1859).

Position 586

**1...g5+! 2.fxg5 hxg5+** Only thus, and not 2...fxg5+. **3.♔h5 ♕xh3+ 4.♕xh3 ♔g7**. There is no defence against 5...♗f7# (Pascual Perez-Cruz Lima, Cuba 1993).
We would note that, if Black had taken with the f-pawn (2...fxg5+?), White would have had the defence 5.♖f1.

Position 587

**1.♞xg7! ♚xg7 2.♝d4+ ♚g8** On 2...f6 there is 3.gxf6+ ♝xf6 4.♖hg1+. **3.g6!** Crowning the attack, whereas 3.♛h6 would allow Black to defend successfully: 3...♝f8 4.♛f6 ♖e5 5.♖hf1 ♛c7. **3...fxg6 4.♛e6**+, mating (Mikhalchishin-Kovalenko, Russia 1992).

Position 588

**1...b4! 2.axb4 ♖xh4 3.gxh4 g3 4.fxg3** The bishop has no pawn protection, and after 4...c3+ 5.bxc3 a3 White resigned in Lund-Nimzowitsch, Christiania 1921.
Even more accurate was reversing the move-order and starting with 1...♖xh4, since in the game White could have refused to take the rook.

Position 589

The problem-like move **1.♛h5!!** puts Black in a hopeless position. The threat is 2.♖g8+. After the capture of the queen, 2.♖g8+ ♚d7 3.e8♛+ and 4.♛xh5 is sufficient for a win. Also after **1...♖xg2+ 2.♖xg2+ ♖xh5 3.♖xb2 ♖xh3+ 4.♚g1** the win is a matter of technique: **4...♖h7 5.♖h2 ♖g7+ 6.♚f2 ♖g8 7.♖h6 ♚f7 8.e8♛+** (Maroczy-Romi, San Remo 1930).

Position 590

**1...♖xb2! 2.♚xb2 ♛xc3+! 3.♚xc3 ♝g7+ 4.♚c4** The same result comes from 4.♚b3 ♖b8+ 5.♚a3 (or 5.♚a4 ♞c5+; 5.♚c4 ♝e6+) 5...♝b2+ 6.♚a4 ♞c5+ 7.♚a5 ♝c3#. **4...♝e6+ 5.♚b4** 5.♚d3 ♞c5#. **5...♖b8+ 6.♚a5 ♝c3+ 7.♚a4 ♞c5+ 8.♚a3 ♝b2#** (Diaz-Gongora, Cuba 1996)

## Position 591

By destroying the enemy king's pawn cover with **1.♘xg7! ♚xg7 2.♖xf7+ ♚xf7**, after **3.♕h7+ ♚f6**, White creates irresistible mating threats with the accurately-calculated move **4.e5+!** followed by **4...♚xe5** (4...♚f5 5.♕h5+) **5.♗f4+! ♚xf4** (the same result comes from 5...♘xf4 6.♖e1+ ♚d4 7.♕e4# or 6...♚f6 (instead of 6...♚d4) 7.♘e4+ ♚e5 8.♕g7+ ♚f5 9.♘g3#, and also 5...♚d4 6.♕xg6) **6.♖f1+ ♚g4** (6...♚g5 7.♘e4+; 6...♚e5 7.♕g7+; 6...♚e3 7.♕h3+) **7.h3+** and **8.♘e4#** (Daudzvardis-Bogdanovich, USSR 1989).

## Position 592

**1.♕g5+! ♗xg5 2.hxg5+ ♚h5**
The g-pawn is pinned, but how to give mate?
**3.♖h8!** Forcing the queen to leave the third rank.
**3...♕xh8 4.g4#** (from a game played in England in 1962)

## Position 593

**1.♖xh6+! gxh6**
If 1...♚xh6, then 2.♕g5+ ♚h7 3.♕h4+ and after 3...♚g6 – 4.f5#.
**2.♕g8+! ♘xg8 3.♗f5#**
(Bauer-Gelner, Berlin 1956)

Position 594

**1.♗c8!**, decoying the rook to c8, with a mating finish: **1...♖xc8 2.♖a8+! ♔xa8 3.♕xc8+ ♖b8 4.♕c6+ ♖b7 5.♕a4+ ♔b8 6.♕e8+** (a somewhat amended position from the game Niedermann-Zucks, 1895)

Position 595

**1.♖xh7+! ♔xh7 2.♕h4+ ♔g6**

(*see next diagram*)

**3.♘xf4+!** Clearing the diagonal of the bishop at d3. **3...exf4 4.e5+ ♗f5 5.♗xf5+ ♔xf5 6.♕h7+!** Now the king has to run to the queenside. **6...♔xe5 7.♖e1+ ♔d4 8.♕e4+ ♔c5 9.♘a4+ ♔b4 10.♕c2** The first 'quiet' move. **10...♔a5** The threat was 11.♕c3+ and 12.♕a3#. **11.♕c3+ ♔a6 12.♘c5+ dxc5 13.♕a3+ ♔b6 14.♕b3+** and **15.♕b5#** (Wade-NN, simultaneous display, London 1958).

Position 596

**1.♗xf6 ♗xf6** On 1...gxf6 there follows 2.♕g4+ ♔h8 3.♕h5, attacking the squares h7 and f7. **2.♕f5!** A manoeuvre which exploits the pin on the e-file. Black has to allow the enemy queen to h7, after which White's attack becomes irresistible.

**2...♗xb2** If 2...h6, then 3.♕h7+ ♔f8 4.♘f5! g6 5.♘xh6. More tenacious was 2...♔f8 3.♕xh7 g6, but Black's defence is not a joyous task here.

**3.♕xh7+ ♔f8 4.♕h8+** Other continuations of the attack are similar to the previous variation and that which occurs in the game: 4.♘f5 g6 5.♘h6 ♗xa1 6.♗b5 or 4.♗b5 ♗d7 (better is 4...g6) 5.♗xd7 ♕xd7 6.♕h8+ ♔e7 7.♕h4+, and after 7...♗f6 – 8.♕b4+ (8...♕d6 9.♘f5+; 8...♔d8 9.♖ad1). **4...♔e7 5.♕h4+ ♗f6** 5...f6 6.♕b4+.

**6.♕b4+ ♔d8 7.♖ad1** Catastrophe along the d-file cannot be averted. After **7...♗c3** (if 7...♗d7, then 8.♗b5 and after 8...♖e7 – 9.♗xd7 ♖xd7 10.♕f8#) **8.♗b5+ ♗d7 9.♕a4 ♖e7 10.♖e3 e5 11.♖xc3** Black resigned in Lebredo-Chaviano, Cuba 1980.

Position 597

There is no time for the manoeuvre ♗a4-b5-a6 or ♕d1-d3-a6 because of the threat 1...g4xh3. By clearing the back rank with the aid of a sacrifice, and at the same time eliminating an important defender (♗d4-b6), White creates an unstoppable mate threat: **1.♗h6! ♖xh6** If 1...♕xh6 White is not threatened with mate, and besides the queen sacrifice which occurs in the game, he wins at once with 2.♕e2, threatening 3.♕a6. **2.♕xd4 exd4 3.♖fb1** Black resigned in Schuppler-Hönig, Mannheim 1948.

Position 598

**1.♗xg6+! ♔xg6 2.♘xe5+! fxe5** If 2...♔xh7, then
3.♕h5+ ♔g8 4.♕f7+ ♔h7 5.0-0-0! with the
threat of 6.♖h1+. Closing the h-file with the
move 5...♗h3 does not save Black from mate
after 6.♖h1 ♕c8 7.g4!. **3.♕h5+ ♔f6 4.♕xe5+
♔f7 5.♕xg7+** mating (Palau-Te Kolsté, London
Olympiad 1927).

Position 599

White eliminates the enemy king's pawn cover:
**1.♖xg6+! fxg6** If 1...♔xg6 2.♕g3+ ♔h6 3.♖xf7
Black is mated. **2.♖f7+! ♔xf7 3.♕xh7+ ♔e6** On
3...♔f8, 4.♘f4 decides. **4.♕xg6+ ♔e5 5.♕g7+
♔xe4 6.♘f6+ exf6 7.♕xd7**. Black resigned. In
saving the rook, he loses his pawns (Ragozin-
Veresov, Moscow 1945).

Position 600

**1.♗xh7+! ♔xh7 2.g6+! ♔g8** On 2...fxg6 there
follows 3.♘g5+ ♔g8 4.♕f3 (this same position
arises later on, by a transposition). And if
2...♔xg6, then 3.♕d3+!. **3.♘g5 fxg6 4.♕f3!**
Threatening 5.♕f7+ and 6.♕xg6, and also 5.♕h3.
If 4...♕d7, then 5.e6; 4...♕e7 5.e6; 4...dxe5 5.♕f7+
♔h8 6.♖e4; 4...♖xe5 5.♖xe5 dxe5 6.♕f7+ ♔h8
7.♕xg6. There is no satisfactory defence.
In the game, Black gave his queen and did
not obtain sufficient compensation: **4...♕xg5
5.♗xg5 dxe5** and after **6.♖ac1 ♖a7 7.♕d3 ♖e6
8.f4 ♘ac4 9.fxe5** he soon capitulated in Spassky-
Geller, Riga 1965.

## Position 601

**1.♗xg6! fxg6 2.♕xg6+ ♗g7 3.♖h8+ ♔xh8**
**4.♕f7!** – mate is unstoppable (Buturin-Kozakov, Lviv 1996).

## Position 602

**1.♗f8!** Clearing the h-file. **1...♖xf8** On 1...♘h5, which, in fact, was the least of the evils, White would play 2.♗xe7, for example 2...♗xc3 (2...♗g7 3.♗xd6) 3.bxc3 ♖xc3 4.♖c1 or 4.♖xh5 ♖xc2 5.♕a5!. **2.♖xh8+** Decoying the king. **2...♔xh8**
**3.♕h6+ ♔g8**

(*see next diagram*)

4.♘d5! Deflecting the knight deprives Black of the defensive move ...♘h5. After 4...♘xd5 there follows 5.♖h1, mating. At the same time, 5.♘xe7# is threatened. Black resigned in Mann-Vajtho, correspondence game, 1983.

## Position 603

**1.♘e7+! ♖8xe7** 1...♖2xe7 2.♕xe7. **2.♖d8+ ♖e8**
**3.♕f8+! ♖xf8 4.♖xf8#** (Chigorin-Znosko-Borovsky, Kyiv 1903)

Position 604

**1.e5!** A series of deflecting sacrifices opens the h-pawn's path to the promotion square. **1...fxe5** After king moves, the simple 2.e6 wins. **2.g5 hxg5** Here king moves are met by f5-f6: 2...♔d7 3.f6 ♔e6 (3...gxf6 4.gxh6) 4.fxg7 ♔f7 5.gxh6

*(see next diagram)*

5...b5 6.♔e4 b4 7.♔d3!, winning.
**3.f6 gxf6 4.h5** This was the finish of Averbakh-Bebchuk, Moscow 1964.

Position 605

**1.♖e8+! ♘xe8** On 1...♖xe8 there follows 2.♖xe8+ ♘xe8 3.♕xf7+ ♔h7 4.♕g8+ ♔g6 5.♕xe8+ ♔g5 (5...♔f6 6.♕f7+; if 5...♔h7, then 6.♗g8+ ♔h8 7.♗f7+ and 8.♕g8#) 6.h4+. **2.♕xf7+ ♔h7 3.♕f5+ g6** If 3...♔h8, then 4.♕f8+ ♔h7 5.♗g8+, mating. **4.♖e7+ ♘g7 5.♕f6** and Black resigned in Uhlmann-Holzhäuer, Kecskemet 1984.

Position 606

White has a pawn more. The attacked pawn on b2 can be defended. But the open h-file proves fatal for Black: **1.♖h7+! ♔xh7 2.♕h1+ ♔g8 3.♕h6 ♘ce5** The only defence against the threat to g6. **4.♖h1 ♘xf3+ 5.♔d1 ♘xb2+ 6.♔c1 ♘d3+ 7.♔b1** and Black resigned in Nguyen Anh Dung-Züger, Moscow Olympiad 1994.

Position 607

White completed his attack with a double rook sacrifice: **1.♖xb7+! ♔xb7 2.♖xc7+ ♔xc7 3.♕xa7+ ♔c8 4.d6!** Mate is unstoppable (Khalifman-Serper, St Petersburg 1994).

Position 608

**1.♗xf7+! ♔xf7 2.♖xg7+! ♗xg7** Or 2...♔xg7 3.♕g4+ ♔f7 4.♕h5+ ♔g7 (4...♔f6 5.♕f5+ ♔g7 6.♘ce6+ dxe6 7.♘xe6#) 5.♘f5+ ♔f6 6.♗g5+ ♔xf5 (on 6...♔e5 there is mate in several ways) 7.♗h4+ ♔f4 8.♗g3#. Declining the rook with 2...♔f6 leads to mate after 3.♕g4 h6 4.♕f5+ and 5.♘ce6+. **3.♕h5+ ♔f8** 3...♔f6 4.♕f5#. **4.♘ce6+** and mate next move (Schlosser-Kanchev, correspondence game, 1967).

Position 609

**1.d5!** Opening the central files is the prelude to the destruction of the kingside. **1...exd5** Or 1...♗xd5 2.♘xd5 exd5, and the king's position is bared by 3.♗xh7+ ♔xh7 4.♕h3+ ♔g7 5.♕g4+ ♔h7. Now it is mate with 6.♖d3 ♗d2 7.♖h3+ ♗h6 8.♖xh6+ ♔xh6 9.♖a3 or straightaway 6.♖a3 ♗xa3 7.♖d3. Black's best move was 1...♗d7. **2.♘xd5 ♗xd5** The least evil was 2...f5 3.♗xf5 ♕h4 4.♗xh7+ ♔xh7 5.♕c2+ ♔g7 6.♕xc6 – White should win without any trouble.
(*see next diagram*)
**3.♗xh7+ ♔xh7 4.♕h3+ ♔g7 5.♕g4+ ♔h7 6.♖d3** and Black resigned (6...♗d2 7.♖h3+ ♗h6 8.♕h5, and mate) in Bruzon-Perea, Cuba 2003.

Position 610

White has an extra pawn. The following combination transforms the position into a technically winning ending: **1...♘xf2 2.♗xf2 ♖xf2 3.♕xf2**

(*see next diagram*)

**3...♘g4!** The point. With the forced series of discovered checks, Black wins three pawns and then the rook. **4.♕xd4 ♗xd4+ 5.♔h1 ♘f2+ 6.♔g1 ♘xd3+ 7.♔h1 ♘f2+ 8.♔g1 ♘xe4+ 9.♔h1 ♘f2+ 10.♔g1 ♘d3+ 11.♔h1 ♘xe1 12.♘d2** Or 12.♘c3 ♘c2 13.♖c1 ♘e3. **12...♘c2 13.♖c1 ♘e3** and Black realised his material advantage in Schmaltz-Vouldis, Fürth 2002.

Position 611

**1.♖e8+** Decoying the king onto the d-file. **1...♔d7 2.♖e3!** Exploiting the pin. **2...♕h4**

(*see next diagram*)

And finally, two decoying sacrifices: **3.♖xd4+! ♕xd4 4.♖d3 ♕xd3 5.♘e5+** and **6.♘xd3**, with an extra knight (Kofman-Sacchetti 1945 – this combination is based on a single journal source and its legitimacy is questioned. It might be a composition).

## Position 612

**1...h5! 2.♕xh5** After 2.g4 Black wins a knight and reaches a winning queen ending with 2...hxg4+ 3.♕xg4 ♕h1+ and 4...♕e1+. If 2.♕b7+ ♔h6, the threat of 3...g4+ is deadly (after 3.♘f1 Black does not even take the knight, but plays 3...g4+ 4.♔h4 ♕c5). **2...♕h1+ 3.♔g4 ♕d1+ 4.♘f3 ♕d7#** (Liutov-Botvinnik, Leningrad 1925) This was the finish of an offhand game, played by the 14-year old Mikhail Botvinnik. In the same year, the composer Sergey Kaminer, together with Botvinnik, composed a study based on the final combination.
*(see next diagram)*

White to play and win:
**1.g4+ ♔h4 2.♗h6!! ♕xh6 3.♕h2+ ♔g5 4.♕d2+** By analogy with the game, after the forced **4...♘f4**, the check on d8 mates.

## Position 613

**1.♗d5! exd5** If Black defends the square e6 with the move 1...♘f8 (1...♘e5! was the only move), White opens the bishop's diagonal: 2.♖xe6! ♘fxe6 3.♖xe6 ♘xe6 4.♗xe6+ ♔f8 5.♕h8+ ♔e7 6.♕f6+ ♔e8 7.♘f5 with unstoppable mating threats (7...d5+ 8.♔h4). **2.♕xg7+! ♔xg7 3.♘f5+ ♔g6 4.♖e6+ ♘f6** 4...♔xg5 5.h4#. **5.♖xf6+ ♔xg5 6.♖ee6! ♖g2+** Otherwise 7.h4#. **7.♔xg2 ♕d8 8.♘e7!** and Black resigned in Rossetto-Cardoso, Portoroz 1958.

Position 614

**1.♗xa4** White clears the c-file with the sole object of exchanging rooks. After this, the rook on c8 proves to be lacking defence, which allows a standard tactical operation: **1...♕xa4 2.♖xc8 ♖xc8 3.♘h6+! gxh6** 3...♔h8 4.♕xf7 ♘f6 5.♕g8+ and 6.♘f7#. **4.♕g4+ ♔h8 5.♕xc8** and Black resigned in Balashov-Bronstein, Tbilisi 1975.

Position 615

The standard breakthrough on the queenside with 1.a4 bxa4 2.♕xa6 favours Black: 2...♕xe5 3.♕xa8+ ♔f7 4.♖f1+ ♖f6 (5.♖xf6+ ♔xf6; 5.♘f5 exf5).

But the kingside is vulnerable: **1.♗g6+! ♖xg6** After 1...♔d7, declining the sacrifice, 2.♗xh5 is sufficient, and Black cannot hold for long. **2.♕xh5 ♔f7 3.♖f1+ ♗f6** *(see next diagram)*

**4.♖xf6+! gxf6 5.♕h7+ ♖g7 6.♕xg7+ ♔xg7 7.♘xe6+ ♔f7 8.♘xc7** and White wins (Tanin-Maximov, Kislovodsk 1949).

**Position 616**

**1.♘xe5! ♗xe2 2.♘d7+ ♔e8**

*(see next diagram)*

**3.♘b8+!** Shutting off the eighth rank. **3...c6**
If 3...♕xb5, 3...♗xb5 or 3...♔f8, then 4.♖d8#.
**4.♘d6+ ♔f8 5.♘d7#** (Najdorf-NN, Buenos Aires 1942).
There was also another winning idea – utilising the unfortunate position of the enemy queen by means of **1.b4** (1...♕a3 2.♘xe5!+−).

**Position 617**

It is obvious that the win can only be associated with the move **1...♘h5+**. But it does not lead to material gains – the rook at g5 turns out to be under attack: **2.♔h4 ♘xf4 3.♔xg5**
Now the study-like move **3...♘g2!** deprives the white king of a retreat square.

*(see next diagram)*

There is no defence against the threat of 4...f6#.

Position 618

In a position resulting from the so-called Max Lange Attack (the previous moves being 1.e4 e5 2.♘f3 ♘c6 3.♗c4 ♘f6 4.d4 exd4 5.0-0 ♗c5 6.e5 d5 7.exf6 dxc4 8.♖e1+ ♔f8? 9.♗g5 ♕d7?), White wins with the elegant move **10.♗h6!** (a form of blockading sacrifice, fixing the h7-pawn) and after **10...gxh6 – 11.♕d2!** with unstoppable mate (analysis by Chigorin, 1902).
The question mark after 8...♔f8 is Chigorin's; after 9.♗g5 gxf6 10.♗h6+ ♔g8 and 11...♗f8, Black survives.

Position 619

**1.e7+! ♖xg4 2.e8♕+ ♕d8 3.♕e6+ ♕d7 4.♕xd7+ ♔xd7 5.♘e5+** and **6.♘xg4**, with an extra knight (Trülsch-Heidenreich, Germany 1935).

Position 620

The queen is attacked, but Black played **1...♖xc3!**. The idea is deflection. After 2.♖xd4 there follows 2...♖c1+ 3.♕f1 ♖xf1+ 4.♔xf1 ♘xd4, and Black has an extra knight. However, the difficulty of the combination lies in the fact that White has the far-from-obvious reply **2.♕f1**. Now, after the queen retreats, White can take the rook without any problem... **2...♖c8!!** 2...♖c2, 2...♖c6 and 2...♖c7 work equally well. **3.♖xd4 ♘xd4** When entering the combination, Black had to assess this, at first sight quiet, position and delve into its tactical nuances. There is a threat to decoy the queen into a fork 4...♖c1 5.♕xc1 ♘e2+. If White tries to prevent this by means of **4.♔h1**, Black inverts the moves with **4...♘e2** (or continues 4...♘b3) and as a result emerges with an extra knight (E. Polyak-Levin, Kyiv 1949).

Position 621

White mates in five moves: **1.♘g5+ ♚h6 2.♖h8+!**
**♗xh8 3.♚g8! ♘d6** Otherwise 4.♘f7#. **4.♚xh8**
Black is in zugzwang and after any knight move,
he is mated on f7 (Study by Alexander Petrov,
1845).

Position 622

**1.♕f8+ ♚h5** If 1...♚g5, then 2.♕f4+ and 3.♕h4#.
**2.♕f4! g5** After the other defence 2...♕e7, mate
comes from 3.g4+ ♚h4 4.h3! with the threat
of 5.♕h6#. If 4...g5 or 4...♕g5, then 5.♕g3#,
whilst in the event of 4...♕g7 there is 5.g5+
♚h5 6.♕g4#. 2...♕f1+ 3.♚xf1 d1♕+ 4.♚g2
♕g4 defends against the mate but allows the
liquidation into a lost pawn-ending. **3.♕f7+ ♚h6**
3...♚g4 4.♕f3#. **4.♕f6+ ♚h5**
*(see next diagram)*
And now what? **5.g4+! ♚h4** If 5...♚xg4, then
6.♕f3+ and 7.♕h3#. **6.♕f3 ♕e4 7.♕xe4 d1♕**
**8.h3! ♕d7 9.♕f3**, and mate is unstoppable
(Kartanaite-Kutanaviciene, Vilnius 1983).

Position 623

Black has a material advantage, but White is attacking with more pieces. The outcome of the game is decided by a combination: **1.♘xf7!** Eliminating a defender and decoying the king. **1...♚xf7** In deciding on the sacrifice, White also had to reckon with 1...♘d4 (if 1...♘f4, then 2.♕e5 ♘g6 3.♕c7; relatively best is 1...♖f8 2.♘xh8 ♖f6). In this case, he would have continued 2.♕e7, and if 2...♕xb5 (after 2...♘f5 there is 3.♕d7), then he has a choice of 3.♘h6+ gxh6 4.♖c7, 3.♘g5, 3.♖c7 or 3.♘d8 with forced mate. After the knight capture 2...♘xb5 White wins by 3.♖e6 ♕d4 4.♕xb7 ♖f8 5.♖e3. **2.♖c6!** Shutting off. **2...♕d8** On 2...♗xc6 the game can be ended with 3.♕xe6+ ♚f8 4.♗xc6, and after 4...♖d8 (or 4...♕d8 5.♗xa8 and the bishop cannot be taken) − 5.♕e7+ ♚g8 6.♗xd5+ ♖xd5 7.♕e8#. It is also possible to save the time spent on 4.♗xc6 and create an immediate mate threat with 4.♕f5+ ♚g8 5.♖e7. There is no defence (5...♗e8 6.♗xe8). **3.♕xe6+ ♚f8 4.♖d6** After 4...♕f6 there follows 5.♕d7. Black resigned in Bareev-Dreev, Azov 1996.

Position 624

The rook on f3 is pinned and attacked. But after **1.♖g2!!** Black had to resign. The threat is 2.♕xh7+ ♚xh7 3.♖h3# and the rook cannot be taken because of 2.♕xf8# (Soultanbeieff-Borodin, Brussels 1943).

Position 625

The pawns on d6 and a5 are undefended, and the move 1.♕c7 is tempting. But White does not need to bother himself with the calculation of the variations resulting from the reply 1...♗e4. I would point out that the hasty 2.♕xd6? would allow Black to draw after 2...♘xd5 3.cxd5 ♗xf3+ 4.♔xf3 ♕e4+.

White demonstrated the virtues of his position by combinative means, with **1.♘c8!**. Deflecting the knight from the seventh rank allows White to land a deadly blow: 1...♘xc8 2.♗h5+! ♔xh5 3.♕xh7+ ♔g4 4.♕h4#. And if 1...♕xc8, then 2.♕xe7, and White should win thanks to the threats 3.♗h5+ and 3.♕xd6. The endgame after 2...♗e4 3.♗xe4 fxe4 4.♕xe4+ is hopeless for Black.

Since the knight on c8 cannot be captured, and the knight on e7 is attacked, there only remains **1...♘g8**. Then comes **2.♘xd6**, and White wins: **2...♕f8 3.♕d7 ♗d3 4.♕e6** (Neibults-E. Kogan, Riga 1957)

Position 626

**1.♘xh7! ♔xh7 2.hxg6+ fxg6** The same variations would follow the king's retreat to g8. **3.♕h5+ ♔g8 4.♗xg6** Both 5.♗g5 and 5.♖d3 are threatened. If 4...♔f8 (and also 4...♕f6 or 4...♘c4), then 5.♗g5.

Black tried to resist with **4...♗c6**, after which there followed the decisive **5.d5! exd5**. After 5...♗xd5 White has the choice between 6.♗g5, 6.♖d4 and 6.♕h7+ ♔f8 7.♖d4. **6.♖d4 ♖e1+ 7.♔h2** and Black resigned in Galliamova-Peng Zhaoqin, Istanbul 2000.

Position 627

**1.b4!** Deflecting the queen. **1...♛xb4**

(*see next diagram*)

**2.♕h5! gxh5** 2...h6 3.♕xh6. **3.♖g3+ ♝g7** **4.♖xg7+ ♚f8** 4...♚h8 5.♖g6#. **5.♖xh7**, and mate is unavoidable (Arkhipkin-Kuznetsov, Kyiv 1980).

Position 628

**1.g4+! fxg3** On 1...♚h4 there follows 2.♚h2! h5 3.♖h6, mating.

(*see next diagram*)

**2.♖h4+! gxh4** 2...♚xh4 3.♖xh6#. **3.♖b5+ ♛xb5** **4.axb5** and the pawn queens (Mieses-NN, Metz 1935).

## Position 629

The pawn on e5 is defended, and it may seem that the king on d4 is safe. But after the sacrifice of rook and bishop by **1...♖xe5! 2.fxe5 ♗xe5+**, he finds himself driven from his refuge and meets his death: **3.♔xe5 ♕c7+ 4.♔f6** There is no way back – after 4.♔d4 there follows 4...♕g7#; 4.♔xe6 ♗d7+. **4...♕g7+ 5.♔g5 ♕e5+**, and mate (W. Mandel-Kurze, Berlin 1968).

## Position 630

**1...♘g3+!**
White resigned. After 2.hxg3 there comes 2...♖a8! with the unstoppable threat of 3...♖h8# (Karpov-Taimanov, Leningrad 1977).

## Position 631

Black's last move was ♗h3-g2, after which there followed **1.♖h8+ ♔f7 2.♗e8+! ♘xe8 3.♔g5!**, and mate is unavoidable (Bondarevsky-Ufimtsev, Leningrad 1936).

## Position 632

White resigned, not seeing a defence against the threat 1...♖c1+. However, there was a defence – indeed, by shutting off the d-file with the move **1.♖d6!!**, White could even have won. If 1...cxd6, there follows 2.f7, whilst **1...♖xd6** deflects the rook from guarding the back rank: **2.g8♕+ ♔d7** 2...♖d8 3.♕xd8+ ♔xd8 4.f7. **3.♕f7+ ♔c6 4.♕e8+ ♔b6 5.♕e3! ♔c6 6.♕xc5+ ♔xc5 7.f7**, and the game ends (this finish could have occurred in a game of Torre Repetto played in New York in 1924).

Position 633

The square f2 is undefended, but White goes over to the attack first: **1.♕e8+ ♔h7 2.♘g5+! hxg5 3.♖h3+ ♔g6**

(*see next diagram*)

**4.♖h6+!** The theme of deflection – 4...gxh6 5.♕g8#, and decoy – 4...♔xh6 5.♕h8+ ♔g6 6.♕h5# – appear again. This was the finish of the game Goltsov-V. Moiseev, Kazan 1970.

Position 634

Looking at the piece formation, it is hard to believe that this position arose in a practical game: Fridman-Thomson, Canada 1949. I have my doubts, but I must draw your attention to the instructive combination, with the help of which White won the opponent's queen: **1.♘b6+! ♔b8** Taking the knight leads to mate: 2.♖a2+ ♔b8 3.♗e5+ and 4.♖a8#. **2.♖h2!** Two decoys, after which a knight fork follows. **2...♕xh2 3.♗e5+ ♕xe5 4.♘d7+ ♔c8 5.♘xe5** with a winning position for White (5...♘e2 6.e7 ♘g3+ 7.♔e1 f2+ 8.♔xf2 ♘e4+ 9.♔e3 ♘f6 and now 10.♔f4! ♘d5+ 11.♔g5 ♘xe7 12.f6 and the f-pawn cannot be stopped, viz. 12...♔d8 13.f7!).
4...♔c8?? was a losing mistake. The correct move was 4...♔c7! with a magnificent study-like draw: 5.♘xe5 ♘e2 6.e7 ♘g3+ 7.♔g1 f2+!! 8.♔xf2 ♘e4+ 9.♔e3 ♘f6 10.♔f4 ♔d6 – zugzwang! White will lose the e-pawn.

Position 635

**1.b4!** Decoying the queen onto the open file. **1...♛xb4 2.♖ab1 ♛xc4 3.♗e2 ♛c2** The queen cannot leave the c-file because of the deadly check on b8. **4.♗d3 ♛c3**, and **5.♖b8+ ♖c8 6.♛xc3** ends the game (Hulak-Romanishin, Moscow 1977).

Position 636

**1.♘f6+!** On 1...gxf6 there follows 2.♔h1+ ♔f8 3.♛d6+ ♖e7 4.♗h6+ and 5.♖g8#, therefore he must retreat the king. **1...♔f8 2.♛d6+ ♘e7**

(*see next diagram*)

White can now take the exchange. 3.♔h1! would have been even stronger. The game move **3.♗h6!** was more striking. If the bishop is taken, the modest move 4.♔h1 sets up an unavoidable mate on g8. **3...♖ed8** But now 3...♛c3! would have made the win more difficult. Now it is the king which retreats: **4.♔h1!** If the queen is taken (or nothing is taken), there follows 5.♗xg7#, whilst if the bishop is taken, there is 5.♖g8#. Black resigned in Nasonov-Chistiakov, USSR 1978.

Position 637

Black's queenside is paralysed. White realises his advantage by creating direct threats on the kingside: **1.♗f6 h6** The threat was 2.♕g5. If 1...gxf6, then 2.♕h6! ♕a4 (2...fxe5 3.♘g5) 3.exf6 ♕g4 4.♕xf8+ (or 4.♘g5), mating. **2.♕f4 ♕xb2** On 2...gxf6 by analogy with the previous variation, 3.♕xh6 wins. **3.♕g4! ♕xf2+** 3...♗xf2+ 4.♔h1 g6 5.♕f4 ♔h7 6.♗e7 ♖g8 7.♖c7!. **4.♔h1 g6** (*see next diagram*)

**5.♕b4! ♗b6** The threat was 6.♕xf8+ and 7.♖d8#. **6.♖d2 ♕e3** 6...a5 7.♕b2 or 7.♕c4. **7.♖c3 a5** Otherwise the queen is lost. **8.♕xf8+!** After 8...♔xf8 9.♖xe3 the rook cannot be taken because of mate on d8. Black resigned in Sax-Sveshnikov, Hastings 1978/79.

Position 638

**1.♗xh7+! ♔xh7 2.♘f6+ ♗xf6** 2...gxf6 3.♕h5+ ♔g8 (3...♔g7 4.gxf6+ ♗xf6 5.exf6+ ♔xf6 6.♕g5+ ♔e6 7.♖fe1+, and mate) 4.gxf6 ♗xf6 5.exf6 ♘e7 6.fxe7 ♖e8 7.♔h2 with mate, or 4...♘e7 (instead of 4...♗xf6) 5.♔h2. **3.♕h5+ ♔g8 4.gxf6 ♘xe5** If 4...♘d8, then 5.fxg7 ♔xg7 6.♔h2. Nor does 4...♘d4 save Black. Then 5.♖xd4 and after 5...cxd4 – 6.♕g5 g6 7.♕h6 ♕g4+ 8.♔f2, whilst if 5...♕h3, then 6.♖d2 ♕e3+ 7.♖ff2. Black is defenceless. **5.fxe5 ♕e6** 5...♖d8 6.fxg7; 5...♕h3 6.♖f3. **6.♕g5 g6 7.♕h6 ♕g4+ 8.♔h2 ♕e2+ 9.♔h3** Black resigned in Zwaig-Martinez, Havana Olympiad 1966.

Position 639

**1...♘xf2! 2.♔xf2 ♘g4+ 3.♔g1 ♘xe3 4.♕d2**
♘xg2! The only way! The point of the knight
sacrifice on f2 (and the attack associated with
it) is the weakness of the light squares on the
kingside. **5.♔xg2**

*(see next diagram)*

**5...d4!** Now the bishop comes into play with
decisive effect. **6.♘xd4 ♗b7+ 7.♔f1** After other
king moves, Black either crowns his attack,
or makes decisive gains. After 7.♔f2 there
follows 7...♕d7 with the threat of 7...♕h3 (for
example: 8.♖ac1 ♕h3 9.♘f3 ♗h6 10.♕d3 ♗e3+
11.♕xe3 ♖xe3 12.♔xe3 ♖e8+ 13.♔f2 ♕f5). Or
7.♔g1 ♗xd4+ 8.♕xd4 ♖e1+! 9.♔f2 ♕xd4+
10.♖xd4 ♖xa1, and Black easily realises his extra
exchange. **7...♕d7!** White resigned because of the
following forced variation: 8.♕f2 (8.♘db5 ♕h3+
9.♔g1 ♗h6) 8...♕h3+ 9.♔g1 ♖e1+! 10.♖xe1 ♗xd4
(R. Byrne-Fischer, New York 1963/64).

Position 640

**1.f5!** Clearing a square. **1...♔xf5** Forced, since
after 1...gxf5 there follows 2.♕f4#, whilst the
queen exchange is impossible: after 1...♕f3
2.♕xf3+ ♔xf3 3.fxg6 the pawns cannot be
stopped, and after 1...♕d4 White wins by means
of 2.♕xd4+ cxd4 3.fxg6 fxg6 4.e6 d3 5.e7 d2
6.e8♕ d1♕ 7.♕e4+ ♔g5 8.♕f4#.
After the f-pawn disappears from the board, it
seems improbable that the e5-pawn on its own
will reach the desired goal.

*(see diagram on next page)*

**Position 641**

*(see next diagram)*

**2.e6!!** Blocking. 2...♕xe6 or 2...fxe6 take the black king's only escape square and are met by 3.♕f4#.

Since 3.e7 is threatened, and on 2...h4 there follows 3.e7 hxg3+ 4.♔xg3 ♕d6+ 5.♔h3, there is nothing else but **2...♕d8** and then **3.exf7 ♔f6** (the threat was not only 4.♕e8, but also 4.♕f3+ and 4.f8♕+) **4.♕e8 ♕d2+ 5.♔h3** and White wins (a variation from the game Mikhailov-Klovans, Riga 1974).

The king is a strong piece in the endgame. As a rule, he does not face any danger, and he can play an active part in the battle. But every rule has its exceptions. In this example (and not only this one), the black king's activity ends in disaster after **1.b4!**. This move deflects the pawn on c5 from control of the d4-square. **1...cxb4** The threat was 2.b5. **2.f4!!** This striking move takes the square e5 from the king and creates a threat of ♖a1-d1-d4#. Black cannot take the g3-pawn because of 3.♖xe7#, nor does 2...♖h7 help, in view of 3.♖xe7+! ♖xe7 4.♖d1, mating. **2...♖c6** The pawn on c4 is attacked. What now? **3.♖d1** and after **3...♖xc4**...

... the stunning **4.♖c7!**. The rook is deflected from the defence of the critical square d4. Black resigned in Keene-Mortensen, Aarhus 1983.

Position 642

In reply to ♗e5+ Black's king can't move to g8 due to ♘h6 mate. But he can give up the exchange. A queen check on d4 is made impossible by the black queen. White's third attacking idea is to get the queen to a1. The problem is solved with a deflecting sacrifice: **1.♖xb5! cxb5 2.♖c8!** After 2...♕xc8 the game ends simply: 3.♕d4+ e5 4.♕xe5+ ♖xe5 5.♗xe5+ ♔g8 6.♘h6#; 2...♖xc3 3.♕a1+ e5 4.♕xe5+ etc. However, it is too early to count one's chickens: **2...♕d5!**

(see next diagram)

Threatening mate on h5, hence White has no time to take the rook on a8. The squares d4 and a1 are both defended, it appears... **3.♕a1+!** The third deflecting sacrifice. The rook cannot leave the back rank: 3...♖xa1 4.♖xf8+ ♔g7 5.♗h6#. **3...e5 4.♗xe5+** Now on 4...♖xe5 there follows 5.♖xa8, but Black has a new possibility of counterplay: **4...♕xe5!**

(see next diagram)

If now 5.♕xe5+ (5.♘xe5? ♖xa1) 5...♖xe5 6.♖xa8, then 6...♖f5; or 5.♕xa8 ♕h5+ 6.♔g1 ♕xg4 7.♖xf8+ ♔g7 8.♖g8+ ♔h6 9.♕f8+ ♔h5. **5.♖xf8+!** A fourth deflection, this time of the rook from the a-file, in order to be able to take the queen 'in comfort'. **5...♔g7 6.♖f7+** The decisive deflection (6...♔xf7 7.♘xe5+; 6...♔g8 7.♘h6+ ♔h8 8.♕xa8+ ♕e8 9.♖f8+). Black resigned in Tietz-Judd, Carlsbad 1898. 6.♖g8+! was also strong. Instead of 2.♖c8, the move 2.♕f1 also wins. If 2...♕d3?, then 3.♗e5+. After 2...♖e4 – 3.♖c8 (3...♖xc8 4.♕a1+; 3...♕xc8 4.♗e5+ ♖xe5 5.♕f6+). 2...♖aa2 does not save Black because of 3.♗e5+ ♖xe5 4.♘xe5 with irresistible threats.

Tietz' opponent was the American consul in Vienna, a strong amateur and a pupil of Steinitz. Even so, the genuineness of this striking combination is open to doubt...

Position 643

**1.♖xd6 ♘xc4** In the event of 1...♕xf5 2.♕e2, the black king is open, and the knight on e5 is unstable – White's advantage is indisputable. But what happens after the text move?
**2.♖xh6+! ♔xh6 3.♕h8+ ♔g5** If 3...♔h7, then 4.♕f6+ ♔h5 5.♕h4#.

*(see next diagram)*

The mating net is completed with the help of two 'quiet' moves: **4.♗e4!** Threat 5.♕h4#.
**4...♕h7 5.h4+ ♔g4 6.♕d8!** There is no defence to the threats 7.♕d1# and 7.♕g5# (Rashkovsky-Gordeev, USSR 1972).

Position 644

**1.♖b7 ♕g8**
After the capture of the rook there follows 2.♘d6+. If 1...♕f8, then 2.♘e5+ ♔c5 3.♘d7+. After 1...♕a8 White wins as in the main variation. **2.♘e5+ ♔c5 3.♖b8! ♕h7** 3...♕xb8 4.♘d7+. **4.b4+ ♔d6 5.♖h8!** Forcing Black to take the rook after all. **5...♕xh8 6.♘f7+**, winning (study by Alexey Troitzky, 1914).

Position 645

**1...♘g3+ 2.hxg3 ♕g7!** After 2...♕f7 White would simply take the pawn on g4. Now the threat is 3...♕h6#. **3.f5**

*(see next diagram)*

**3...♕g6!**
If the queen is taken, it will be mate. Meanwhile, there is a threat against h5.
**4.♖f2 ♗xf2 5.♕g1**

*(see next diagram)*

Here 5...♗xg1 was already possible (but not 5...♗xg3? in view of 6.♕c5+ and 7.fxg6): 6.fxg6 ♗f2, and also 5...♕h5+ 6.♕h2 ♕xh2+ 7.♔xh2 d4. But the most precise move is **5...♗b6!**.
After **6.fxg6** (6.♕xb6 ♕h5+ and 7...axb6) **6... hxg6+ 7.♕h2** White is mated: **7...♖xh2+ 8.♔xh2 ♖h8+**
Also hopeless is 6.♕h2 exf5, whilst after 6.♖f1 the simplest is 6...♖df8.
In the game Becher-Brückner (West Germany 1986), the possible finish of which we have been examining, the game ended with the move 3...♕g6.

Position 646

**1.♕xf8+!!**
The two exclamation marks reflect not the move itself, which is quite obvious, but the whole combinative thought that underlies it.
**1...♕xf8 2.♘e7+ ♚h7 3.♖xf8**
White wins a piece, but surely the b-pawn queens...
**3...b2**
On 3...♖e1 White also wins in very striking fashion: 4.♚f5!, and if 4...g6+, then 5.♚e5 b2 (5...♚g7 6.♖g8+ ♚h7 7.♖b8) 6.♖xf7+ ♚h8 7.hxg6 ♖xe4+ 8.♚f6!. And if 4...♖f1+ 5.♚e5 b2, then 6.♘g6!. Nor does 5...♖f6 (instead of 5...b2) save the game. Then 6.♘d5 ♖b6 7.♘c3 and White realises his material advantage.
*(see next diagram)*

**4.♘g6!!** and Black resigned in Miles-Schneider, Philadelphia 1980.

Position 647

Without paying any attention to the a4-pawn, Black deals with the jumbled-up pieces on the back rank: **1...♗b5!** There followed: **2.axb5 ♘hg3+!** Clearing the h-file. **3.♘xg3** 3.hxg3 ♘xg3+ does not change matters. **3...♘xg3+ 4.hxg3 hxg3+ 5.♚g1 ♖h1+** Decoying the king. **6.♚xh1 ♖h8+ 7.♚g1 ♗c5+ 8.bxc5 ♖h1+ 9.♚xh1 ♕h8+ 10.♚g1 ♕h2#** In several publications, it is claimed that the above combination occurred in a game played in London in 1948. However, there seems little doubt that the whole of this finish (an excellent textbook example, one must admit) was invented.

Position 648

**1.♖c8!!** The pawn on d7 is attacked twice and not defended at all, and the square c8 is also under Black's control, yet he cannot take on either d7 or c8. However, he has nothing else but to take: **1...♖xc8** On 1...♕xd7 there follows 2.♕f8+ (the queen and rook combine with the help of an 'X-ray'). **2.♕e7!** The conclusion of a study-like idea. Black resigned in Alekhine-NN, simultaneous display, Trinidad 1939.

Position 649

**1.♖g7+! ♔xh8 2.♖h7+ ♔g8 3.g7!** and after any capture of the rook, there is 4.gxf8♕, whilst if the black rook retreats, 4.♖h8+ (a study by Szaja Kozlowski, 1929).

Position 650

**1.♖a6!** A combination requiring deep calculation. Twelve moves later, a piece up, Black resigns. **1...♖d1+** 1...bxa6 2.♗xc6+. **2.♘e1 ♖xe1+ 3.♕xe1 ♗xe4** 3...♖xe4 leads only to a transposition of moves. **4.♖xe4 ♖xe4 5.♕xe4 bxa6 6.♕xc6+ ♕b7 7.♕e8+ ♕b8 8.♕e4+ ♕b7** Perhaps Black thought the game would end in perpetual check?... **9.c6 ♕c7 10.♕e8+ ♕b8** (see next diagram)

**11.♕d7!**
The final 'quiet' move. The black knight is too far away, and the c-pawn is unstoppable.
**11...♕b1+ 12.♔h2 ♘f5 13.c7**
There are no checks, so Black resigned in Tarrasch-Gunsberg, Frankfurt am Main 1887.

339

Position 651

**1.罝d8+ 含g7 2.h6+ 含f6** And what now? **3.罝d6+! 豐xd6 4.盒g5+ 含e5 5.盒f4+ 含f6** If the queen is taken, it will be stalemate. Instead, **6.e5+! 豐xe5 7.盒g5#!** (study by Velimir Kalandadze, 1966).

Position 652

Give mate: **2.豐xf7+! 罝xf7 3.匂g6#** (Zhunusov-Khamraev, Alma Ata 1994)

Position 653

The move **1.c5** is the decisive mistake, because of **1...豐xf4**. The queen cannot be taken because of 2...盒d4+ (Alterman-Avrukh, Tel Aviv 1999). White should have played 1.匂f1, 1.豐b3 or 1.盒xg3.

Position 654

White loses, because after the spectacular **1.匂f7+ 罝xf7 2.豐d8+** Black does not take the queen (2...罝xd8? 3.罝xd8+ 盒xd8 4.罝e8+ mating, Borta-Pustovoitov, Moscow 2005), but defends effectively with the modest move **2...罝f8**.

**Position 655**

Taking the b7-pawn loses. Black replies **1...♘b4!**, simultaneously threatening 2...♘xa2# and 2...♛xb7. This was the finish of the game Földi-Florian, Budapest 1958.

**Position 656**

Winning! After the deflecting sacrifice **1...♖h1+! 2.♔xh1**, the move **2...exf2** creates threats of 3...fxe1♛+ and 3...♖h8+ (the finish of a simultaneous game by Nimzowitsch, Copenhagen 1925).

**Position 657**

**1.♛f4 ♘xd3? 2.♛f6!** and Black resigned in Karstens-Ullrich, Germany 1932.

**Position 658**

After **2.♛h6!** Black is mated (Marin-Kiselev, Bucharest 1997).

Position 659

The move **1...♘e5?**, played in the game Miles-Timman, Amsterdam 1985, led to defeat after **2.♗xe5 fxe5 3.♕d5+** (3...♕xd5 4.♘xe7+ and 5.♘xd5).

Position 660

The move **2.♕h6!** forced Black to resign in Bednarski-Nouisseri, Siegen Olympiad 1970.

Position 661

White has not blundered. After **1...♕xf3?** it will be mate: **2.♕g7+ ♚h5 3.♕xg6+! hxg6 4.♖h8#** (Cortlever-Van der Weide, Beverwijk 1968)

Position 662

He wins by **1.♖d7!** (1...♖xd7 2.♖xc8+ ♚h7 3.♘f8+; 1...♖e8 2.♖xc8 ♖xc8 3.♘e7+), Tal-NN, simultaneous display, Tbilisi 1965.

Position 663

No, he shouldn't. White wins by **2.♘d5!**
(2...♕xd2 3.♘xe7+ and 4.♘xd2), Sikorova-
Modrova, Karlovy Vary 2004.

Position 664

By giving mate: **1...♗xg5+! 2.♔xg5 f6+ 3.♔f4
g5#** (Khagurov-Volkov, Krasnodar 1998).

Position 665

The mate threat can be met by 1.h4 or the
sacrifice of the bishop for three pawns: 1.♗xf7+
♔xf7 2.♖xg5, then winning the h-pawn.
With the move ...♔g6 Black set a trap. The
tempting **1.♗b1** does not escape the mate: **1...
h4+ 2.♔g4**

*(see next diagram)*

**2...f5+!** Black breaks the pin on the rook in an
original way. **3.♖xf5 ♖g2#** (Tavernier-Grodner,
France 1952)

Position 666

No. In the game Maric-Gligoric, Belgrade 1962, after **1.♖xf5** there followed **1...♖b3!**, and White had to resign.

Position 667

Only on a6, since **1...♘c6?** loses to **2.♘xc6 ♗xc6 3.b4 ♗d6**

*(see next diagram)*

**4.♕d3** The bishop is attacked. It can be defended by **4...♖ad8**, but after **5.♕c3!** (this manoeuvre would also have followed a bishop retreat) simultaneously attacking g7 and the bishop on c6, leads to material gains (Konstantinopolsky-Byvshev, Moscow 1952).

Position 668

No. The routine move in such positions, **1.♘xe5**, leads to the loss of a piece, since after **1...♘xe5 2.♕xh5** (2.d4! ♗g4 3.f3 is better, but no picnic either) **2...♗g4** the queen has no retreat.

*(see next diagram)*

This was the game Busvin-Birnberg, London 1924.

Position 669

White mated in two: **2.♘b5+!** The c-file must be opened, to stop the king hiding on c7. **2...cxb5 3.♘b7#** (Lokasto-Zakrzewski, Augustow 1974)

Position 670

**1.♖xh7+ ♔xh7 2.♕h3+ ♔g6** 2...♔g7 3.♕h6#. **3.♕h6+ ♔f5 4.♕h7+ ♖g6** The same mate follows after 4...♔g4. **5.♕h3#**, Torre-Yates, Baden-Baden 1925.

Position 671

The move **1.♘f4** is wrong because of **1...♘f3+! 2.gxf3 ♕g5+ 3.♘g2 h3 4.♕xg7+ ♕xg7 5.♗xg7 hxg2**, and White ends up a piece down (a variation from the game Euwe-Romanovsky, Leningrad 1934).

Position 672

No. After **1.♕b5+** Black replies **1...♕d7**, and the capture of the pawn – **2.♕xc5?** leads to the loss of the queen after **2...♘f5 3.♕a5 b6** (W. Adams-G. Kramer, New York 1945).
If 1.dxc5, then 1...♘ec6, immediately regaining the pawn (for example, 2.♕g3 or 2.♕e3 – 2...♘d7; 2.♕b5 ♕d7 3.f4 ♘xe5).

Position 673

Black wrongly agreed to a draw. He could have given mate by means of **1...♖h3+ 2.♔f4 ♖f3+! 3.♕xf3 ♕e5#**. This could have been the conclusion of the game Stoltz-Pilnik, Saltsjöbaden 1952.

Position 674

**1...♗xd5! 2.♘xf6+** If White had foreseen Black's knight jump on move 5, shutting off the first rank, he would probably have tried to put up some sort of resistance, by playing 2.♗xf6. However, after 2...♗c4+ 3.♔g1 ♘e2+ 4.♔f1 ♕d7 5.♘d2 ♘g3+ 6.♔g1 ♘xh1 7.♔xh1 ♗d5 Black has a clear advantage.
**2...♕xf6! 3.♗xf6** White has an extra queen, and he also threatens mate. But Black delivers mate first: **3...♗c4+ 4.♔g1 ♘e2+ 5.♔f1 ♘c1+! 6.♔g1 ♖e1#** (Eckhardt-Tarrasch, Nuremberg 1888).

Position 675

**2.♖h8+! ♔xh8 3.♖xc8+ ♖xc8 4.♕h3+ ♔g8 5.♕xc8+ ♖f8 6.♕e6+ ♔h8 7.♕h3+** and mate next move (Benini-Reggio, Rome 1911).
It is also possible to invert the moves – 2.♖xc8+ and then 3.♖h8+, whereas the continuation 2.♕xe5 leads only to a draw: 2...♗xh3 3.♕xd5+ ♔f8 4.♕d6+ (4.♕xa8+? ♕e8) 4...♔g8 5.♕d5+.

Position 676

The sacrifice is incorrect. After **3...♕xe4+** White replies **4.♕e2** and after **4...♕xh1** (otherwise White has an extra pawn) gives discovered check with **5.♘g6+**, obtaining a decisive material advantage.

Position 677

After examining the natural variation with checks – **1...♖g8+ 2.♔h6 ♕xh2+ 3.♖h5**, Black decided that there was no follow-up to the chase of the white king (and White has an extra rook), and she took the rook instead: 1...♕xf1. In the end, the game was drawn (Ivanka-Lazarevic, Yugoslavia 1972).

*(see next diagram)*

However, the game could have been decided in the above variation by an unnoticed deflection sacrifice: **3...♕d2+!** and **4.♕xd2 ♖g6#**.

Position 678

No. By playing **1...♛xc2?**, Black falls into the trap: after **2.♞f6+!** he would have to resign. After 2...gxf6 there comes 3.♛e8+ (not 3.♖g3+? on account of 3...♚f8) 3...♚h7 4.♖g3. The same result comes from 3...♝f8 4.♖g3+ (P. Dely-Lengyel, Hungary 1973).

Inverting the moves is also possible: 2.♛e8+ and after 2...♚h7 – 3.♞f6+ ♚g6 4.♛g8.

Position 679

If the rook were not on a8, Black would be mated. Hence, **1.♝c8!**.

By shutting off the rook's actions, White threatens both 2.♛f8# and 2.♖e8#. After 1...♖xc8 there follows, of course, 2.♛xc8+ ♞xc8 3.♖e8#. The only chance to defend the back rank is **1...♛d8**. But then there follows **2.♛c3!** with the threat of 3.♖e8+ ♛xe8 4.♛xf6#. After **2...♞d5** (if 2...♝b5, then 3.♖eg5, and on 2...♛f8 – 3.♖e8) **3.♖xd5 ♛e7 4.♖f5** Black resigned in Van Scheltinga-Orbaan, The Netherlands 1954.

Position 680

**5.♞xg6 hxg6 6.♝xf7+! ♚xf7 7.♛c4+ ♚f8 8.♞h6!** and Black resigned in Puiggros-Pedrosa, Buenos Aires 1972.

## Position 681

The move **1...e5!** includes the second rook in the attack. After **2.fxe5** (or 2.dxe5) Black plays **2...♗xb2!**.
If 3.♖xb2, then 3...♖xb2+ 4.♔xb2 ♖b6+, and White is mated. Mate also follows 3.exf6 ♗xc3+. White resigned in Ostertag-Kosintseva, Vladimir 2002.
It would have been inaccurate to sacrifice the bishop first by 1...♗xb2 2.♖xb2 ♖xb2+ 3.♔xb2, and only now to play 3...e5. After the pawn is taken, the attack is crowned by 4...♖b6+, as in the game; 4.♕e1 meets the threat (4...♖b6+ 5.♔a1) but Black is still winning after 4...♖a6. Best for White is 4.♔a1, but Black remains better after 4...♖a6 followed by 5...♕xc3+ if the knight moves.

## Position 682

In an inferior position, White overlooked his opponent's combination. After **1.♘c7?** there followed **1...♖xa4!**, deflecting the rook from the defence of the back rank, after which White had to resign. After 2.♖xa4 Black wins by 2...♗h3! 3.♖xh3 ♕xf3+ 4.♔g1 (4.♔g2 ♕d1+) 4...♗xc3, attacking the queen and at the same time threatening 5...♗d4# (Lputian-Ivanchuk, Montecatini Terme 2000).

## Position 683

With the move **1...♗f1!**. After **2.♗xf1** (2.♕xf1 ♘g3+) **2...♘g3+** White has to give up his queen, to avoid 3.♔g1 ♘e2+ 4.♔h1 ♖g1# or 3.♔g2 ♘e4+ 4.♔h1 ♘f2+: **3.♕xg3 ♖xg3** and Black realised his material advantage in Barcza-Antoshin, Sochi 1966.

Position 684

No. After **3.罩d8+!** Black is mated: **3...罩xd8 4.罩xd8+ 含xd8 5.營g8+** (Juarez-Sanguinetti, Argentina 1950).

Position 685

Draw after **1...奧g1+! 2.營xg1 營e2+ 3.營g2 營xg2+ 4.含xg2 奧e4+** and **5...奧xb7** with a completely equal ending (Lilienthal-Tolush, Parnu 1947).
Another path is 1...奧xg3+ 2.營xg3 營e2+ 3.含g1 營d1+ 4.含f2 營d2+, also with a draw.

Position 686

The choice of retreats is not great – to h5, g7 or h7 (1...含f6? 2.②d5+). The active-looking **1...含h5** leads to defeat:

*(see next diagram)*

**2.g4+ 含xh4 3.含g2!** There is no defence to the threat 4.②f5# (Jansson-Ivarsson, Uppsala 1973). Correct is the retreat to g7 or h7.

Position 687

**1...♞xe5 2.dxe5?** Correct is 2.c5. **2...♝c5+ 3.♔h1** Or 3.e3 ♝xe3+ 4.♖f2 ♛d8 5.fxe4 fxe4 with a decisive material advantage. **3...♞xg3+**, and after **4.hxg3 ♛h6+** White is mated. This was the finish of the game Grünfeld-Torre, Baden-Baden 1925.

Position 688

**1.h4!** Played without worrying that Black will take this pawn. **1...♖b4+ 2.♔xe5 ♖xh4**

*(see next diagram)*

**3.f4** Decoying the rook. **3...♖xf4 4.♖xg7+** Deflecting the king. **4...♔xg7 5.♖xg5+** and **6.♔xf4**, winning (Khalomeev-Isakov, Simferopol 1947).
The same result occurs if White starts with the move **1.f4**: **1...♖b4+** 1...exf4 2.h4. **2.♔xe5 ♖xf4** 2...♖b5+ 3.♔d6. **3.♖xg7+**

Position 689

The move **1...♖a8** is wrong. After **2.♛xb6 ♖xa1 3.♖xa1 ♛xb6 4.♖a8+ ♔f8 5.♖xf8+ ♔xf8 6.♞d7+** and **7.♞xb6** White has an extra knight (Szöllosi-Boguszlavszky, Budapest 1981).

Position 690

After **1...♗xd1** Black is mated: **2.♗xg7+ ♔g8 3.♗h8!!** (Tal-Rantanen, Tallinn 1979)

Position 691

**1.♖xg7+! ♔xg7 2.♖g1+ ♔h8**
After 2...♔f6 there follows 3.♕h4+ ♔f5 4.♕g5+, 5.♖e1+ and 6.♕g3#, whilst in the event of 2...♔h6 there is 3.♕h4#.

*(see next diagram)*

**3.♕xe5+! dxe5 4.♗xe5+ f6 5.♗xf6+ ♖xf6 6.♖g8#**
(Hartlaub-Testa, Bremen 1913)
If in reply to 1.♖xg7+ Black retreats his king, he is also mated: 1...♔h8 2.♖xh7+ ♔xh7 3.♕h4+ and 4.♖g1+.

Position 692

**2.♕xf8+!** After 2.♕f7+ ♖xf7 3.♖xf7+ ♕xf7 4.♖xf7+ ♔g8 5.♖xb7 ♖xh5 6.♖xa7 ♖h6 7.g7 White still has to realise his advantage in the rook ending. **2...♖xf8 3.♖xf8 ♕xf8 4.h6+!** Only so. After the naïve 4.♖xf8 ♔xf8 the pawn ending is drawn. Black obtains a second passed pawn by means of ...e5-e4, after which the white king cannot support his g- and h-pawns. Now, however, it is over: **4...♔g8 5.h7+ ♔g7 6.♖xf8** (Tarrasch-Janowski, Ostend 1907)

## Position 693

After 1.fxg4 it's mate in three: **1...♕xh2+! 2.♔xh2 ♘g3+ 3.♔xg3 3.♔g1 ♖h1#. 3...f4#** (Kosolapov-Nezhmetdinov, Kazan 1936)

## Position 694

**1...♕xf3! 2.gxf3 ♖dg8+ 3.♗g3 ♖xg3+! 4.hxg3 ♗xf3**, and mate next (Johansson-Ekenberg, Sweden 1974).

## Position 695

Rather than exerting positional pressure (1...♖fg8 or 1...♖gf7), Black preferred a tactical decision: **1...♖xf3! 2.♔xf3 ♗xe4+! 3.♔xe4 ♖xg3**

(see next diagram)

The Achilles Heel of White's position is the square e3 – the threat is 4...♕a2. 4.♖hg1 does not save him, since after 4...♕a2! 5.♖xg3 (5.♕xa2 ♖e3#) 5...♕xd2 White's situation is hopeless because of the weak position of his king. If he defends the square e3 by means of 4.♖he1, the trouble comes from the other side – 4...♕a8!, with the threat of 5...b6# (5.♖a1 ♕g8!). In the game, **4.♖a1** was played, and **4...♕b2** ended the game (Palatnik-Kruppa, Kyiv 1984).

Position 696

**1.♖xc4 bxc4 2.♖f5!**
The rook cannot be taken: 2...gxf5 3.♕xf5+
♔h8 (3...♔h6 4.♕h5#) 4.♕h5+ ♔g8 5.♕g6+
and 6.♕g7#. Meanwhile, there is a threat of
3.♖h5+ and 4.♕xg6#. Black resigned. All of his
pieces are just spectators (Tal-NN, simultaneous
display, The Netherlands 1976).

Position 697

**1...♘d5+ 2.♗d2 ♕b6! 3.♕xa8+ ♔d7**
The threat is 4...♘c7. 4.a4 ♘c7 5.a5 does not help
White, because of 5...♕xb2.
**4.0-0 ♘c7 5.♗a5 ♘xa8 6.♗xb6 ♘xb6**
Black has won two pieces for a rook and duly
realised his advantage in Nimzowitsch-Alekhine,
Bled 1931.

Position 698

White's tactical operation is mistaken. After
**1...♖8xd5! 2.♗xd5 ♗xd5 3.♕d8+ ♔h7 4.♖xd5**
the double attack **4...♕d2** wins a rook for Black
(Kozlov-Labutin, Kaluga 1968).

Position 699

Black overlooked an important zwischenzug:
**1...♔h8? 2.♗xe6 ♖xd1**

*(see diagram on next page)*

**3.♕a8+! ♔h7 4.♗xf7**, and Black could only resign (Bilek-I. Farago, Hungarian Championship 1974).

Position 700

He has to take the bishop. After **1.♕xg5** (1.♕xe5+ ♗f6) **1...♕b1+** (1...♕xc3+? 2.♕d2) **2.♔d2 ♕b2+ 3.♔d3 ♕b1+ 4.♔c4! ♕xe4+** (4...♕a2+ 5.♔xc5 ♕a3+ 6.♔b6) **5.♔xc5 ♕d5+ 6.♔b6 ♕xd7**, White, having a breathing space, played **7.♕xe5+**.

Wherever the king retreats, White exchanges queens and obtains an easily winning endgame: **7...♔h6** (7...♔g8 8.♕b8+ and 9.♕c7) **8.♕e3+!** and Black resigned in Gavrilov-Lukin, Lviv 1984.

Position 701

After 2.dxe4 Black was ready to play 2...♕g4+. However, by clearing the long diagonal for his queen, White gives mate: **2.♖g6+! fxg6 3.♕h8+ ♔xh8 4.♖xf8#** (Basman-Balshan, Ramat Hasharon 1980)

The correct continuation was 1...♕e7.

Position 702

**1.♖xf6! ♗xf6**
On 1...♖xb7 there is 2.♗g7+ ♔xg7 3.♕h6+ ♔h8
4.♖f7 with mate.
If the sacrifice is declined by 1...♘f5, then 2.♖xf5
♗xf5 3.♕g5, and mate. Or 2...♖xb7 (instead of
2...♗xf5) 3.♕c3! and Black is defenceless.
**2.♕g5 ♗f3+**
Taking the queen allows mate on g7.
**3.♔g1**
And Black had to resign in Rautenberg-
Schlensker, Bad Nauheim 1948.
Another choice is 1.♗g7+! ♔xg7 2.♖xf6. After
2...♔xf6 there is mate after 3.♕h6+ ♔f5
4.♕xh7+. In the event of 2...♔h8 White wins
by 3.♖f7. There is also the move 2...♘f5. Then
3.♕g5+ ♔h8 4.♕xg4 (4.♖f7?! ♖xb7 is unclear).

Position 703

**1.♗xd7** After 1.♘xd7 ♘xd7 2.♕xd4 ♘f8 Black
holds. **1...♘xd7 2.♘xh5! gxh5 3.♕g5+ ♔f8**

*(see next diagram)*

**4.♘g6+! fxg6 5.♖xe6 ♕c5**
The threat was both 6.♕e7+ and 6.♕h6+. If
5...♕xc2, then 6.♖de1!.
**6.♕h6+ ♔f7 7.♕xg6+ ♔f8**, and now the final
'quiet' move **8.♖de1!**, after which Black is
defenceless (Levenfish-Ravinsky, Leningrad
1928).

Position 704

In this position, the combination with the bishop sacrifice on h7 and the subsequent transfer of the heavy pieces to the h-file does not work. After **1.♗xh7+ ♚xh7 2.♕h5+ ♚g8 3.♗xe5 ♘xe5 4.♖h4** Black went over to the counter-attack with **4...♘f3+ 5.♕xf3 ♗xg5**.

*(see next diagram)*

Both rooks are attacked. After the attempt to create threats by **6.♖g4 ♗xd2 7.♕f6** Black replies **7...♗h6** (or 7...♗e3+ and 8...g6) and after **8.♕xh6 – 8...♖e1+**, winning: 9.♔f2 ♕xc2+ 10.♔xe1 (or 10.♘d2 ♕f5+) 10...♖e8+ (Nunn-Csom, Moscow 1977).

Position 705

**2.♖h8+ ♚g6**

*(see next diagram)*

**3.♖xh6+!**
3.♕e8+ (3...♕f7 4.♕e4+ ♚g5) was a false trail. Now, however, White wins the queen. After 3...♚xh6 there follows 4.♕h8+ ♚g6 5.♕h5+ ♚f6 6.g5+ and 7.♕xf3. The same happens after 3...gxh6 4.♕g8+ ♚f6 5.♕f8+. Declining the rook sacrifice is impossible: 3...♚f7 4.♕c7+ ♚g8 5.♕c8+ ♚f7 (5...♕f8 6.♖h8+) 6.♕e6+ and 7.♖h8# or 3...♚g5 4.♕e5+ with mate. Black resigned in Bronstein-Korchnoi, Moscow 1962.

## Position 706

The weakening of the black kingside allows a forcing operation, beginning with the move **1.♗a6!**.
**1...♗xa6** Or 1...♕c8 2.♘xc6 ♕xc6 3.♗xb7 ♕xb7 4.♕h4 ♔g7 5.♗h6+; 1...♘a5 2.♗xb7 ♘xb7 3.♘c6 ♕c7 4.♘xe7+ ♕xe7 5.♕h4. **2.♘xc6 ♕e8 3.♘xe7+ ♕xe7 4.♕h4 ♔g7 5.♗h6+** White has won the exchange and duly realised his material advantage in Klaman-Smyslov, Leningrad 1974.

## Position 707

After **1...cxd4 2.cxd4** the tempting move **2...♘xd4** (counting on winning the exchange) leads to defeat: **3.♘xd4 ♕c3+**

*(see next diagram)*

**4.♕d2! ♕xa1** 4...♕xd4 5.♗b5+ and 6.♕xd4.
**5.c3!** Cut off from its remaining forces, the black queen is caught and the threat of 6.♘b3 is unstoppable. White can even play 5.0-0 and catch the queen later (Booth-Fazekas, London 1940).

## Position 708

**1.♖h4** and after **1...♕a3 2.♕xg7+! ♔xg7 3.h8♕+ ♖xh8 4.♖g4+ ♔h6 5.♖h1#** (N. Zhuravlev-V. Zhuravlev, Liepeja 1961).

Position 709

**1.♘b6! ♘xb6** If 1...h5, then 2.♕e4 (2...♘xb6 3.♕xg6+ ♗g7 4.♘xe6). **2.♖c7!** By deflecting the knight and queen from the defence of the kingside, White crowns his attack energetically. **2...♕xc7**
Declining the sacrifice does not save the game either. After 2...♕e8 Black is mated by 3.♕xe6+ ♚h8 4.♗b2+. In the event of 2...e5 White achieves his aim by 3.♖xd7 ♖xd7 4.♕e6+ ♚h8 5.♘f7+ ♚g7 6.♗c1!. Finally, after the intermediate move 2...h5 there follows 3.♕e4 (3...♚g7 4.♘xe6+ ♚f7 5.♖xd7 ♖xd7 6.♘f4 or 5...♘xd7 6.♕d5).
**3.♕xe6+ ♚g7 4.♗b2+ ♚h6 5.♕h3+ ♚xg5 6.f4#**
(Smirnov-Rotstein, USSR 1976)

Position 710

White forces a draw in a most unexpected way:
**1.b4! ♖xb4** 1...♖xd6? 2.bxc5. **2.d7 ♖d4** If 2...♖b8, then 3.♚c4 and then 4.♚xc5. **3.b4!** After 3...♖xd7 4.bxc5 Black has to give up his rook for the pawn. Draw (Helmertz-Wernbro, Lund 1973).

Position 711

**1...♖xf4! 2.♕xf4 ♖f8 3.♕g3 ♖xf2! 4.♕xf2** 4.♖xf2 ♕e1#; 4.♕h3+ ♚g8 5.♕b3+ ♖f7+. **4...♕e4!**
The conclusion of the combination – White is mated (Mestrovic-Basagic, Sarajevo 1972).

Position 712

The exchange of knights and sacrifice of the central pawn is the prelude to a standard combination, known since the time of the old game Lasker-Bauer (Amsterdam 1889).

**3.♗xh7+ ♔xh7 4.♗xg7 ♔xg7**

If 4...f6, then 5.♕h6+ ♔g8 6.♗xf8 ♖xf8 7.♕g6+ ♔h8 8.♖d3 or 6...♘xf8 7.♖d3. There is no counterplay with 4...♗a2+, because of 5.♔xa2 ♖xc2+ 6.♔b1.

**5.♕g5+ ♔h7**

Apart from these trivial moves, White had to have foreseen the finish (unless he was prepared to settle for a draw by perpetual check). The black king is bare, and, just on general considerations, he should be mated. But White cannot win just as he pleases. He can only do so with the help of a concrete forcing variation:

**6.♕h5+ ♔g7 7.♕g4+ ♔h6**

(*see next diagram*)

**8.♖d3 ♖c3 9.♕h4+ ♔g7 10.♕g3+ ♔h6** Or 10...♔h7. **11.♖f4!**

He could take the rook with 11.♖xc3, retaining a very strong attack (after 11...f5 there follows 12.♖f4 ♘f6 13.♖h4+ ♘h5 14.♖c7, whilst in the event of 11...♗e4, there comes 12.♕h4+ ♔g7 13.♖g3+ ♗g6 14.♕d4+ e5 15.♕xd7). But the move 11.♖f4! is more convincing.

(*see next diagram*)

If now 11...♕d8, then 12.♖h4+, winning the queen and the rook. After 11...♗a2+, White can simply take the bishop since the checks soon run out: 12.♔xa2 ♕xa3+ 13.♔b1 or 12...♖xc2+ 13.♔b1. Note that the white queen checked in such a way that e1 was defended after the move ♖f4. Thus, in the event of the straightforward 6.♖d3 (instead of 6.♕h5+ and the subsequent checks) 6...♖c3 the move 7.♖f4 would have been a mistake, because of the counterattack 7...♖b3+!

(*see diagram on next page*)

8.♖xb3 (or 8.cxb3) 8...♕e1+, winning.
The game Fogel-Klisch (correspondence, 2002),
the finish of which we have been examining,
ended after **8.♖d3** – Black resigned.

## Position 713

After 1...♖c1, there follows 2.♕f3. In this critical
situation, Black is saved by the idea of stalemate:
**1...♖c6!**
If the rook is taken, then **2...♕d5+ 3.♕xd5**
(3.♗xd5) **3...b3+** and a draw (Minic-Savic,
Yugoslavia 1989).
2.♗f7 ♖xg6 3.♗xg6 ♕d5+ 4.♕xd5 b3+ is the
same motif.
If 2.♕f7?, Black, no longer satisfied with a draw
(2...♖xe6 3.♕xe6 ♕d5+), continues 2...b3+!
3.♗xb3 (3.♔xb3? ♕d1+) 3...♖f6 and 4...♖xg6.

## Position 714

**1.♗xh7+ ♔xh7 2.♖h4+ ♔g8 3.♕h3 fxe5 4.♖h8+
♔f7 5.♕h5+ g6 6.♖h7+**
If 6.♕h7+, then 6...♔f6 7.♕h4+ g5 8.♖h6+ ♗g6,
and White's attack, having sacrificed two pieces,
misfires.
**6...♔g8** But not 6...♔f6? 7.♕f3+ ♔g5 8.h4#.
**7.♖h8+** The white queen is also under attack,
therefore there is nothing better. After **7...♔f7**
the opponents agreed a draw in the game Tal-
Nei, Tallinn 1979.
Since White has the initiative in the initial
position, we can conclude that there was no need
for the sacrifice on h7.

Position 715

A deflection of the queen serves as the prelude to the typical double bishop sacrifice combination:
**1.♖xa3! ♕xa3** and then **2.♗xh7+ ♔xh7 3.♕h5+ ♔g8 4.♗xg7 ♔xg7.** He has to take the bishop, since after 4...f5, 5.♕g6 wins. **5.♕g5+ ♔h8** 5...♔h7 loses at once because of 6.♖e4. **6.♖e4**

*(see next diagram)*

When calculating the combination, White had to take into account the attempt by Black to give up his queen for a rook by means of **6...♕a1+ 7.♔h2 ♕b1.**
Now after 8.♖h4+ there follows 8...♕h7, after which White has to content himself with perpetual check (9.♖xh7+ ♔xh7 10.♕h5+). However, White wins with the preliminary **8.♕h6+ ♔g8** and only now **9.♖h4!** After the only defence **9...f6** there follows a king chase: **10.♖g4+ ♔f7 11.♖g7+ ♔e8 12.♕h5+ ♔d8 13.♕c5! ♗d7 14.♕xf8+ ♔c7 15.♕c5+ ♔d8 16.♖g8+,** mating (Belyaev-Pavlov, Russia 1992).

Position 716

In a winning position (after the methodical 1...♖e4 2.♕c8+ ♔f3 3.♕c3+ ♖e3 4.♕c6+ ♘e4 the game would end) Black went in for a mistaken combination:
**1...♔h3**
Expecting after **2.♕xf4** to decide the outcome of the game by decoying the queen into a fork:
**2...g2+ 3.♔f2**
3.♔g1 ♖e1+.
**3...♖f6**
After 4.♕xf6 there would have followed 4...♘e4+. However, the surprising move **4.♔g1!** saved the game (Zagoryansky-Tolush, Moscow 1945).

## Position 717

Black's combination is wrong. There followed **6.♘g6+! hxg6 7.♖xf8+ ♔h7**

(see next diagram)

Now the simple capture on b7 wins, but more spectacular is the deadly blow **8.♕h6+!** (8...♔xh6 9.♖h8#; 8...gxh6 9.♖xb7+ mating; N. Popov-Novopashin, Beltsy 1979).

## Position 718

**1.♘xe6!** Clearing the queen's path to a4 and opening the f-file for the rook. **1...fxe6 2.♕xa4+ ♕b5**

Things are not changed significantly by 2...♔e7 3.♕h4+ ♔e8 4.♕g4, and Black cannot defend one of his pawns on e6 or g7.

**3.♕g4 ♕c6 4.♕xg7 ♖f8 5.♖xf8+ ♗xf8 6.♕xh7 ♖c8** More tenacious is 6...♗c5, but this does not change the result. **7.♕g6+**

After 7...♔e7 there follows 8.♖d6 ♕c4 9.♕h7+ or 9.♕f6+. Black resigned in Spassky-Darga, Varna Olympiad 1962.

Position 719

**1.♗g5!**
The bishop cannot be taken with either the pawn (1...hxg5 2.♘g6! with mate on h8) or the queen (1...♕xg5 2.♕xf7+ ♔h7 3.♕g8#).
**1...♕d7 2.♖ad1 ♗d6**

*(see next diagram)*

**3.♗xh6!**
Destroying the king's pawn cover. The entry of the rook on e1 allows White to give mate.
**3...gxh6**
If 3...♘xb3, then 4.♗xg7 ♔xg7 5.♘f5+.
**4.♕g6+ ♔f8 5.♕f6 ♔g8**
The threat was 6.♘g6+ ♔g8 7.♕h8#.
**6.♖e3**
Or 6.♘f5. Black resigned in Geller-Portisch, Moscow 1963.

Position 720

The tempting move **1...♗xc3+** loses. After **2.bxc3 ♕xc3+** White continues **3.♕d2!**, and after **3...♕xa1** he replies...

*(see next diagram)*

**4.♗b1!**
The black queen is trapped. There is no defence against the threat of 5.♗b2 (Nezhmetdinov-Konstantinov, Rostov-on-Don 1936).

Position 721

Black cannot take the bishop with the knight, because of 2.♘xf6+ and 3.♘xd7. But with the rook, he can take. After **1...♖xc4 2.♘xf6+ ♚h8** (only so) **3.♘xd7** he wins with the help of a combination:

*(see next diagram)*

**3...♘f3+! 4.gxf3 ♖g8+ 5.♚h1 ♛xh2+ 6.♚xh2 ♖h4#** (a variation from the game Furman-Ubilava, USSR 1971)
Therefore, instead of 3.♘xd7? White should play 3.f4. Then there could follow 3...♗e6 4.fxe5 ♛xe5 5.♖a5 with a complicated, double-edged position.

Position 722

White had anticipated his opponent's combination. After **3.b4 cxb4** he played not 4.♘xg5, nor 4.hxg5, but...

*(see next diagram)*

**4.♛xh7+!** And mate in the familiar way: **4...♚xh7 5.hxg5+ ♚g6** Or 5...♚g8. **6.♘e7#** (Casas-Piazzini, Buenos Aires 1962)

Position 723

On move 4 White is not obliged to take the pawn on d6.

By sacrificing queen and bishop, he saves the game by virtue of stalemate: **4.♗e4+! ♛xe4 5.♕g7+!** (Sliwa-Doda, Poland 1967)

Maybe Black should not have brought his king to g6, and should instead have played 3...♚g8 ? But then too, White achieves stalemate: 4.♕e8+ ♞f8 *(see next diagram)*

5.♗d5+ ♛xd5 6.♕xf8+!.

The winning idea in the starting position is 1...♛b2+! (instead of 1...♛a2+) 2.♔h3 and now 2...♛e5! 3.♕e7+ ♚g6 4.♕e8+ ♚f6 5.♕h8+ ♚e7 6.♕xh6 ♞d4 7.♕h7+ ♚d8 8.♗e4 a5 and now White can resign.

Position 724

**5.♞xe6! ♚xe6**

*(see next diagram)*

**6.♕d5+! ♞xd5 7.♗g4+** The black king is escorted by a convoy, into the enemy camp.
**7...♚e5 8.♖f5+ ♚d4** 8...♚e6 9.exd5#. **9.♖xd5+ ♚c4 10.♗e2+ ♚b4 11.a3#** (Shulman-Feldmus, Riga 1986)

## Position 725

After **1...♕h3 2.♕f1 ♕xh2+ 3.♔xh2 ♖cg8** White resigned, in view of the deadly threat of 4...♖h5+. This was the finish of the game Samarin-Antoshin, Berdiansk 1985.

*(see next diagram)*

Even so, instead of resigning, White could have won, by defending the threatened mate with the move **4.e6!**. A shut-off, at the same time clearing the fifth rank and preparing the following rook sacrifice. **4...♗xe6** 4...♖h5+ 5.♕h3. **5.♖xc5! bxc5 6.♖xc5** Mate has been averted, and White has queen for rook – it is Black who must resign! Consequently, Black should have refrained from the rook sacrifice and played 2...♕h5!.

## Position 726

The exchange of queens leads only to a draw. We therefore examine the attempt to exploit the position of the Black king, by means of **1.g4+ fxg3 2.♕xf5**.

*(see next diagram)*

If 2...♕e1+ 3.♔g2 ♕e2+ 4.♔xg3 ♕xa6, there follows 5.♕f7+ ♔g6 6.♕f3+ g4 7.hxg4+ ♔g5 8.♕f4#. But what happens if we ignore the rook and go for stalemate with **4...♕e5+!** ? This saves the game (Green-Aitken, England 1966). And there is more. Instead of 2...♕e1+, we can play 2...g2+ 3.♔xg2, and now not 3...♕g3+? (when taking the queen leads to stalemate, but 4.♔f1! prevents this), but 3...♕e2+!, and a draw. Thus, neither the exchange of queens nor 1.g4+ gives White a win.

Position 727

White considered the move **1...♘xd4** to be impossible, because of the variation **2.♖c7 ♘e2+ 3.♔f1 ♘xc1 4.♖xb7** with two threats – 5.♗xc1 and 5.♖b8+.

*(see next diagram)*

However, there followed **4...♘xa2!**, and White realised that he had miscalculated – the passed pawns decide the outcome of the game. He played the 'spite check' **5.♖b8+** and after **5...♔d7** resigned in Barendregt-Portisch, Amsterdam 1969. He could have played on a little longer: 6.♖xh8 b3 7.♖d8+ ♔c7 8.♖d6 b2 9.♗d8+ ♔c8 10.♖xb6 ♘b4, and the pawn reaches its goal. One small detail. Instead of 5.♖b8+ White could have set a 'desperation trap', by giving a different check: – 5.♖e7+.
*(see next diagram)*

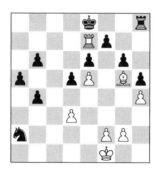

Black must step into another check with 5...♔d8, after which 6.♖xe6+ ♔c7, or 6.♖xf7+ ♔c8 or 6.♖b7+ ♔c8 give him an easily winning endgame. But if 5...♔f8?, 6.♗f6! and White wins!

Position 728

In calculating the variation, the opponents assessed this position differently.

'If,' thought the black player, 'White takes the bishop, I can immediately re-establish material equality: 7.♔xf1 ♕h1+ 8.♔e2 ♕e4+ and 9...♕xe7. There is nothing else, since mate is threatened and the rook is attacked. If he closes the diagonal with the move 7.♖d5, then the bishop retreats to h3, and 8.♖h5 does not work because of the mate threat on g2...'

But the move **7.♖d5** was played, and Black resigned! (Lengyel-Sliwa, Szczawno Zdroj 1966) There is a threat, missed by Black in his calculations, of mate by 8.♕xh7+ ♔xh7 9.♖h5#, which would follow after 7...♗h3. This means that he loses a bishop.

Position 729

**3.♕h6 ♘xf6 4.♘g5** White threatens the manoeuvre ♖h3-f3xf6. During these three tempi, Black can defend the square f7 and free his rook for the manoeuvre ...♖f8-g8-g7. After this, the knight on f6 is ready to cause White serious trouble, as the queen on f6 will be in danger. Thus, **4...♕e7 5.♖h3 ♖g8**. In the event of 5...♔g8 6.♖f3 ♖d8 the threat of a sacrifice on f6 forces 7.♖ee3 (7...b5 8.♖xf6 ♕xf6 9.♕xh7+ ♔f8 10.♖f3; 7...♘e4+ 8.♖xe4 f6 9.♖ef4). **6.♖f3 ♖g7** The square h7 is defended, and both 7...♘xg4 and 7...♘g8 are threatened. But the outcome of the game is decided by two deflecting blows.
(see next diagram)

**7.♖xf6!**

If it were not for this move, Black would be winning the game. Now, however, he has to resign. After **7...♕xf6** there follows **8.♘xh7!**, and in order to avoid mate, Black has to surrender his queen: 8...♕xf2+ (8...♖xh7 9.♕f8#) 9.♖e2 ♕xh4 10.♕xh4 ♖xh7, after which further resistance makes no sense (Neishtadt-Szeiler, correspondence game, 1963/64).

### Position 730

By playing **1.d7!** White gives up a pawn, but creates a mating net, exploiting the weakness of the dark squares.
**1...Rd8**

*(see next diagram)*

**2.Qf6!**
If now 2...Qxd7, then 3.Bg5!, first driving the rook from the d-file (so that Black will not have the move ...Qd7-d4), and then 4.Bh6.
But after **2...Rxd7 3.Bh6** the move **3...Qd4** is possible. What then?

*(see next diagram)*

**4.Re1!** and after **4...Be4** (4...Rd8 5.Qxd4; 4...Be6 5.Rxe6!) – **5.Rxe4** Black resigned in Dobierzin-Bänsch, Halle 1977.

Position 731

Black was not afraid of the move **8.♗xf7+**. By giving up his queen with **8...♔xf7 9.♕xd8**, he gets a new one: **9...cxb2+ 10.♔e2 bxa1♕** and as a result, establishes a large material advantage.

(see next diagram)

Here Black stopped calculating... and found himself being mated: **11.♘g5+ ♔g6 12.♕e8+ ♔h6** Or 12...♔f6 13.♖f1+. **13.♘e6+** This was the finish of the game Tatai-Mariotti, Reggio Emilia 1967/68. Thirty years later, the whole line was repeated in V. Ivanov-Bataev, St Petersburg 1999. Instead of taking the bishop, Black should settle for loss of castling, by playing his king to e7. The conclusion from this opening catastrophe is that instead of 5...exd4, Black should follow Nimzowitsch's old advice and play 5...♗e6!.

Position 732

The paradoxical move **1.♗g8!** wins.
Mate is threatened on h7, so there is no choice –
**1...♖xg8**

(see next diagram)

**2.♔f7! ♖xg6 3.fxg6**, and mate in three moves (study by Berthold Lasker).

Position 733

By means of a piece sacrifice, Black penetrates the enemy position with his queen. Then by bringing up the reserves, he crowns the attack:
**1...e5!**
Chasing the king out with the pieces currently available fails: 1...♕h1+ 2.♔e2 ♕g2+ 3.♔e1 ♕xg3+ 4.♔d2 ♘xe3 (1...♕xe3 5.♔c2) 5.♖f3 ♕xg5 6.fxg5 ♘xd1 7.♔xd1. Or 3...♘h2! (instead of 3...♕xg3+) 4.♕e2 ♕xg3+ 5.♔d1 ♘xf1 6.♕xf1, with equality.
**2.dxe5 ♘dxe5+ 3.fxe5 ♘xe5+ 4.♔f4 ♘g6+ 5.♔f3**
*(see next diagram)*

With such an enemy king, Black is naturally not satisfied with the perpetual check on e5 and g6. Now his hitherto slumbering queen's bishop comes into the game.
**5...f4! 6.exf4**
6.gxf4 ♘h4# or 6...♘e5#.
**6...♗g4+! 7.♔xg4**
White could have avoided mate by giving up his queen, but of course, this would not have saved the game.
**7...♘e5+ 8.fxe5 h5#**
(Glücksberg-Najdorf, Warsaw 1929).
'The Polish Immortal', as Tartakower dubbed the game.

Position 734

There followed **3.♘d5 ♕d7**. On 3...♕d8 (3...♕xc2? 4.♘xe7+ and 5.♕xh5+) there comes 4.♖xc8 ♗xc8, and 5.g6! wins: 5...fxg6 (5...exf3 6.♘xe7+; 5...♗f6 6.♘xf6+ exf6 7.♕xh5 fxg6 8.♕xg6+ ♔h8 9.♕h5+ ♔g8 10.♔h1) 6.♘xe7+ ♔f7 7.♘g5+ ♔xe7 (7...♔e8 8.♖xf8+ ♗xf8 9.♘xc8 ♕xc8 10.♕xe4+ or 8...♔xf8 9.♕f4+ ♗f5 10.♘xg6+) 8.♘f7+ and 9.♘xd8. But 3...♗xd5!? 4.♖xc7 ♖xc7 may be less clear.

*(see diagram on next page)*

**4.♘f6+!** The knight must be taken, after which the g-file is opened. As distinct from the previous variation, here 4.g6 does not work – Black replies 4...♗xd5. After 5.♕xh5 fxg6 6.♕xd5+ e6 7.♕xb3 ♖xc2 8.♕xc2 exf3 he has a material advantage. **4...exf6 5.gxf6** The rook on c2 and the knight are attacked, but Black must defend against 6.♕g5. **5...♕f5** If 5...♗xf6 6.♕xf6 ♖xc2, then 7.♗h6 and Black is mated.
(see next diagram)

**6.♘e1!** The most decisive continuation of the attack. It may be that the following head-spinning variation is also favourable: 6.fxg7 ♖fe8 7.♘d4 ♘xd4 (7...♕e5 is relatively better: 8.♖xc8 ♗xc8 9.♘xb3 exd3 10.♗d4 ♕d5 with a double-edged position that should favour White) 8.♖xf5 ♘xf5 9.♕xh5 ♘xg7 10.♖g2 exd3 11.♕g4 ♗xg2 12.♗h6 ♔f8 13.♗xg7+ and 14.♔xg2, but the tempting 6.♖g2 exf3 7.♖xg7+ ♔h8 8.♖g5 meets a refutation: 8...♖g8 9.♕xh5+ ♕h7. 8.♗g5 (instead of 8.♖g5) also fails. Then 8...f2+! 9.♖xf2 ♗f3 10.♕xh5+ ♗xh5 11.♖fxf5 ♖c5, and here Black also wins. The continuation 6.♘g5 ♕g6 7.fxg7 ♖fe8 8.♖xc8 ♗xc8 9.dxe4 (9.♖xf7 exd3) 9...♖e5 or 9...f5 is unclear.
**6...♕e5 7.♖g2 ♘d4** Or 7...exd3 8.♖xg7+ ♔h8 9.♖g5 ♕xe3+ 10.♔h2 ♕e2+ 11.♖f2, and Black cannot avoid mate. **8.♖xg7+ ♔h8 9.♗xd4 ♕xd4+ 10.♖f2 ♖c5** If 10...♕e5, then 11.d4!.
(see next diagram)

Black has defended against mate on h5, but after **11.♕f4** he has no defence against the mate on h6. (Neishtadt-Abramov, Moscow 1953).
The combination which occurred in the game could have been prevented by playing, instead of 2...fxe4, the move 2...♕d7.

Position 735

White cannot make a new queen because of 3...♖c1+, and he is still threatened with 3...d1♕#. He has perpetual check, it is true, by decoying the enemy king to f8: 3.♕f8+ ♔xf8 4.d8♕+ ♔g7 5.♕d4+ or 3.♕a1+ ♔h7 (3...f6 4.♕xf6+ and 5.d8♕+) 4.♕h8+ ♔xh8 5.d8♕+ ♔h7 6.♕h4+. However, White has more than just a draw. (*see next diagram*)

**3.♕xf3**

Suicide? No, a win! Black resigned, without waiting for 3...♖c1+ 4.♕d1! (whilst apparently just stopping the enemy pawn promoting, White forces transition into a technically winning pawn ending!) 4...♖xd1+ 5.♔e2 ♖b1 6.d8♕ d1♕+ 7.♕xd1 ♖xd1 8.♔xd1, and the healthy extra h-pawn renders further resistance pointless (Ermenkov-Sax, Warsaw 1969).

# Index of names

(numbers refer to pages)

Modrova . . . . . . . . . 343
Moiseev,O.. . . . . . . . . 91
Moiseev,V. . . . . . . . . 330
Mondolfo. . . . . . . . . 70
Moritz . . . . . . . . . . 291
Morphy . . . . . . . . . .311
Mortensen . . . . . . . 334
Movsesian . . . . . 94, 259
Mross . . . . . . . . . . . 267
Mukhina . . . . . . . . . .217
Munk . . . . . . . . . . . 293
Muraviov . . . . . . . . . 287
Murey . . . . . . . . 201, 248
Murugan . . . . . . . . . 263

**N**
Naegeli . . . . . . . . . . . 226
Nagy . . . . . . . . . 220, 250
Naipaver . . . . . . . . . 277
Najdorf . . . . . . .272, 283,
          289, 323, 372
Nakhimovskaya . . . 286
Napolitano . . . . . . . . 21
Naranja . . . . . . . . . . 210
Nasonov . . . . . . . . . . 331
Naumkin . . . . . . . . . 298
Naumov . . . . . . . . . . 197
Navarovszky . . . . . 309
Navrodsky . . . . . . . . 105
Nazarenus . . . . . . . . 261
Nedeljkovic . . . . . . . 301
Nei . . . . . . . . . 214, 361
Neibults . . . . . . . . . . 327
Neiksans . . . . . . . . . 299
Neiman . . . . . . . . . . . 76
Neishtadt . . . . . . 63, 94,
          369, 373
Nenarokov . . . . . . . . 78
Nesis . . . . . . . . . . . . 254
Nette . . . . . . . . . . . . 38
Neumann . . . . . . . . 122
Nezhmetdinov . . . . .55,
          287, 353, 364
Nguyen . . . . . . . . . 318
Niedermann . . . . . . 314

Nikolac . . . . . . . . . . 309
Nikolaev . . . . . . . . 284
Nikolic,P. . . . . . . . . 310
Nikolic,Z. . . . . . . . 259
Nikolov . . . . . . . 97, 260
Nikonov . . . . . . . . . 292
Nimzowitsch . .69, 106,
          312, 341, 354, 371
Ninov . . . . . . . . . . .300
Noordijk . . . . . . . . . 254
Nouisseri . . . . . . . . . 342
Novopashin . . . . . . 363
Novotelnov . . . . .11, 279
Nowrouzi . . . . . . . . 56
Nugent . . . . . . . . . . . 86
Nunn . . . . . . . . . . . 357

**O**
Ojanen . . . . . . . . . . . 47
O'Kelly . . . . . . . . . . 227
Olafsson . . . . . . . . . 279
Olariu . . . . . . . . . . 261
Olsen . . . . . . . . . . . 215
Ongemakh . . . . . . . 193
Opocensky . . . . . . .290
Oraevsky . . . . . . . .306
Orbaan . . . . . . . . . .348
Orienter . . . . . . . . . .209
Orlov . . . . . . . . . . . 218
Ormos . . . . . . . . . . . 250
Ornstein . . . . . 90, 248,
                  289
Ortueta . . . . . . . . . 109
Ostertag . . . . . . . . .349
Oszvath . . . . . . . . . . 37

**P**
Pacheco . . . . . . . . . 295
Paeren . . . . . . . . . . 233
Palatnik . . . . . . . . . 353
Palau . . . . . . . . . . . 316
Panchenko . . . . 77, 274
Panczyk . . . . . . . . . . 19
Pankratov . . . . . . . . 92
Panno . . . . . . . .192-193

Panov . . . . . .22, 251, 311
Paoli . . . . . . . . . . . . 198
Paramonov . . . . . . . 192
Parma . . . . . . . . . . . 210
Paromov . . . . . . . . . .271
Parr . . . . . . . . . . . . . 71
Pascual Perez . . . . . .311
Patience . . . . . . . . . . 108
Pavey . . . . . . . . . . . 253
Pavlenko . . . . . . . . .217
Pavlov . . . . . . . . . . . 362
Pawelczak . . . . . . . . 245
Pedrosa . . . . . . . . . 348
Peev . . . . . . . . . . . 264
Pelaez . . . . . . . . . . . 199
Pelts . . . . . . . . . . . . 275
Peng . . . . . . . . . . . . 327
Penrose . . .61, 202, 300
Peptan . . . . . . . . . . . 194
Perea . . . . . . . . . . . 319
Pereira,R.. . . . . . . . 269
Pereira,S. . . . . . . . . 269
Perenyi . . . . . . . . . . 231
Peresipkin . . . . . . . . 295
Perez . . . . . . . . . . . 296
Perlis . . . . . . . . . . . .111
Petkevich . . . . . . . . 23
Petrosian . . . . . . 55, 214
Petrov . . . . . . . . . . . 97
Petrov,A. . . . . . . . . 325
Petrushansky . . . . . 197
Petursson . . . . . . . . 276
Piazzini . . . . . . . . . . 365
Picco . . . . . . . . . . .290
Pidorich . . . . . . . . . . 85
Pietzsch . . . . . . 218, 249
Pigits . . . . . . . .120, 206
Pihajlic . . . . . . . . . . 207
Pillsbury . . . . . . . . . 238
Pilnik . . . . . . . . . . .346
Pimenov . . . . . . . . .118
Pinkas . . . . . . . . . . 223
Pinter . . . . . . . . . . . 288
Piotrowski . . . . . . . .211
Pirc . . . . . . . . . . . .36, 68

# Glossary of Terms

**Attack**
When a piece is threatened by capture or a king is threatened by checkmate.

**Back rank**
The first rank (for White) or the eighth rank (for Black).

**Blitz game**
Quick game in which each player gets five minutes (or less) for all his moves.

**Capture**
When a piece is removed by an enemy piece, which then takes the place of the captured piece.

**Castling**
A move by the king and the rook that serves to bring the former into safety and to activate the latter. The king is moved sideways two squares from its original square. At the same time, a rook moves from its original square to the adjacent square on the other side of the king.
A player may castle to the kingside or to the queenside, but only if both the king and rook in question have not moved before in the game, if his king is not in check, and if his king does not pass a square on which it would be in check.

**Check**
When a king is under direct attack by an opposing piece.

**(Check)mate**
When a king is under direct attack by an opposing piece and there is no way to deal with the threat.

**Combination**
A clever and more or less forced sequence of moves which usually results in an advantage for the player who starts the sequence.

**Connected pawns**
A number of fellow pawns on adjacent files; they can protect each other and are usually less vulnerable than isolated pawns.

**Correspondence game**
A game between two players who send each other each move in turn by mail or (in recent years) by e-mail.

**Diagonal**
A line of squares running from top left to bottom right or the other way round (e.g. 'the a1-h8 diagonal').

**Doubled (tripled) pawns**
Two (three) pawns on the same file (the result of a capture by one (two) of these pawns).

**Endgame/Ending**
The final phase of a chess game, when there are only few pieces left on the board.

**En passant**
When a pawn which has just moved forward two squares from its original square, is captured by an enemy pawn standing immediately

beside it. This capturing pawn then occupies the square behind the captured pawn, as if it had made a normal capture.

**En prise**
When a piece is under attack and threatened with capture.

**Exchange**
1) When both sides capture pieces that are of equal value. A synonym is trading or swapping pieces.
2) The surplus in value of a rook above a minor piece (a bishop or a knight).

**Fianchetto**
The development of a bishop to the second square of the adjacent file of the knight (to b2 or g2 for White, to b7 or g7 for Black).

**File**
A line of squares from the top to the bottom of the board (e.g. 'the e-file').

**Fork**
When two (or more) pieces are attacked simultaneously by the same opposing piece.

**Fortress**
A defensive formation designed to prevent the opponent from breaking through.

**Fritz**
A computer programme with which games can be analysed.

**Isolated pawn**
A pawn which does not have any fellow pawns on adjacent files. It cannot be protected by another pawn and therefore may be vulnerable.

**Kingside**
The board half on the right (e-, f-, g- and h-files).

**Liquidation**
When the next phase of a game is entered by an exchange of a number of pieces.

**Major piece**
A queen or a rook.

**Mating net**
A situation where a king is attacked by enemy pieces and eventually cannot escape the mate threat.

**Middlegame**
The phase of the game that follows immediately after the *opening.

**Minor piece**
A bishop or a knight.

**Open file/rank/diagonal**
A file, rank or diagonal whose squares are not occupied by pieces or, especially, pawns.

**Opening**
The initial phase of the game.

**Opposition**
A situation where two kings are facing each other with one square in between. The king that is forced to move 'loses' the opposition and has to make way for the opponent. When the distance between the two kings is larger, but one of the two cannot avoid 'losing' the opposition, the other is said to have the 'distant opposition'.

**Overburdening/Overload**
When a piece has to protect more than one fellow piece or square at the same time and is not able to maintain this situation satisfactorily.

**Passed pawn**
A pawn that has no enemy pawns on the same or an adjacent file. Its promotion can only be prevented by enemy pieces.

**Perpetual (check)**
An unstoppable series of checks that neither player can avoid without risking a loss. This means that the game ends in a draw.

**Pieces**
All chessmen apart from the pawns. In this book, mostly queen, rook, bishop and knight are meant because many tactical motifs (sacrifices, for instance) cannot be carried out by a king.

**Pin**
An attack on a piece that cannot move away without exposing a more valuable piece behind it. Pins can take place on a rank, file or diagonal.

**Promotion**
When a pawn reaches the 8th rank, it is turned into a more valuable piece (knight, bishop, rook or queen).

**Queenside**
The board half on the left (a-, b-, c- and d-files).

**Rank**
A line of squares running from side to side (e.g. 'the third rank').

**Rapid game**
Quick game in which each player gets fifteen to thirty minutes for all his moves, sometimes added with a number of seconds after each completed move.

**Sacrifice**
When material is deliberately given up for other gains.

**Sealed move**
A move which was written down and kept in cover when a game was 'adjourned'. When the arbiter opened the cover, the game was resumed starting with the sealed move. In the meantime, the players were allowed to analyse the position.

**Simultaneous display**
An event where a strong player takes on a number of weaker players on a number of boards at the same time.

**Square**
One of the 64 sections of the chessboard that can be occupied by a pawn, piece or king.

**Stalemate**
When a player who is not in check has no legal move and it is his turn. This means that the game ends in a draw.

**Tempo**
The duration of one move made by one side. A tempo can be won or deliberately lost by several methods, see e.g. 'Triangulation'.

**Triangulation**
A manoeuvre where the king first moves sideways and only then forward, in order to 'lose' a tempo, for example to gain the opposition.

**Underpromotion**
The promotion of a pawn to a piece of lesser value than the queen. This is quite rare.

**Wing**
Either the kingside or the
queenside.

**Zugzwang**
When a player is to move and
he cannot do anything without
making an important concession.

**Zwischenschach**
An intermediate check, disrupting
a logical sequence of moves.

**Zwischenzug**
An intermediate move with a point
that disrupts a logical sequence of
moves.

# About the author

Born in Moscow in 1923 and raised there, Yakov Isayevich Neishtadt became a living legend in Russian chess. He was already a first-category player at the beginning of World War II, but then he had to serve his country in battle. After the war he started to play in tournaments again and became a master of sports of the USSR as well as a world-class correspondence chess player and an arbiter.

But Neishtadt was best known as an outstanding chess journalist. He has written more than twenty opening books, which have been published in a dozen languages. From 1955 to 1973 he was secretary of the magazine *Chess in the USSR*, and from 1977-1979 an editor of the famous Soviet chess magazine 64.

In 1992 Neishtadt moved to Israel with his family. There he kept writing books. In March 2023, he passed away at 99 years of age. Genna Sosonko, in the article 'Yakov Neishtadt at 80' in his book *Smart Chip from St. Petersburg* (New In Chess, 2006), called him 'a living treasure-trove of history, anecdotes, incidents, events, memories of people, sketches.'

# Explanation of symbols

**The chessboard**
**with its coordinates:**

| | |
|---|---|
| ± | White stands slightly better |
| ∓ | Black stands slightly better |
| ± | White stands better |
| ∓ | Black stands better |
| +− | White has a decisive advantage |
| −+ | Black has a decisive advantage |
| = | balanced position |
| ! | good move |
| !! | excellent move |
| ? | bad move |
| ?? | blunder |
| !? | interesting move |
| ?! | dubious move |
| # | mate |
| ch | championship |
| zt | zonal tournament |
| izt | interzonal tournament |
| ct | candidates tournament |
| tt | team tournament |
| ol | olympiad |
| m | match |
| cr | correspondence |

❑ White to move
■ Black to move
♔ King
♕ Queen
♖ Rook
♗ Bishop
♘ Knight

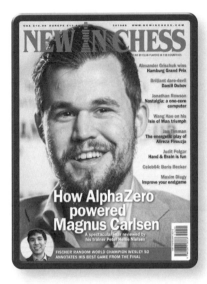